To Sr. Celly Ann, w[hen you read?]
in this book, you [...]
it 100 times — teaching
children to speak out.

R P Irvine

FORGOTTEN CHILDREN:

A True Story of How Politicians Endanger Children

Written by

Roberto P. Treviño, M.D.

• DR. ROBERTO P. TREVIÑO •

PRESA PUBLISHING

Presa Publishing, LLC.
1103 S. Presa
San Antonio, Texas

All Rights Reserved
Copyright © 2009 by Presa Publishing, LLC.
This book may not be reproduced or portions thereof
in any form without the permission of the author in accordance
with U.S. Copyright Law.

Cover design by ESD & Associates
Interior design by Mark Mayfield

ISBN 978-1-936109-00-5
Printed in the United States of America, Litho Press Inc.
First Printing July 2009

ACKNOWLEDGEMENTS

This book would not have been written if it wasn't for so many past and present Social and Health Research Center staff members who worked hard, alongside with parents, food service staff, teachers, and school officials, to change favorably the health outcomes of children. Without these positive health outcomes, the Social and Health Research Center would not have survived the giant adversaries.

The first draft of the story was written with anger because of the injustices witnessed. This is where the editors Ron Donaghe and Elizabeth Zack came in and turned on the lights. Ron cleared the language and refined the grammar, and Elizabeth asked the hard questions, and rearranged the answers. The answers to her questions—When did it take place? Who was there? How was it done? Why would they do it? And where is the evidence?—were important to build the story on solid ground.

I am grateful to my mother, Elva, for showing me to love all humans and to my father, Roberto, for telling me to fight against injustices.

The most important humans I love, my wife, Maria del Carmen, and my children, Bianca Michelle and Robert Emerick, made an enormous sacrifice. Not only did they have to do without me during many of our family activities, they also shared the frustration I experienced witnessing the injustices toward children of color and those living in poverty.

• DR. ROBERTO P. TREVIÑO •

Forgotten Children: A True Story of How Politicians Endanger Children

FORGOTTEN CHILDREN:

A True Story of How Politicians Endanger Children

Table of Content

		Page
	Abbreviations and Main Characters	vi
	Author's Note	x
I.	A new disease	1
II.	Commissioner 'Stonewall' Archer	15
III.	State control turns federal	35
IV.	Texas "Burrocrats" centrally planning children's health	63
V.	Perry sets mechanisms in place for withdrawals	71
VI.	The brown one turns his back	95
VII.	Perry and Sanchez are unmasked	113
VIII.	A foe more formidable than the TDH	125
IX.	The bulldozer legislative bill	139
X.	Not making the grade. How the TEA 'flunked' the Bienestar program	159
XI.	Under investigation	179
XII.	The Buildup to Attack the TEA	191
XIII.	They have politics, SHRC has science	211
XIV.	Ambush	227
XV.	Protecting the border children: The House	239
XVI.	Protecting the border children: The Senate	259
XVII.	Who was responsible? Interest groups, bureaucrats, or politicians	283
Appendix A		
	Recommended Reading	287

Abbreviations

CATCH, Original	The Child and Adolescent Trial for Cardiovascular Health
CATCH, Texas	Coordinated Approach to Children's Health
CDC	Centers for Disease Control and Prevention
CTN	CATCH Texas Network which consist of Houston's UTSPH, Flaghouse Inc., and *others* (a TDH document states *others* but does not specify)
DSHS	Texas Department of State Health Services, formerly the Texas Department of Health
ESC	Education Service Centers; a branch of the TEA
HB	House Bill
HHS	Texas Senate Health and Human Service committee
Houston's UTSPH	Houston's University of Texas School of Public Health
ISD	Independent School District
LULAC	League of United Latin American Councils
MALDEF	Mexican American Legal Defense and Educational Fund
MMH	Macmillan McGraw-Hill

NIH	National Institutes of Health
PE	Physical Education
SAISD	San Antonio Independent School District
SB	Senate Bill
SBOE	State Board of Education
SHRC	Social and Health Research Center
TAPHERD	Texas Association for Health, Physical Education, Recreation and Dance
TEA	Texas Education Agency
TDC	Texas Diabetes Council; a department within the TDH
TDH	Texas Department of Health, and later, the DSHS
TMA	Texas Medical Association
UTHSCSA	University of Texas Health Science Center at San Antonio

• DR. ROBERTO P. TREVIÑO •

Main Characters

Alen, Maria	McAllen physician and former chairwoman of the Texas Diabetes Council
Anderson, David A	Texas Education Agency Legal Counsel
Anderson, David D	TEA Director of Curriculum & Professional Development
Archer, William III	Texas Department of Health, Commissioner of Health
Bell, Charles	Acting Commissioner at the Texas Department of Health and then Deputy Commissioner for the Texas Health and Human Services
Bernal, Joe	State Board of Education board member and former state senator
Bush, George W	President of the United States and former governor of Texas
Cribb, Peter	Houston's UTSPH staff; Texas CATCH program coordinator
Fleming, Tommy	TEA Director of Health and Physical Activity
Garcia, Oralia	Social and Health Research Center, Director Evaluation Department
Gonzalez, Hector	Director of the City of Laredo Health Department
Guillen, Ryan	State Representative D-Laredo, Co-Author H.B. 3618
Hernandez, Irene	SHRC, Associate Director
Hoelscher, Deanna	Houston's UTSPH professor and Texas CATCH program coordinator

Forgotten Children: A True Story of How Politicians Endanger Children

Huang, Philip	TDH Chief Bureau of Chronic Disease Prevention and Control
Kelder, Steve	Houston's UTSPH professor and Texas CATCH program coordinator
Kloster, Jeff	TEA Associate Commissioner, Department of Health and Safety
Madla, Frank	State Senator D-San Antonio
Murray, Tinker	Texas State University professor and TAKE 10 program coordinator
Nelson, Jane	State Senator R-Grapevine
Ozias, Jan	Texas Diabetes Council Director
Perry, Rick	Governor of Texas
Raymond, Richard	State Representative D-Laredo; Author H.B. 3618
Rodriguez, Roger	San Antonio ISD, Director of Health Curriculums
Saldaña, David	SHRC marketing consultant
Salinas, Albert	SHRC financial director
Sanchez, Eduardo	TDH Commissioner of Health (after Archer)
Shapleigh, Eliot	State Senator D-El Paso
Treviño, Maria del Carmen	Treviño's wife
Treviño, Roberto P.	SHRC Director
Van de Putte, Leticia	State Senator D-San Antonio and pharmacist
Zaffirini, Judith	State Senator D-Laredo

• DR. ROBERTO P. TREVIÑO •

Author's Note

For years I've lived, worked and raised a family in America, and there are many things wonderful about this country, and its culture. It's comprised of a lot of different people, groups, and beliefs. I appreciate so much that it is comprised of a lot of different people, groups, and beliefs.

Yet often those beliefs can oppose one another, and often drastically. This is quite apparent through two main movements afoot in America today: the conservative and liberal movements. This country needs both political ideologies to keep it in orbit. If either one vanishes or succumbs to the other, our nation will lose its gravitational force and stray into chaos.

But like in every group, there are subgroups with extreme ideologies. Extremist members of the conservative and liberal movement I call they-group and them-group, respectively. The movement that keeps them in check I call the US-group. Following is a description of the three groups.

THEY-GROUP

The main conservative establishment is good, and I'm glad it exists. The conservative establishment is important to maintain a balance in American society. The conservative establishment's primary belief is in individual freedom (from government influence). Individual freedom and self-reliance are tenets of conservative ideology. But sometimes this ideology can be taken to an extreme where an individual's success comes at the expense of equality. An example of this is increasing corporate profits at the expense of decreasing workers' conditions.

For the purpose of discussion in this book, my experience as a physician, researcher, and community activists have helped me identify and define who is they-group. The subgroup, they-group, has little regard for equality, and it places cultural superiority as its main force. Culture comprises physical, linguistic, religious, and economic traits, and the culture of they-group is white, English-speaking, Christian, and capitalist. There is absolutely nothing wrong with this culture except for when it uses illicit means to gain superiority. It is the hypothesis in this book that to gain superiority, they-group used a disease to make a profit and to deprive members of a different culture from receiving effective preventative healthcare.

This book will be presenting events that show how they-group endangered children's health, particularly children of color and those living in poverty. The occurrences will show that they-group used illicit means to provide children at-risk for diabetes with a school health program never shown to decrease blood sugars, and to keep one that has away.

Why? Diseases are a big industry, and diabetes is among the most profitable. One in ten health care dollars will be spent on diabetes care. Diabetes affects disproportionately more people of color and the poor. According to the Centers for Disease Control and Prevention (CDC), one in two people of color and the poor will develop diabetes over their lifetime compared with one in three for non-Hispanic whites. This is a major public health concern, since diabetes is the leading cause of blindness, limb amputation, kidney failure, and stroke. Because diabetes is a $174 billion a year industry and affects disproportionately more people of color and the poor, it is this book's purpose to test the hypothesis that diabetes is used to make a profit and to endanger a population that is different in culture and appearance than they-group.

THEM-GROUP

The main liberal establishment is good too, and its existence is important to maintain a balance in American society. Their primary belief is in social equality. Social equality is to go beyond self-interest for the good of the group. Social equality provides services and opportunities for the poor and underserved. But sometimes this ideology can be taken to an extreme where it can encumber individual freedom. An example is sustaining welfare programs at the expense of overtaxing the private enterprise.

While the subgroup them-group presents a front for social equality, inside it is egoism that drives them. Public policy levied by them-group on the American populous are developed by and for those with the financial means. Because the poor and underserved are generally unable to contribute to them-group's political campaigns, their concerns and needs are hardly met. This circumstance weakens the commitment them-group has to the constituents they are meant to represent.

This book will reveal those occasions when them-group were approached and told of the injustices produced by they-group. Them-group members were provided with information and documentation about the unethical and unfair conduct of they-group members. On all these occasions, however, them-group members turned their faces the other way and on some occasions, even supported the conduct of they-group. This leaves what I call the US-group—to whom we have recourse to protect vulnerable populations from they-group and them-group.

US-GROUP

US-group is the American people and their cause is freedom and equality. Freedom is the ability to self-determinate and to move up the economic ladder, and equality is the compassion to give a hand to those who are falling behind. If freedom threatens equality, then US-group will shift the pendulum to swing toward equality. If equality threatens freedom, then US-group will shift the pendulum to swing toward freedom. US-group is the embodiment of the pendulum that swings from side to side to keep American society in balance.

The American people have a strong will, and are kind. It is the few in the they- and them-groups that give US-group a bad reputation around the world. The freedom enjoyed by individuals has made US-group the wealthiest, strongest, and most influential country in the world. The equality valued by American society has made US-group contribute the highest amount of U.S. dollars for humanitarian aid to developing countries. According to the United Nations, the four highest contributors in 2006 were the USA, United Kingdom, Japan and France. Each contributed $23 billion, $13 billion, $12 billion, and $10 billion, respectively, for humanitarian aid.

A SERIOUS THREAT

There is a serious threat to Americans. One in four, or 75 million Americans, are affected by pre-diabetes and diabetes. Pre-diabetes is fasting blood sugar between 100 and 125 milligrams per deciliters (mg/dl) and diabetes is fasting blood sugar above 125 mg/dl. Normal should be less than 100 mg/dl. Thirty years ago the annual rate of diabetes was less than five percent, and now it is twenty-five percent.

The increasing rate of diabetes has little to do with race and a lot to do with culture—the cultures of poverty and technology. Culture, like genetic traits, is transmitted from one generation to the next along family lines. A 2001 study from the Harvard School of Public Health showed that ninety-one percent of all causes for diabetes were eating little dietary fiber; eating lots of animal fat and refined sugars; sedentary lifestyles;

lack of exercise; and being overweight. A 1999 study from San Antonio, Texas showed that the more socially deprived the neighborhood was, the higher were the rates of diabetes. This is because populations living in poverty have less access to healthier messages, foods, and physical environments. It so happens that people of color are overrepresented in the poverty bracket, and this is what explains their higher rate of diabetes.

The other cause is technology. Technology has given the US-group processed foods and remote controls. Refined sugars and synthetic trans-fatty acids are the processed foods that wear down the body organ (the pancreas) responsible for manufacturing the hormone (insulin) that keeps blood sugar in check. Once the pancreas is exhausted, diabetes ensues. Technology also has given US-group screens to rub because pushing buttons has gotten too hard. Because there is lots of money to be made in processed food, technology, and disease, we are on a self-destructive course.

But there is a solution—early-age interventions. Chronic diseases are programmed developmentally during early ages, and early-age interventions might decrease rates of disease. Unless we invest in early-age interventions and quantify the results, diabetes rates and medical care cost will remain uncontrolled.

WHAT THIS BOOK WILL DO

As mentioned earlier, this book will present events and documents that question the kind of health care being provided to children of color and those living in poverty. Children of color and those living in poverty are at higher risk for diabetes, and it has come to my attention that certain individuals deliberately performed acts to deprive these children of a potentially effective diabetes control program and give them one that was not. The program they-group forced onto children at-risk for diabetes was the Texas Coordinated Approach to Child Health Program (Texas CATCH) school program. The Texas CATCH program was originally designed to prevent cardiovascular disease, but failed to decrease cholesterol, blood pressure, and obesity. It was not designed to prevent type 2 diabetes; and thus it is incorrect to pitch it ever as a diabetes control and/or prevention program.

In this book, the name Texas CATCH is used to distinguish it from the scholarly National, Heart, Lung, Blood Institute original CATCH program. The group behind the Texas CATCH program is the CATCH Texas Network (CTN). The CTN is comprised of Houston's University of Texas School of Public Health (UTSPH), Flaghouse Inc., and *others* (a TDH document states *others* but does not specify). Flaghouse Inc. is a nationwide sports equipment distributor and the *others* are never mentioned. The individuals, ultimately responsible for facilitating the acts of CTN, were then Texas Governor George W. Bush and present Governor Rick Perry. The hypothesis of this book is that children at risk for diabetes were endangered by politicians who tried to implement, through central planning, a school health program targeting the medical condition of youth-onset type 2 diabetes without the program having any evidence behind it of decreasing blood sugar levels. High blood sugars levels, in type 2 diabetes, is the single most important marker known to damage the human body.

In the chapters that follow, I am going to recreate the entirely-true events that occurred to real people and real children living in the state of Texas between the years of 1997 and 2007. Please note that I changed the name of children and patients to protect their identity, and referred to myself in the third-person throughout as I tell the story.

Forgotten Children: A True Story of How Politicians Endanger Children

Chapter 1

A NEW DISEASE

WHAT'S HAPPENING TO OUR CHILDREN
The phone rang at 7:40 a.m. on a warm morning in San Antonio, Texas at the house of Ms. Gonzalez.

The caller spoke first, in response to Ms. Gonzalez's "Hello?"

"Good morning, Ms. Gonzalez. This is Diana Cortez with the Social and Health Research Center, and I am calling to give you Adam's blood sugar result."

At the time, Adam was nine years of age, and a fourth grade student at Storm elementary school in San Antonio. His mother, Ms. Amelia Gonzalez, was a single parent who cleaned houses to support her three boys aged seven, nine and eleven. She had signed a school consent form to screen Adam for diabetes, but was surprised to get a call about it so early in the morning.

"Is everything okay?" Ms. Gonzalez asked nervously.

"Everything may be okay," Diana Cortez replied in a subdued tone of voice, "but I need to ask you some questions first."

"What questions?" Ms. Gonzalez asked, a bit confused.

"Did Adam have anything to eat or drink this morning before his test?"

Ms. Gonzalez thought back to earlier in the morning, when Adam had gotten up and went to school.

"No," she responded thoughtfully. "Just water, like the form explained." Diana Cortez continued asking questions, which were related to the symptoms of diabetes, Adam's present medication intake and his past medical history. There was nothing noteworthy or unusual about any of Ms. Gonzalez's answers.

"Adam's blood sugar was 148 this morning, Ms. Gonzalez," Cortez finally said. "Normal should be less than 100. We recommend you take Adam to your doctor for a complete medical exam."

"What do you mean, his blood sugar was 148?" Ms. Gonzalez said anxiously. She needed an answer now! "Does it mean he has diabetes?"

"No, no, no" Cortez responded soothingly. "Our test was only a screen for diabetes, and not a diagnosis. What it does mean is that he needs to see his doctor for a more complete medical examination."

Taking Cortez's advice, Ms. Gonzalez took Adam to the Texas Diabetes Institute two days later to see Dr. Daniel Hale, a pediatric endocrinologist with the University of Texas Health Science Center at San Antonio (UTHSCSA).

Dr. Hale had an arrangement with the Social and Health Research Center (SHRC) to provide medical examinations to children with high blood sugars, and usually from uninsured families, at no cost to the parents. He had a research grant from the National Institutes of Health (NIH) to study the effect of treatments in youth with type 2 diabetes, and the grant covered medical examinations and blood test. This was, in fact, why Ms. Gonzalez had taken her son to Dr. Hale; she did not have health insurance or a private physician.

After repeated testing at the pediatrician's office, Adam showed high blood sugars and Dr. Hale diagnosed the young boy with type 2 diabetes. When the pediatric endocrinologist informed her of the diagnosis, Ms. Gonzalez was alarmed. She knew something of the horrors of the disease because she had just lost her father to diabetes complications. Frantically she asked Dr. Hale about whether her young son now would be going blind, losing limbs or needing dialysis as a result of the disease.

AN OLD DISEASE, A NEW HOST

Initially, type 2 diabetes was an adult-onset disease and it was unheard of in youth in previous decades. In 1998, however, three studies from California and Arizona confirmed the new suspicion that children as young as eight years of age were developing the disease. The studies discovered the condition in Mexican-American and Native-American children.

Before 1998, it was estimated that only two percent of children had type 2 diabetes; after 1998, the estimation grew to sixteen percent. This discovery soon became a major public health concern, because it was found that children with type 2 diabetes were three times more likely to die prematurely than children without the disease.

Information from the National Health and Nutrition Examination Survey conducted in 1999 through 2000 estimated that there are approximately three million children in the U.S. with type 2 diabetes. Many of these children were already showing diabetes complications such as heart and circulation disease.

Most of the children who get the illness live in low income and uninsured households, and depend on public facilities to receive their medical care. Because of this, youth-onset type 2 diabetes is a significant cost to the U.S. government (or us), and specifically provides, as of this writing, $26 billion in annual revenue to the health care industry. *They*-group might argue that it is up to the individual to work hard, be successful, and move out of poverty but these are children being afflicted, and they did not choose their household or neighborhood.

A TOXIC SOCIETY

It was Sunday morning June 1999 on the Southside of San Antonio where Las Cazuelas restaurant was busting at the seams with customers. The crowd at the restaurant was loud and happy, and full of familiar faces. The Valadez family, who owned the restaurant, offered a good selection of healthier northern Mexico cuisine as breakfast possibilities.

On this particular morning, Roberto Treviño, a physician who grew up in the near Southside of San Antonio, and his family were customers in the restaurant. The Treviño and Valadez families were friends since high school.

While Treviño was waiting to order, the physician noticed a man, a woman and two children at the table next to his. The obese man had a dark tan skin, and his hair combed back. He boasted a tattoo on his left forearm, and was wearing jeans and a blue t-shirt. The woman had light skin, and her hair was dyed blonde. She too was wearing jeans, was obese, and seemed to be doing most of the talking. The boy and girl at their table were between six and nine years of age and were also obese.

Despite the din in the restaurant, it was fairly easy for Treviño to overhear their conversation.

"Next Saturday they are having Joey's birthday at Chema's house," the woman said. "They're going to barbeque briskets and ribs."

Not stopping his chewing, the man mumbled, "*A que hora va hacer?*" ("At what time will it be?")

Instead of answering his question, the woman kept on with the thread of her conversation.

"You know, Chema makes great briskets. He marinates his briskets with a special sauce made from scratch," she said.

The young boy had just finished eating two tacos de *carne guisada* (beef strips on sauce) on a flour tortilla.

"*Quieres otro dos tacos?*" ("Do you want another two tacos?") the man asked the boy. "*Alcabo que si no te los acabas yo me los hecho.*" ("If you don't finish them, I'll finish them.") The child took time to contemplate the offer before he said, "Okay, but I want them to have sausage *con huevo.*" ("with egg")

At this, the man stopped chewing to look up and flag down the waitress.

Treviño who had been listening closely, looked across the table at his wife, Maria del Carmen. He then shook his head and compressed his lips in a gesture of disgust at the excessive order of high calorie food.

Maria del Carmen responded by lowering her head and raising her eyebrows slowly, giving Treviño a signal to calm down.

When Treviño looked over at the table again, the waitress had just served the young girl another large glass of iced tea. The mother then started pouring sugar into the glass.

"*Tambien compraron un large screen TV y van a ver el Cowboy's game,*" ("They also bought a large screen TV and they are going to watch the [Dallas] Cowboys game,") she said as she let sugar pour like water out of a broken faucet into her daughter's glass. "*Les dieron un buen deal por la television en Sam's. Let's go to Sam's despues de aqui nada mas pa ver.*" ("They got a good deal for the television at Sam's. Let's go to Sam's after here just to see.")

The woman continued talking without even glancing at the steady stream of sugar that by now had started whitening the tea.

Treviño's face started to turn red, the red of a plum tomato. "*La van a matar!*" ("They're going to kill her!") he whispered to his wife before he started to turn around to talk to the couple.

Maria del Carmen immediately grabbed him from the arm, pulling him back to his previous position.

"This is not the right place," she told him in a stern voice. "You cannot go around at every place and tell people how to raise their children."

Treviño, not softening his expression, turned back to face his wife and then murmured, "*Que brutos son unos padres.*" ("How ignorant can some parents be.")

A TOXIC ENVIRONMENT

In 1998, when Adam was a fourth grade student at Storm Elementary in San Antonio, Texas, their school cafeteria was serving him and his fellow students foods that had thirty-eight percent fat instead of thirty-five percent of total daily kilocalories (fat should make up less than thirty-five percent of total daily kilocalories).

A study conducted by SHRC investigators and published in *Diabetes Care* in 1999 showed that children attending schools located in low-income neighborhoods were consuming 1.2 servings a day of fruits and vegetables instead of the recommended five servings a day. These children were attending schools where fresh fruits and vegetables were replaced by canned pears dripping with sugary syrup and French fries full of trans-fatty acids; and recess and physical education (PE) were removed from the daily schedule. The schools were failing these children.

Adam and his classmates live in a city where the public resources are distributed unevenly. For example, from downtown San Antonio to Storm Elementary, a stretch of five miles along Guadalupe Avenue, there is only one public park. Yet from downtown San Antonio to Cambridge Elementary, which is also a five mile stretch along Broadway Boulevard, there are five public parks. You see, Storm is located in a poor, high crime area, while Cambridge is located in an affluent and highly secured area. The children living around Storm Elementary cannot play outside during the day because of the high crime, infrequent police patrols and fewer playgrounds. Yet there is absolutely nothing wrong with the residents around Cambridge; they are role models who work hard and are successful. What is wrong is the uneven distribution of public services. And the government is part of that problem.

Because the Storm Elementary children cannot play outside their homes for fear of crime, they stay indoors watching an average of three hours of TV a day. This means they spend an equal amount of time a year sitting in front of a TV as they do sitting in front of a teacher.

Not only is this sedentary lifestyle harmful, but so is the kind of commerce supplied through the television. Investigators from Case Western Reserve University found that the Public Broadcasting Service, Nickelodeon and Disney channels averaged 1.4 food advertisements every half-hour, with the majority of these commercials being for fast-food chains and sugar-added foods. Now, these are the "decent" well-regarded TV channels. Can you imagine the *in*decent ones?

The neighborhood's Latino mothers around Storm Elementary usually buy groceries at H.E.B. Las Palmas. H.E.B. is a dominant Texas grocer that makes aggressive marketing efforts to reach the Latino customer. For example, as of this writing, outside the H.E.B. Las Palmas store are large signs, written with red markers on white paper, at the drive-by eye level. They announce the sale of *chorizo* (pork sausage), Big Red sugar-added beverages, and flour tortillas.

When mothers like Ms. Gonzalez walk into H.E.B. Las Palmas, to the left is the produce area. The produce area has 660 square feet of a few, not-so-fresh, fruits and vegetables. Compare this to the produce area in the H.E.B. Central Market near Cambridge, which boasts 7,500 square feet of fresh produce from around the world. All this has nothing to do with the Cambridge area specifically; what it has to do with is commerce providing messages that differ according to the socio-economic class of the client. Many times, the messages aimed at the disadvantaged are not the most favorable.

Parents, schools, government, and commerce are providing the children of the disadvantaged with all the wrong messages. And these messages are reaching the children during their formative years, when biological set points are being programmed.

A socio-environment providing high doses of toxic messages to the pregnant mother and to the child from birth to nine years of age can create unhealthy behaviors that program a child's fat cells to proliferate incessantly. This developmental defect needs to be corrected early, because later on in life it will be nearly impossible to do so.

How can these messages be countered with more healthful ones?

THE BEGINNING

Back in 1993, in an old wooden house belonging to the Catholic parish of St. Philips of Jesus in San Antonio, Treviño was observing his wife, Maria del Carmen, run a youth ministry session.

She was standing in front of fourteen adolescents between the ages of fifteen and seventeen.

"Everyone get off their chair and sit on the floor," she said. "Get in a circle because we are going to play the wishing-well game."

"Miss, what is that?" questioned a young boy with big round brown eyes. The others were also wondering what this was all about.

As Maria del Carmen passed around colored paper and markers, she responded, "You'll see. Now everyone, please write down any sad or unhappy things that happened to you last week. But don't write your name on the paper. When you're done, fold it and throw it in the middle of the circle."

The children took a minute to write down some words, and then, as instructed, folded up and tossed their papers into the middle of the floor.

After all the notes were thrown into the middle, Maria del Carmen,

Forgotten Children: A True Story of How Politicians Endanger Children

gathered them together and shuffled them to make sure they would remain anonymous. She then politely asked a girl with caramel-colored skin and long black hair to pick a note and read it aloud.

After the girl considered the message, she sported a frown on her face as she read out loud, "My father came in late one night and started arguing with my mother. They started screaming at each other so loud I got scared and started crying."

Many of the children's faces started to reflect a similar look to that of the girl's. Maria del Carmen took over, and asked everyone to give examples of what could have been done to improve that difficult situation.

"I would have painted flowers and birds on two cards, one for each of my parents, to show them how much I love them," said a boy in khaki pants and a brown sweater.

A girl who was kneeling and resting on her heels raised her hand swiftly. Maria del Carmen looked over, and pointed at her.

"I would have grabbed their hands tightly and started kissing them. I would have started climbing on their laps and hugging them," she said. "I would have told them how much I love them and how important both were in my life."

Concerned about their classmates' issues, all the children eagerly started becoming a part of the discussion that ensued to help their classmates, and themselves, begin to understand and learn insightful and creative ways to navigate difficult situations.

As the discussion continued, a light bulb went off in Treviño's head. Treviño had reviewed much of the health behavior modification literature, and had seen that most programs at that time had shown failure because scientist were using health education classes to teach knowledge to adults. As a physician he knew that changing health behaviors late in life was too late.

The method of instruction Maria del Carmen was using in this experience gave Treviño a new idea for a better way to design school-based health interventions. Traditional health behavior interventions use knowledge-based instruction, but in Maria del Carmen's method, she was using emotion-based instruction to get a message across, and the approach seemed to inspire each child to care about what was being discuss. Treviño instead decided to use games and fun activities in the school education program he was planning to stir the emotions, in order to facilitate new healthful behaviors in the children.

This is how the Bienestar program was initially conceptualized: start it early; make it interactive; and work the emotions.

THE NEED FOR A SOLUTION

Although poor as a child, Treviño had worked hard, and succeeded at school. He received his medical degree from the *Universidad Nacional Autonoma de Mexico* under an exchange scholarship between the United States and Mexico. He then went to Chicago where he studied internal medicine at the University of Health Science/Chicago Medical School and Critical Care Medicine at Chicago's Institute of Critical Care Medicine.

He wanted to help the underprivileged; so it was in San Antonio back in 1991 that Drs. Roberto Treviño and Roberto Ross founded the San Antonio Institute of Medicine and later the South Alamo Medical Group. One of the group's first clinics opened up in a medically underserved area—two blocks away from the housing project where Treviño grew up.

At this time, Treviño and others of his colleagues noticed that despite the opening up of more primary care clinics in low-income neighborhoods, the number of people with type 2 diabetes wanting to come through his front door was increasing. More worrisome was that the medicines available only slowed, not stopped, the progression of diabetes complications. A study correlating that observation was published in 1999. It showed that the incidence of type 2 diabetes and its complications in San Antonio was increasing by nine percent per year.

Dissatisfied with the diabetes outcomes in the current medical model, Treviño started experimenting with early-age diabetes prevention programs in the schools. For this reason he founded the SHRC in 1994 to study the effect of the Bienestar ("Well-being" in Spanish) school health program on diabetes control.

THE FRAMEWORK

The Bienestar's theoretical model is based on Social Capital Theory. In the field of sociology, it is believed that financial, human, and social capitals are resources for human development. *Financial capital* is household income, *human capital* is educational attainment, and *social capital* is the exchange of messages among individuals and groups of individuals (organizations). Because social capital has value, it is also referred to as social currency.

The effects of these capitals on human development are independent of each other, but the lack of one might cause an imbalance in lifestyle that leads to unhealthy behaviors and disease. Yet while financial and human capitals inherent in the individual, social capital lies in the relationship among individuals and organizations. Thus, a set of parents may be low-income and uneducated but they may still be able to inculcate positive values in their children.

The reverse is true too. Because highly compensated and educated parents might get home late and tired if they have been working all day, they might not have the time and energy to provide positive values to their children. Like money, social capital is exchanged in social interactions, and these exchanges can change behavior and one's predisposition to disease.

When studying health outcomes, scientists usually exclude social capital from the analysis and only incorporate financial and human capitals combined to form a poverty index. Poverty, as measured by household income and educational attainment, has been shown to be associated with heart disease, cancer, high blood pressure, diabetes and death among adults; and with unhealthy behaviors, decreased preventive practices, low-birth weight, overweight, and death among children.

Poverty (being poor and uneducated) is a good predictor of disease, but it does nothing to resolve health problems. Scientist cannot design health interventions that give away college degrees or generous salaries. Fortunately, there is one capital remaining that is available to the poor—one likely to favorably impact their health behaviors and decrease their predisposition toward disease. That capital is social capital.

The Bienestar program incorporates social capital in its intervention process. The aim of the program is to provide sessions of health programming—messaging—to students, parents, teachers, food service staff, and after-school caretakers who are working with students living in homes that lack financial and human capital. The program's healthful messages—decrease animal fat; decrease refined sugars; increase fruits, vegetables, and whole grain foods; and increase physical activity—are delivered through cultural, colorful and age-appropriate health textbooks published by Macmillan McGraw-Hill (MMH). The healthful messages are delivered to modify the children's home, health class, physical education, school food service and after-school care environments. These environments are the ones that have the most impact on children's health behaviors. The Bienestar's health class and physical education curriculums are designed to educate children in kindergarten through eighth grades.

THE FIRST EXPERIMENTS

In September 1995, Irene Hernandez, Associate Director of the

SHRC, was standing in front of the fourth grade class at St. John Berchmann to operate the school's first after-school health club. St. John Berchmann is located on the Westside of San Antonio, an area characterized by high poverty levels.

Hernandez is tall and slim in stature. She has wavy black hair that falls to her waist, and her large smile easily attracts the attention of children.

On this particular day, Hernandez moved from side to side in front of the class, her eyes roving the room to ensure they made contact with the eyes of each of the twenty-six children in the room.

"Please grab your desk and drag it to the side of the room to make space in the middle," she asked the students.

As the children scrambled to perform this task, one young girl so tiny she was not even the size of the desk she was pulling stopped suddenly, and looked over at Hernandez.

"Miss, I want to learn about diabetes so I can teach my grandfather how to take care of himself," she said.

"Does your grandfather have diabetes?" Hernandez asked.

"Yes," she responded. "He is in a wheelchair because the doctors had to cut off his leg."

The whole class stopped what they were doing. It got so quiet you could hear a pin drop.

"My mother is so sad and worried about him because he's also going blind. She had to stop working to take care of him," the little girl confided.

Hernandez took a look at the children's suddenly-stricken faces, and asked the class who else had family members with diabetes. Over half the class raised their arms.

She nodded her head, and sat down to begin to educate the children about the benefits of healthful eating and exercise.

VERIFIABLE RESULTS

The child's positive response to Hernandez's question was consistent with the findings of a study conducted by SHRC staff. It showed that near sixty percent of the students where the Bienestar program operates have first- or second-degree family members with diabetes. And, as indicated by the little girl in Hernandez's class, the children who live with family members being consumed by diabetes are impacted greatly by the hideous experience.

Fortunately, as the program's health education activities are imparting, choosing a better diet and engaging in physical activity are important health behaviors that can prevent the onset of, and/or control, type 2 diabetes.

Investigators for the SHRC conducted a study of fourth-grade children at risk for diabetes during the 1996-97 school year. They wanted to observe the effects of the Bienestar program on dietary intake. Before implementing the program, they measured the children's daily dietary intake over three days and analyzed the information with a nutrition-analysis software. The Bienestar was implemented from September to April of the school year, and then the children's dietary intake was measured again.

Children who had been involved in the program significantly decreased their dietary fat intake from 7.4 to 5.5 servings, and increased their fruit and vegetable intake from 2.5 to 3.1 servings.

In a separate study, SHRC investigators studied the impact of Bienestar on children's physical fitness. This study was conducted among 561 fourth-grade children from nine Texas elementary schools. Ninety-seven percent of the children were Mexican-American, and ninety-five percent were from disadvantaged households. Children from five elementary schools participated in the Bienestar programming sessions; students from four other elementary schools did not. A fitness score for a child was calculated by having the children step up and down on a one-foot-high stool for five minutes and counting the number of heart beats per minute after the test.

The children's fitness scores improved by +2.9 units in the participating schools, and worsened by -.2 units in the non-participating schools. This difference between students in participating and non-participating schools was significant.

CHANGING BEHAVIORS AND BIOLOGY TO PREVENT DISEASE

It is important to recognize that modifying health behaviors is a means—and not an end—in terms of preventing disease. Because the aim of the Bienestar program is to prevent disease, it therefore must impact both health behaviors and biological endpoints. The biological endpoints are to decrease body fat, blood sugar, blood cholesterol, and blood pressure. All of these conditions can cause strokes, heart attacks, blindness, amputations, and kidney failure.

The value of health programs that modify health behaviors without improving biological endpoints is uncertain. Fortunately and impressively, the Bienestar program has been shown to impact both health behaviors and biological endpoints.

For example, between 1999 and 2002, the staff of the SHRC conducted screenings for type 2 diabetes among children residing in socially deprived neighborhoods. Nearly five percent of nine-year-olds were found to have high blood sugar levels. This was alarming because such children will suffer the complications of diabetes and die at an earlier age. The positive findings, however, were that receiving the Bienestar programming was enough to: 1) restore the children's blood sugars to normal if the blood sugars were high; and 2) prevent the children's blood sugars from increasing if the blood sugars were currently normal. The results of these preliminary studies show Bienestar's potential to treat and prevent type 2 diabetes in youth.

RIGOROUS TESTING AND MORE APPLICATION

A hallmark study published in the *Archives of Pediatric and Adolescent Medicine* in September 2004 examined the Bienestar program using a randomized controlled study. This method is the most rigorous scientific design to test an intervention for effectiveness.

This study included nearly 1,400 children. The study found that nearly 700 children who participated in the Bienestar increased their fitness levels and fruit and vegetable intake and decreased their blood sugar levels. The nearly 700 children who did not participate in the Bienestar had the opposite effects: decreased fitness levels, decreased fruit and vegetable intake, and increased blood sugar levels. Mean blood sugars decreased by .20 mg/dl among students in participating schools and increased by .52 mg/dl among students in non-participating schools (a significant difference!).

While originally the Bienestar program was designed with culturally appropriate material for Mexican-American children, it was translated afterwards to the African-American culture and experience because African-American children also have high diabetes risk factors. This program, put together by African-American investigators at SHRC, was named NEEMA ("Well-being" in Swahili) school health program.

A study published in the *Journal of the National Medical Association* in 2007 showed that African-American children who participated in the NEEMA program significantly increased their fitness levels by forty-five percent and decreased their blood sugar levels by six percent.

DON'T FORGET THE CHILDREN

Children of color and those living in poverty have the highest rates of diabetes, yet as of this writing the Bienestar and NEEMA programs are the only programs in Texas modifying these children's unhealthy behaviors, and controlling their blood sugar levels. If these children do not receive effective early-age interventions, the impact will be considerable and devastating. They will suffer serious medical consequences by adolescence and many will die before adulthood from the disease.

• DR. ROBERTO P. TREVIÑO •

Forgotten Children: A True Story of How Politicians Endanger Children

Chapter 2

COMMISSIONER 'STONEWALL' ARCHER

From January 17, 1995 to December 21, 2000, George W. Bush, who went on to become president of the United States for two terms, served as governor of Texas. In September of 1997, he approved the nomination of Dr. William Reyn Archer, III to the position of Texas Health Commissioner. Dr. Archer is a physician and specialist in Obstetrics and Gynecology. He was in private practice before he was named Commissioner.

Like Governor Bush, Archer III was raised in Houston, Texas. He too was son of a prominent Republican politician—in this case, retired U.S. Representative Bill Archer.

The young Archer is a good-looking man, standing about five feet six-inches tall. Slim in physique, and a fast talker, he wears beautifully tailored suits that feature embroidered initials on the shirt sleeve. This last detail only adds to the impression Archer makes on many people: one of wealth, and arrogance. At business meetings, Archer would lean back in his chair, put his elbows on the armrest, clinch his hand in front and move his mouth almost incessantly, so as to provide others with no opportunity to speak. Many times he spoke before he thought—a habit that got him into trouble.

In 1998, the *Houston Chronicle* quoted Archer as having said, "We need to figure out why it is when blacks were more segregated and had less opportunity that they did better on cultural measures than they do in that sense today." Governor Bush supported him through this particular controversy, and it was eventually forgotten by most.

A FATEFUL MEETING

It was a pleasantly warm day in Austin in September 1998 as Treviño walked through the parking lot to the Texas Department of Health

• DR. ROBERTO P. TREVIÑO •

(now the Department of State Health Services) building, where he had a meeting with Archer. The meeting was held in the Commissioner's ornate wood-paneled conference room.

Treviño was planning on protesting the unfair grant review process that had been conducted recently by the Texas Department of Health (TDH) staff (see page 20).

Attending the meeting (in addition to the Commissioner of Health and Treviño) were Dr Maria Alen, the chairwoman of the Texas Diabetes Council, a branch of the TDH; Jacquie Shillis, Archer's chief of staff; and Gloria Moreno, the TDH Director of Governmental Relations.

Alen had set up the meeting. She was suspicious of the doings of the TDH staff when it came to the grant review process.

The meeting convene with these words from Treviño

"Good afternoon, Dr Archer. I want to thank you and your staff for taking time from your busy schedule to meet with me. I'm worried about the rates of diabetes in Texas, and how it's affecting mostly minority and poor populations. Lifestyles practiced by the poor are putting an enormous burden on the pancreas, and—"

"Dr. Treviño, how can we help you?" Archer interrupted, rolling his eyes upward. He seemed disinterested in the topic at hand.

In response to this somewhat brusque interruption, Treviño dropped any pleasantries and got right to his complaint.

"Dr. Archer, how is it that Pete Hoffman, one of your staff members, gets paid by the Texas Department of Health to travel around the state to promote the Texas CATCH program, and is also responsible for writing the guidelines and putting together the review committee members of the Diabetes Education in the Elementary Schools grant announcement? There's clearly a conflict of interest here."

"*El problema no es el gobierno,*" ("The problem is not the government,") Archer said, in nearly perfect Spanish, "*el problema es la creencias de la gente Hispana. Lo que ha pasado es que los Hispanos estan perdiendo la fe en Dios y han dejado sus valores morales.*" ("the problem is the beliefs of the Hispanic community. What has happened is that Hispanics have lost their faith in God and have forgotten their moral values.")

Treviño, who had been expecting to receive a discourse in science, and not religion, was surprised at Archer's response, but he attempted to keep a smile on his face. He listened to Archer go on for at least twenty minutes about the need to reestablish faith and family values into the Hispanic culture. This, Archer suggested, would correct unhealthy lifestyles and control the rise of disease—diabetes in particular—in the

Hispanic community.

Treviño attempted several times to interrupt Archer's monologue, but each time he did so, Archer would raise his voice and simply not let Treviño speak. Treviño, however, had driven an hour and a half from San Antonio to Austin for this single meeting. He was not going to go back without being heard.

"You need to listen to me now," Treviño finally managed to cut in with a forceful tone of voice. "We have children as young as eight years of age who will go blind, lose limbs, or be in dialysis if we do not implement evidence-based programs to stop diabetes. For your staff to make decisions based on personal preference and not on the best proven practices will be deleterious to these children. I wish you could visit San Antonio and see the Bienestar diabetes program operate in the schools. You need to see how well it is received by both students and teachers."

Archer's face got red at these words. He sat up on his chair and leaned forward, putting his hands firmly and deliberately down on the table.

"You will never have the Bienestar program operating in Texas schools," he declared. "You need to get used to the CATCH program, because that is the only program that will be operating in Texas schools."

As soon as Archer finished uttering these words, he got up and walked out of his office. Treviño had no chance to respond.

THE DAY AFTER

The following morning Treviño walked into his office. He was greeted by Albert Salinas, the SHRC's financial director.

Albert is of short stature, with dark brown skin and hair. He sports a flattop with plenty of gel. The expression on his face was hopeful and optimistic until he asked Treviño how it had gone with the Commissioner of Health.

"It didn't go too well," Treviño responded despondently.

"What happened?" said Salinas. He pulled up a chair, and sat down in a gesture of solidarity.

"Doctor Archer did not want to hear about poor children, or about Bienestar. In fact, he told me straight out the Bienestar program would never be implemented in Texas schools!"

"Albert, I drove back disheartened by what the Commissioner said! I didn't feel like I'm going to be able to change his mind. He was so set and determined—so narrow-minded. He didn't want to hear any of the evidence that shows the Bienestar program's effectiveness in the schools, and in the children themselves. It was so depressing that I felt like just walking away from it all, and not going through all the effort that will be necessary to try and change his mind! After all, I have a successful private practice and a wonderful family. Why should I go through all this stuff?" he groused.

"Dr Treviño, you simply can't walk out on these kids!" Salinas responded in a trembling voice, and with a shocked frown.

"No, no, Albert, of course I'm not going to walk out on the children! Like I said, I had all these awful thoughts on my drive home from Austin," Treviño confided ruefully. "But as my car trip was ending and I was approaching San Antonio, I made myself drive straight to the skating party we had planned for the families in our Bienestar program. When I got there, I saw a long line outside SkateTime, the rink where the party is. I went up to the line, and asked if they were there for the Bienestar skating party. When they said yes, it was as if a shot of positive energy had been injected into my body. The people in line were mostly poor, Mexican-Americans, and they all seemed so happy and excited.

"I then asked the adults if their children were making better health choices, or practicing better health behaviors as a result of their school education program. And do you know what a short man in a cowboy hat and boots told me?" *Margie nos levanta los Sabados temprano pa caminar. Esta es la unica manaña que dormimos tarde y esta huerca quiere que a fuerzas nos levantemos a caminar.* ('Margie gets us up early Saturday morning to go out and walk. This is the only day we sleep late and this brat forces us to get up and walk.')

"'Oh no, listen to her,' I told him. 'She's learning a lot of new, healthy information, and she wants you to be healthy too.

"Then another lady who had two kids with her told me, '*Cuando vamos al grocery store, Wille me saca la comida del cart y lee los labels. Despues me dice que los cheerios que tengo no tienen fiber y me los cambia.*' ('When we go to the grocery store, Wille pulls the food off the cart and reads the food labels. Then he tells me that the cheerios I have do not have enough fiber, and he exchanges them for others. Note: In the Hispanic community cheerios is sometimes used as a generic term for all cereals'.)

"Albert, these are eight- and nine-year-old children who are telling parents what to do! They've taken what they've learned in the program, and are starting to transform their lives, and their family's lives, for the better! They're amazing. Of course we will not let them down!"

"But what can we do, Dr Treviño? How do we change the

Commissioner's mind?" Salinas respectfully inquired.

Treviño paused a moment, squinted his eyes, and looked pensive before he said carefully and open-mindedly, "The first thing I need to do is learn more about the Texas CATCH program. Maybe it does have value and is the best thing for children."

THE ORIGINAL CATCH

The Child and Adolescent Trial for Cardiovascular Health (original CATCH) was a study funded by the National Heart, Lung, and Blood Institute (NHLBI). It was conducted in four different sites around the country. The purpose was to examine if a set of elementary school health curriculums could improve the heart and circulation health of children. As with the Bienestar program, its approach was to modify the environments that might have an impact on children's health behaviors. In the original CATCH program, these environments were: the health classes, food service, physical education classes, and home. The home component, however, was weak because of the fewer number of classes and the low parent participation.

The original CATCH program involved 5,900 third grade students that were followed up to fifth grade. Its goals were to have more favorable cholesterol, body fat, and blood pressure levels in children participating in the original CATCH program, as compared to children not participating in the program. CATCH's other goals were to improve students' health behaviors and knowledge and the schools' food service and classroom environments.

The original CATCH program was well-designed, well-funded, and staffed by some of the best investigators in school-based health programs in the country. It had nearly $25 million designated to implement and evaluate the program.

The original CATCH program showed that children's diet and physical activity improved (as reported by the children in the program themselves), and that this self-reported information was sustained after a three-year period. The health program also worked to decrease the levels of fat found in the food served in school cafeterias, and improved the length of time spent in physical education. All of these were indeed favorable findings, but as it turned out, CATCH's main goals were not met: to decrease actual cholesterol, body fat and blood pressure levels.

As mentioned earlier in this book, programs that improve self-reported behaviors, but do not improve physiologic measures, have uncertain value in medicine. Nonetheless, the original CATCH study was a formidable project that set the standards for how other school health programs could be designed and evaluated.

TEXAS CATCH IS NOT THE CATCH

A problem started when the NHLBI turned over the running of the program to Houston's UTSPH because of its ineffectiveness in altering blood cholesterol, body fat, and blood pressure. The original CATCH was taken over by Dr. Steve Kelder, a professor at Houston's UTSPH; Dr. Deanna Montgomery, a professor at Houston's UTSPH (who later became Deanna Hoelscher, and then Kelder's wife); and Peter Cribb, a member of the study staff at Houston's UTSPH.

Peter Cribb was, effectively, the Texas CATCH's salesman. Being athletically built and verbose, with a strong Australian accent, made him an attractive salesman for the program. But instead of selling the Texas CATCH to schools, it turns out he and others like him were best at selling it to bureaucrats and politicians.

Houston's UTSPH also partnered up with Flaghouse, Inc., a school equipment distributor, and others (a TDH document states "others" but does not specify who are they) to form the CATCH Texas Network (CTN). The CTN changed the CATCH acronym to mean "Coordinated Approach to Children's Health." And mechanisms were set in place to protect the Texas CATCH program from any and all competition. Here's what started happening.

THE START OF CENTRAL PLANNING

Author's note: The following event is what led to the meeting with Archer presented earlier on page 15.

Earlier in the year, in February 1998, Treviño travelled to Austin to make a presentation to board members of the Texas Diabetes Council (TDC). The TDC is a branch of, and funded by the TDH, and its purpose is to conduct diabetes surveillance and fund community-based diabetes control programs. Roberto Ramirez, SHRC's statistician, accompanied Treviño.

Treviño and Ramirez got to the TDH early and decided to pay Pete Hoffman a visit first. They had met Hoffman at a conference a month ago. Hoffman was the TDH's school health curriculum specialist. What this long title meant, they later found out, was a TDH staff position whose objective was to centrally plan the implementation of the Texas Catch program.

When the two men knocked on Hoffman's door, Hoffman, a short and stout man, immediately welcomed them in.

As Treviño and Ramirez entered the room, they noticed a Texas

CATCH program cap on the desk; a Texas CATCH T-shirt on the credenza; and two Texas CATCH posters on the wall of the office.

Somewhat thrown off by this display of favoritism, Treviño and Ramirez, both knew they had somewhat nervous smiles on their faces. The TDH, a mammoth and supposedly impartial state agency, appeared to employ Hoffman to disseminate only one school health program.

"Pete, how are you doing?" Treviño said in a casual manner, trying to recover his equilibrium. "We're presenting the Bienestar program at today's Texas Diabetes Council meeting, and decided to stop by beforehand to say hello. But you seem to be very busy; what are you up to?"

"I'm finishing a brief presentation for the Council meeting too," Hoffman said.

"What are you presenting?" Treviño asked.

"A draft of the Diabetes Education in the Elementary Schools grant proposal."

"What is that?" Ramirez asked with interest.

"The Texas Diabetes Council is releasing a request for a grant proposal. It is to fund an elementary school diabetes education program."

"That's very interesting," Ramirez continued.

Treviño, however, immediately started to realize that there was a conflict at play when a state employee was planning a grant—and yet he had one specific program's promotional materials all over his office.

"The CATCH is a good program," Treviño slowly offered as he looked around at the Texas Catch items. "Where did you hear about it?"

"From Peter Cribb," said Hoffman. "I think it has a lot of good qualities."

"No doubt," responded Treviño calmly, although inwardly his mind was considering the apparent conflict that had arisen. "But there are other programs out there. I do hope the Texas Diabetes Council considers them too."

Hoffman stared at the gentlemen, but did not respond. He seemed in a rush, so Treviño and Ramirez wished him well and went on to the meeting. There Treviño was cut short, given only five minutes to present the Bienestar program.

Afterwards, he and Ramirez walked outside to the parking lot. When they arrived at Treviño's pickup truck, they started to laugh. It wasn't exactly a happy laughter, however.

"*Chingao* (damn), did you see that Texas CATCH material plastered all over Pete's office?" Treviño ventured loudly.

"It looked like the Texas CATCH bookstore in there," Ramirez said, laughing so hard he almost tripped.

"I can't believe what we walked into," said Treviño. Now his tone became serious, and his demeanor reflected the change in his voice.

"That's downright scary, Dr Treviño," Ramirez reaffirmed. "It's obvious that the Texas CATCH people seem to have a tight grip on the Texas Diabetes Council. It just seems those guys will get whatever they want, and there's nothing we can do."

By now, Ramirez had lost his smile. His face showed an expression of consternation. No doubt Ramirez suspected that with the TDH behind the Texas CATCH, the Bienestar program had no chance when it came time to compete for the grant.

"Well, we don't know," Treviño said in a reassuring tone, trying to calm Ramirez. "We will compete for that grant as best and fairly as we are able, and we will follow the Diabetes Council's decision process closely."

As Treviño and Ramirez drove to San Antonio, they were wondering just how they were going to keep the Bienestar program operating if they did not receive the necessary funding. Unlike the people at CTN, they never considered the strategy of lobbying state bureaucrats for program support.

The next month, the TDH and the TDC commissioned a study to compare the Texas CATCH and the Bienestar programs. Hoffman was selected to direct and organize that study.

During the process, no one from the TDH ever contacted the SHRC staff or even requested the latest Bienestar studies. Cribb, on the other hand, was getting faxes from Hoffman asking him to specify the merits of the Texas CATCH program.

The programs were evaluated on: policy, institutionalization, systems, and other such 'official-dom' terms. Curiously, a very important component was missing from the evaluation criteria: **health outcomes**. Despite the Texas CATCH program never having measured a child's blood sugar (nonetheless having lowered one), this program received all the merits and the Bienestar received none.

The TDH/TDC Diabetes Education in the Elementary School grant announcement was released in May 1998; applications for the funding were due July of that year.

Two TDH community health employees, Janice Briester and Victor Limon, were sent to school districts in San Antonio to promote the Texas CATCH program while the competition was on-going. Bienestar received no similar employees from the TDH to promote their program.

In July, when it was past the award notice date, the SHRC had not received any notification, so Treviño called Mary Thomas. Thomas was a program specialist with the TDC, and she had previously provided TDC staff with favorable reports about the Bienestar program. The current rumor being heard by the staff of the SHRC was that the Texas CATCH program had been awarded $149,351.

Thomas, an African-American who had grown up in public housing, was sensitive to the health of high-risk children. She was someone whom Treviño could trust to get him information about the inside workings of the TDC, and his phone conversation with her went something like this.

"Mary, this is Dr. Treviño. How are you doing?" he asked warmly.

"Oh, Dr. Treviño, I'm doing fine. It's nice to hear from you," she answered.

Treviño did not take long to get to the point of his call.

"Mary, I'm calling to get an update on the grant awards. We heard that the Texas CATCH program had been funded, and I am interested to find out how the Bienestar did."

"Dr. Treviño, can you wait a minute? Let me ask if I can release the information."

Thomas put Treviño on hold, and after two minutes she returned to the phone.

"Dr. Treviño, Pete does not want the information to be released yet," she informed Treviño.

"Did you say, Pete, as in Hoffman?" Treviño queried.

"Yes, Pete was in charge of the selection process," Mary offered.

"But Mary, Pete has Texas CATCH posters all over his walls! It's obvious they've been lobbying him for support. So how can he be in charge of the selection process for the grant? That's very unfair!"

"I know, I know," agreed Thomas, lowering her voice. "Pete is an enthused proponent of the Texas CATCH program."

"Can you do me a great favor?" Treviño asked thoughtfully.

"What is it?"

"Can you fax me the list of the persons that sat in on the review process?"

"Of course, but please don't tell anyone I sent you this list. Just give me your fax number."

When the list of reviewers for the diabetes grant proposal was faxed over, Treviño studied it carefully. It was carpeted with the names of

TDH/TDC staff—and at the head of the list were Pete Hoffman and Tommy Fleming. Fleming was health curriculum director for the Texas Education Agency (TEA) and also a strong proponent of the Texas CATCH program. (He will get his own chapter later.)

Something was not feeling quite right about the whole thing, so the same week he called Alen directly to inquire about the review process. She was also an individual Treviño knew he could trust. When Alen took his call, Treviño started with a few pleasantries, then got right to business.

"Dr. Alen, I just got notice that the Texas CATCH program was selected for the Diabetes Education in the Elementary School grant. I have a concern here. It is that Pete Hoffman is paid to give Texas CATCH talks, and yet he may have been the person in charge of selecting the program. That clearly is a conflict of interest."

"Last I knew, Hoffman was responsible for writing the grant proposal. I don't think he supervised the selection process," Alen replied.

Treviño pleaded, "Can you please check, Dr. Alen, as to whether he was involved with the selection process?"

"Sure. Let me make some calls, and I will call you back."

As chairwoman of the TDC, Alen had many reliable sources inside the TDC to whom she could call, and from whom she would get accurate answers.

Two days later she called back.

"You were right," she said quietly but firmly. "Hoffman was put in charge of planning the grant, selecting the reviewers and choosing the program for funding. That was unfair. I will try to get you an appointment with Dr. Archer, the Commissioner of Health, to discuss the matter."

It was not until August 28, 1998, that the SHRC finally got the formal notification letter stating they were not selected for funding. Treviño, who was upset about the entire review process by now, felt he could not wait any longer for Alen to set up the appointment with Archer.

He took matters into his own hands, sending Archer the first of several letters on August 31, 1998. Noteworthy excerpts from the first letter read as follow:

> ...The Texas Diabetes Council (TDC) must judge grant applications by the highest standards and fund those that demonstrate results based on effectiveness measures rather than funding projects based on personal

preferences. Despite the Bienestar being the only diabetes prevention program in the State of Texas to modify behavior and biological risk factors associated with diabetes, the TDC has preferred to misspend public money by funding a more costly and less effective school-based program (CATCH). Dr. Archer, give us the opportunity to meet with you so we can reveal other unfair grant review practices by TDC staff.

Treviño copied Dr. Philip Huang, TDH Chief Bureau of Chronic Disease Prevention and Control and a person also assigned to protect and promote the Texas CATCH program, and TDC board members Maria Alen, Judith Haley, Victor Gonzalez, Gene Bell, Stuart Fitts, Lawrence Harkless, Richard Hayley, and Tommy Fleming on this letter.

It was this letter, as well as Alen's request, that led to the September 1998 meeting with Archer described at the start of this chapter.

Despite the depressing outcome of that meeting (see page 15), in October 1998, Treviño sent Archer two letters inviting him to visit the San Antonio schools where the Bienestar program was being implemented. This would give Archer opportunities to observe first-hand the response and enthusiastic reception of children and teachers participating in the program.

The months went by, and Archer never responded to these invitations.

INVOLVING THE OPPOSING PARTY

Treviño is a dedicated and passionate man, so even though his overtures were being met with negative responses from Archer, he decided to preserve as best he could. It was critical that attention could be brought to the unfair reality that a potentially effective early-age diabetes prevention and education program was being denied an opportunity to compete fairly for funding. Treviño was determine to have Archer explain to elected officials how the state was going to address the increasing rates of type 2 diabetes among children of color living in poverty. The Republican Party controlled the politics of Texas, and seemingly were opposing the Bienestar program, so he decided to approach members of the opposing party.

In early September 1999, Treviño turned to Pancho Velasquez. Velasquez, a heavy-set man who sported a big Stetson hat and expensive western-style Lucchese boots, was well connected to the Democratic Party. Treviño planned to ask Velasquez to get state senators and representatives to influence Archer to open up to other school health programs. Treviño arranged to meet Velasquez for breakfast at Mi Tierra restaurant located in downtown San Antonio's historic Mercado district.

Velasquez was already aware of Archer's intention to keep the Bienestar program away from the school system, and at the breakfast, he assertively told Treviño, "If a group of Republicans restrain the Bienestar program, then a group of Democrats should relieve it."

"I sure hope so," Treviño said, somewhat despondently. *"Ya van tres cartas y dos llamadas al Archer y nada."* ("It has already been three letters and two phone calls to Archer and nothing.")

"A ese vato le vale madre," ("That guy don't give a shit,") Velasquez said, releasing a sarcastic smile.

"What did you think of the meeting with Leticia?" Treviño then asked Velasquez.

Treviño and Velasquez had met with State Senator Leticia Van de Putte (D-San Antonio) the week before hoping she could set up a meeting between them and Archer.

"She's a pharmacist," Velasquez responded quickly, "so she should see that there is something wrong with society when the sales of diabetes drugs are going up every month."

"I sent her, State Senator Frank Madla, and State Representative Robert Puente a letter to inform them about Archer's intention to exclude the Bienestar program from competing for state funding," Treviño said.

Both men were democrats from San Antonio.

"I also asked them to help us set up another meeting with Archer," Treviño continued. Treviño felt that if this time he walked into the meeting with Archer with elected state officials, who controlled Archer's budget, Archer might be more receptive to hear about other school health programs.

"I think Leticia's staff will get us an appointment with Archer," Velasquez said optimistically.

Two weeks later, Treviño received a response from Leticia. The state senator had come full circle—and was now requesting that Treviño be responsible for setting up the appointment himself.

Treviño tried again, but there was still no response from Archer.

In November 1999, Treviño sent Archer a report showing that the SHRC had conducted a screening for diabetes in Texas's Bexar County. They found that five percent of the children tested had undetected pre-diabetes condition (blood sugars above 100 mg/dl). These children were from poor families, and they needed immediate attention. An excerpt from Treviño's letter read:

> While in Bexar County the incidence of diabetes has increased by 9% per year for the last 8 years and the new cases of type 2 diabetes diagnosed in children has increased every year for the last 5 years, Texas Department of Health has done nothing to address this expanding health problem in Bexar county. On the contrary, the TDH has attempted to support a more expensive and less effective school-based program than the current Bienestar health program.

In this letter, Treviño asked Archer to develop a grant process where evidence-based diabetes programs could compete fairly for TDH funding. Treviño sent copies of this letter to the state senators and the state representatives from Bexar County. These recipients were: Frank Madla, Leticia Van de Putte, John Longoria, Robert Puente, Arthur Reyna, Judith Zaffirini, Leo Alvarado, Carlos Uresti, and Juan Solis. All were from the Democratic Party, and none responded to Treviño's letter.

However, a month later, Archer finally responded with a letter highlighting the original CATCH's behavioral achievements. He completely avoided mention of the fact that the Texas CATCH program had never lowered a blood sugar or any other biological marker.

Treviño responded to Archer's letter in January 2000 with his own. This letter read as follows:

> As you know, the Bienestar is the only school-based diabetes prevention program in the state shown to modify diabetes risk factors in low-income Mexican American children. The TDH, in turn, is supporting a scaled-down version of the CATCH cardiovascular prevention program that has not been tested for cost-effectiveness in South Texas populations. Although the "authentic" CATCH program showed limited individual benefits, regionally it may be ineffective because of its cultural irrelevance to South Texas children. The "authentic" CATCH was written for Minnesota children. Nonetheless the rational for TDH supporting the "modified" CATCH over Bienestar was because of "modified" CATCH's

cheaper cost per student ($1.07). Despite the TDH spending millions of dollars for unsuccessful diabetes control programs, it is beyond understanding how the "modified" CATCH will control diabetes with $1.07 per student. Could this be a misunderstanding?

In your letter it is mentioned that the "modified" CATCH would be implemented in San Antonio parochial and public schools. According to the TDH, these school districts were the San Antonio Independent School District and the Archdiocese Catholic Schools. For the TDH's information, neither the SAISD nor the Archdiocese is implementing the "modified" CATCH, and both school districts are committed to the Bienestar. Could this be misinformation?

Lastly is a question of how the TDH has appropriated funds for diabetes prevention programs. The San Antonio Diabetes Awareness and Education in the Community is an agency originally funded by TDH and now is receiving public funds to implement the "modified" CATCH program. The concern is that TDH funded an agency with an apparent exorbitant overhead (84%) and funded an agency without even a Bexar County school district in which to implement the "modified" CATCH. Could this be misappropriation?"

This letter was copied to the same state senators and representatives as those listed for Treviño's November 1999 letter.

When more than a month had passed with no response from Archer, Treviño sent a letter to thirteen Democrat and Republican state senators and representatives from Bexar County to complain about Archer's unfairness when it came to consideration of the Bienestar program for implementation in schools. They were: Frank Corte, Frank Madla, Leticia Van de Putte, Jeff Wentworth, Ken Mercer, John Longoria, Robert Puente, Elizabeth Ames Jones, Ruth McClendon, Arthur Reyna, Judith Zaffirini, Leo Alvarado, and Carlos Uresti. The letter started with these two paragraphs:

Diabetes in South Texas children is increasing and we (SHRC) implement an effective school-based diabetes prevention program. The Bienestar is a culturally relevant curriculum written for South Texas children and is the only behavior modification program in Texas shown to modify diabetes risk factors in low-income, predominately Mexican-American, children populations. Despite the Bienestar being the most effective and most culturally appropriate program for South Texas children, Dr. William Archer, Commissioner of Health, has tried to implement a scaled down CATCH (Child and Adolescent Trial on Cardiovascular) health program in South Texas schools. Although the original CATCH showed limited individual benefits, regionally it may be ineffective because of its lack of cultural irrelevance to South Texas children. The original CATCH was written for Minnesota children.

Dr. Archer is diligently devoted to expanding the Houston's UTSPH-sponsored CATCH program. This zealous effort may explain why the TDH staff's professional conduct may have bordered on unethical and unfair practices. In 1998, the CATCH and Bienestar competed for TDH's *Diabetes Education in the Elementary School (DEES)* grant. A conflict of interest may have occurred when Mr. Pete Hoffman was assigned to design the grant, and review and select applicants for the DEES grant. Mr. Hoffman is a TDH employee paid to implement the CATCH program in Texas schools, and it was to his best interest that TDH continued funding the CATCH program. Furthermore, while the grant review was in process, TDH staff from Region 8 in San Antonio visited school districts where the Bienestar was being implemented. In these school districts, TDH staff unfairly and unsuccessfully tried to convince school officials to adopt the CATCH over the Bienestar as their health program.

Twelve of the thirteen elected officials did not bother to question Archer's position. One, however, did stand up: Frank Madla, a senior state senator who took a strong stance on issues that affected his Southside constituents. The Southside consisted of mostly Mexican-American and poor residents.

Madla was a short man with a round face, and he spoke with a strong accent because of his Mexican upbringing. He wrote Archer the following letter:

• DR. ROBERTO P. TREVIÑO •

As you know, our office has been contacted by Dr. Treviño of San Antonio who operates Bienestar, a diabetes prevention and education program for elementary students in San Antonio. You and your staff have been very responsive to my requests for information and I greatly appreciate your efforts to provide Dr. Treviño with information on other grant opportunities and technical assistance to improve his grant proposal.

I understand that Dr. Treviño's program was originally funded under a waiver by the Department and that waivers no longer exist. Each program to receive funds for diabetes education and prevention must compete through a competitive grant process. I appreciate the importance of this process as the Department is responsible for providing every program with the opportunity to compete for funding.

As you know, the CATCH program was awarded funds through the Diabetes Education in the Elementary Schools (DEES) grant, over the Bienestar program. According to your staff, one of the major reasons for the selection of the CATCH program was a standardized curriculum and a statewide implementation schedule. I believe that the Department was looking to adopt a program that could provide effective services to the greatest number of children, and I support the grant award.

I am concerned though with the slow pace in which the program is being implemented in San Antonio. We currently are in the last half of the school year and the Districts in San Antonio have only recently been trained to implement the program. Hopefully implementation will start soon and this region will begin to see some benefits from the program. I am also concerned with the weak evaluation component of the grant. Your staff was very forthright in discussing with my staff that the CATCH program will need to improve several components of their grant especially in implementation and evaluation.

I write today to ask for your commitment to closely monitor the progress of these improvements, and to ask that if this program is not successfully implemented on a regionally consistent manner that you will see to it that in the regions where the CATCH program is weak, that other programs will have the opportunity to receive funds to supplement or substitute services.

I understand completely the value of standardization and the goals of implementing CATCH, however, I have learned that sometimes one size does not fit all. I hope that the Department and the Diabetes Council have the wisdom to support the growth of a successful system of diabetes prevention and education, and not just the expansion of a system developed for the sake of standardization.

Again, let me thank you, your staff, the Texas Diabetes Council and their staff for all of the hard work and consideration you have put into helping Texans with Diabetes and preventing the spread of disease. Please contact me should you have any questions.

Madla sent copies of his letter to Senators Leticia Van de Putte and Judith Zaffirini (D-Laredo), but at the time, after receipt of the letter, both senators decided to stay on the sidelines and not get involved.

Archer responded to Madla in a letter, saying that evaluation was measured by the number of trainings provided to school staff to implement the Texas CATCH. Yet these "trainings" were, in actuality, only *presentations* made by Houston's UTSPH's Peter Cribb and his staff, who traveled through the state using state money and political clout. These "trainings" were thereafter referred to in Cribb's, and other staff members' progress reports as, "schools adopting CATCH."

Archer never commented to Madla on the importance of a program being able to decrease blood glucose, cholesterol, or blood pressure, which at abnormal levels will kill children.

ARCHER TAKES HIMSELF OUT

Treviño found himself unable to understand why he kept getting stonewalled by Archer when it came to SHRC's diabetes education program. Over time though, it became apparent to him that perhaps Archer's reluctance to aid San Antonio's poor and Mexican-American population might be due less to the specifics of the Bienestar program and more to the fact that, internally, Archer possessed a strong bias against minority and poor populations.

This bias started to reveal itself when the *Houston Chronicle* reported in October 2000 events that occurred surrounding the firing of a TDH administrator.

Dr. Demetria Montgomery, an African-American, had a high-level administrative position with the TDH before she was fired by Archer. After her firing, Montgomery set up a meeting with Archer to discuss the demotion. She secretly recorded the conversation. Her tape recording revealed that Archer had strong opinions of, and perceptions about, people's race. Could this ultimately be tied to his irrational dislike for the Bienestar program?

For example, Archer said to Montgomery, among other things, that spiritual problems were the cause for her demotion; that because she was fair-skinned as a black woman, she got certain privileges in the white culture; and that she use her brains instead of her heart to advance her career, because that is how white people do it. He also made reference to lynching. These words were spoken in February 1998, although not made public at that time.

Archer's mouth and prejudicial beliefs did not stop there. In April 1998, the *New York Times* quoted him as saying: "Texas's high teen-age pregnancy rate is due to Hispanics lacking the belief that getting pregnant is a bad thing. If I… to go to a Hispanic community and say, 'Well, we need to get you into family planning,' they say, 'No, I want to be pregnant.'"

The same month, Archer was quoted in the *Austin American-Statement* as saying: "Society values pregnancies in teen-agers as bad, but certain communities within society may feel differently. I think the Hispanic community generally thinks that pregnancy is a positive thing. They tend to be less judgmental toward a teen-ager who's pregnant than the Anglo or African American communities."

After verbalizing these demeaning opinions, Archer was asked by some Texas legislators to attend cultural competency classes. Governor George W. Bush, nonetheless, continued supporting him despite these backward views.

Archer's 1998 opinions on teen pregnancy re-surfaced again in 2000 in the *San Antonio Express-News*. This time he was confronted by some Texas legislators and community leaders asking for his resignation. He ducked the firing by promising to attend cultural sensitivity classes.

After reading about Archer's opinion, Treviño asked his daughter Bianca, then fifteen years of age, what she thought of Dr. Archer's comments regarding teen pregnancy among Hispanics. Her simple response was, "He's crazy."

So Treviño continued to fight the good fight in the hopes of positively impacting the health outcomes for poor Texan and minority children. On October 3, 2000, he sent Archer an eighth letter. Some excerpts from that letter follow:

> ...We (SHRC) estimate that 15,000 Bexar County children have abnormal glucose levels and are not aware of it. These children, low-income minorities, will suffer from blindness, amputations, and dialysis in the near future if we do not intervene now.
>
> Although the rates of complications of diabetes in South Texas alone are higher than any other U. S. state and the cases of type 2 diabetes in children is growing, the Texas Department of Health has attempted to implement a program that is culturally inappropriate for minority children.
>
> Our center has responded to two TDH request for grant proposals, and both times have been denied. Earlier this year we applied for a National Institutes of Health grant and competed nationally against some of this country's best institutions. Last week the Bienestar, the same program your department rejected twice, received a high score and was awarded $2 million. There is no doubt that our center has an unparallel commitment to the problem of diabetes among low-income, high-risk children in Texas. However, we are highly concerned of your department's evident inadequacies in dealing with this issue. We urge you once again to reexamine your position and convene at the earliest time possible a meeting with our researchers, political, and civic leaders of the Latino and African American community.

Copies were sent to the following state senators and representatives: Frank Madla, Leticia Van de Putte, John Longoria, Robert Puente, Arthur Reyna, Irma Rangel, Elliot Naishtat, Royce West, Eduardo Lucio, Yvonne Davis, Mario Gallegos, Juan Hinojosa, Carlos Truan, Judith Zaffirini, Mike Villarreal, Carlos Uresti, Leo Alvarado, Ruth Jones McClendon, Garnett Coleman, Rod Ellis, Gonzalo Barrientos, Henry Cuellar, Roberto Gutierrez, and Vilma Luna.

Soon after the sending of Treviño's letter, Archer's biased, unfair opinions of people based upon ethnicity or gender started to work against him. On October 16th, 2000, the *Houston Chronicle* reported on Archer's February 1998 meeting (page 32) with Montgomery, publishing the racial slurs he had uttered at that moment for the first time. Archer was put on leave; on October 23rd he resigned.

The morning the news broke out about Archer's resignation, the SHRC staff began gathering together in one of their buildings. It was a relief for everyone to know that state capitol matters would not be interfering with their daily work in the schools. The staff began shaking hands, and giving high fives.

Linda Edwards, a Bush spokeswomen, would say these words about Archer's resignation, "The governor appreciates Dr. Archer's steadfast commitment to quality health care…Gov. Bush thanks Dr. Archer for his dedicated service to the people of Texas."

To this day, Archer's picture still hangs on the entrance hallway of the Department of State Health Services (formerly TDH). Underneath the picture is a brief honorable description of him.

Chapter 3

STATE CONTROL TURNS FEDERAL

Dr. Charles Bell, the number two person at the TDH, was appointed Acting Commissioner after Archer's resignation.

Bell was African-American, robust and always had a smile on his face. He was the complete opposite of Archer. He listened to what others had to say with an open mind, and was courteous and soft-spoken.

Treviño, who had met Bell at a TDH meeting prior to his appointment, had already had positive exchanges with him. So he was able to swiftly set up a meeting with him in November 2000. The topics were to be: accountability and diversity of school health programs.

A SHUT DOOR OPENS
The day was chilly but sunny when Treviño walked into the main TDH building. Walking into those buildings when Archer was Commissioner had triggered in Treviño an increased heart rate, and a rapid breathing reflex. But now that Archer was gone, the physiologic response was gone too.

Treviño entered the conference room where he was greeted cordially by Bell and two other TDH staff members.

"Good morning, Dr. Bell," Treviño began. "Thanks for giving me this opportunity to meet with you."

"Good morning, Dr. Treviño," Bell replied pleasantly, "What can we do for you?"

Because of his prior exchanges with Bell, and his belief in the man's inherent goodness, Treviño decided to give Bell the benefit of the doubt.

"You may or may not know this but we were treated unfairly by the Texas Department of Health when Archer was the Commissioner.

So the reason we are here today is to ask that the Texas Department of Health be inclusive in their selection of school health programs. We believe that by including us and other school health programs out there, we can more effectively control the problem of type 2 diabetes and obesity among youth."

"We value early-age interventions, and your program has shown positive results," Bell responded in a serene tone of voice. "There is no reason for the Texas Department of Health to exclude a good program like yours."

At these words, Treviño visibly relaxed. He smiled as he pointed out, "It's not just my program, Dr. Bell. This is the work of many people and institutions working together unselfishly to raise healthier children. I think that the key to designing a successful program is collaboration. We need to work closely with the Texas Department of Health and other institutions to make sure our children are receiving the best programs available."

"We are on the same page there," Bell responded with a grin.

"As you know, the original CATCH program was a hallmark study that set the foundation for other school health programs," Treviño went on. "Although it was a colossal undertaking, it had its own share of shortcomings."

"To my knowledge, it has changed some health behaviors, and positively impacted the offerings of PE classes and the food in some cafeteria environments. These are some accomplishments, are they not?" Bell queried, although he obviously expected an agreeable response from Treviño to be forthcoming.

"I agree, Dr. Bell, but as physicians we cannot be satisfied with giving a patient with diabetes a questionnaire and assuming that because they answered it correctly that their disease is controlled," Treviño pointed out.

It was very important to Treviño that Bell understand this point and agree with it, as this had been one of the main problems in terms of the Texas CATCH program.

"We need to measure physical or biological values, and demonstrate that these were improved upon," Treviño elaborated. "Measuring and evaluating improvements based upon answers to self-reported questionnaires is not sufficient. This does not offer clinical evidence that a disease has been controlled."

"No doubt, the CATCH program had no effect on biological markers," said Bell smoothly. "But regardless of the results of one program or another, I believe that the science of school health programs is in its early stages and there is no perfect program out there."

And then he said directly, as he met Treviño's eyes, "The Texas Department of Health should not be pruning programs from the school to protect one program."

"That is what we at SHRC ask: to let the programs themselves show their results, and to let the schools make choices based upon the results," responded Treviño. "I think competition among programs is good, and it will encourage us all to produce better curriculums."

"In that system, children will be the winners at the end," Bell added. "We at the TDH are with you," Bell assured Treviño.

With this matter seemingly settled, Treviño moved onto the other issue at the forefront of his mind.

"The other concern I have, Dr. Bell, is that the Texas CATCH program may not be culturally or medically appropriate for South Texas children. The Texas CATCH program was developed as a cardiovascular prevention program and it is not bilingual. In south Texas, diabetes is affecting children, and many of these children are Spanish-speaking."

Bell looked up at the ceiling before he regarded Treviño with a steady gaze.

"I will look into forming a review panel to evaluate the Texas CATCH program for cultural appropriateness," he promised.

To make sure that Bell fully understood the necessity of this, Treviño decided to make his point hit a little closer to home. "Also, I don't know if you know this, Dr. Bell, but African-American children in the original CATCH program were more likely to drop out and increase their blood pressure and body fat than African American children who were not in the program. So these might be indications that in health behavioral interventions, one size does not fit all."

At Treviño's words, Bell's eyes widened, and he appeared visibly startled. "No, I didn't know that," Bell responded.

The two men exchanged a few more words before Treviño left, reassured that Bell had made a commitment to open up the process to other more culturally appropriate programs.

MORE GOOD NEWS

The furor over Archer's racial slur remarks continued. State Senator Frank Madla, who was still upset over Archer's racial remarks, obviously had made a personal commitment that he was not going to let the Texas CATCH program be the only game in the state. He sent Bell, as Acting Commissioner of the TDH, the following letter in November 2000:

• DR. ROBERTO P. TREVIÑO •

Over the past year I have been monitoring the Department's implementation of the grant received by the Coordinated Approach to Child Health (CATCH) diabetes prevention and education program. I have expressed concerns that the CATCH program may not provide culturally appropriate information to students in Bexar County and South Texas. Additionally, I have concerns with the timeline for the CATCH program's implementation.

At this point I request an update on the progress of the implementation of the CATCH grant, specifically in Bexar County. How many children are receiving CATCH services? How many school districts are participating in CATCH? What is the current funding status of the CATCH grant? More importantly, however, I am concerned that the CATCH program cannot provide the culturally appropriate information that will make the program's efforts successful in areas with high minority populations. I am aware that the Department is conducting an evaluation of educational material for cultural relevance. I understand that the Department, by implementing CATCH, is attempting to develop a statewide and consistent approach to diabetes education and prevention. However, the needs of persons, especially children, who are at risk for diabetes are not consistent statewide. I believe that continuing to fund programs that cannot effectively take into consideration the important differences between demographic groups would be irresponsible.

I thank you in advance for your efforts on this matter. I hope that I can count on you and the Department to continue to examine this important grant to ensure that CATCH is meeting all of our children's needs. Please contact me should you have any questions or require any additional information on this issue. I look forward to meeting you and working with you during the upcoming legislative session.

The TDH would be unable to answer the questions of how many students and school districts were truly receiving the Texas CATCH program, because the Texas CATCH program measured encounters simply by the name and school district of the individual who signed up to attend any of their presentations. But for the question of cultural appropriateness, Bell asked a panel of reviewers to evaluate the Texas CATCH program for cultural competence.

After a two-day review, the recommendations came back and they were not good for the CTN people. The recommendations from reviewers were the following:

1) Encourage greater community participation in the implementation of the program,
2) Establish guidelines for community partnerships, such as diabetes education and intervention programs,
3) Strengthen the CATCH program by explicitly addressing community concerns, i.e., diabetes in minority populations,
4) Disseminate best practice and address cultural competency issues at training of school districts to ensure activities are culturally appropriate, and
5) Continue to include minority researchers in program-design modification and evaluation to ensure cultural aspects are addressed.

In December 2000, the TDH gave the SHRC $50,000 to collect physical measures on children and demonstrate the effectiveness of the Bienestar program. At last, the TDH had shifted from murky and exclusive practices to ones of transparency and inclusiveness.

This, however, would not last. While in November of 2000 the Texas CATCH program was evaluated for cultural appropriateness and found to be lacking; and in December of 2000 the TDH provided SHRC with $50,000 in funding, this attempt at transparency and inclusiveness was to last for only two months.

MISLEADING INFORMATION

George W. Bush, formerly Governor of Texas, got elected President of the United States in November of 2000, and as soon as January 2001, TDH Acting Commissioner Bell, received a letter from Dr. James S. Marks, Director of the Centers for Disease Control and Prevention (CDC). The CDC Director responds to the U.S. Secretary of Health, and the U.S. Secretary of Health responds to the President of the United States. A tie between the U.S. Secretary of Health and CTN people is presented later in page 78.

The letter Bell received from Marks read as follows:

> I am writing to applaud the efforts of the Texas Department of Health and the Texas Diabetes Council to support the dissemination of the Coordinated Approach to Child Health (CATCH) in Texas. The Centers for Disease Control and Prevention (CDC) is providing funding for studying the diffusion of the CATCH program as part of its Prevention Research Center program to the University of Texas Health Science Center at Houston, School of Public Health, Center for Health Promotion and Prevention Research. We feel strongly that CATCH is very important for the prevention of chronic diseases such as cardiovascular disease, cancer, and diabetes because of the program's positive impact on children's physical activity and healthy eating.
>
> The nation and CDC are eager to learn from the Texas experience on how to effectively disseminate coordinated school health programs such as CATCH. CATCH is one of the few elementary school programs of proven efficacy that closely meets many of the CDC Guidelines for School Health. CATCH exemplifies model implementation of one of the recommended strategies outlined in the upcoming report on physical activity of the U.S. Community Preventive Services Task Force. We anticipate the Texas model of dissemination will spread to other regions of the country and significantly impact many children, ultimately reducing the burden of chronic disease.
>
> On behalf of CDC, I wish the state of Texas continued success in the dissemination of this important child health program.

When Treviño saw this letter, he was shocked. Through this letter, he believed the CDC was providing misleading information, and in so doing, protecting the Texas CATCH program from competition.

Specifically, Marks mentioned in the letter the "positive impact" the Texas CATCH program had on children's physical activity. Well, the investigators of the original CATCH program measured physical activity by two methods: A questionnaire and a fitness test. A questionnaire is unreliable, because the questionnaire measures self-reported perceptions, while a fitness test is exact, because it measures exercise physiology. The original CATCH program showed improvement in terms of *only* the questionnaire; there was **no improvement found as a result of the fitness test.**

It perplexed Treviño that a noteworthy and esteemed medical professional by background such as the Director of the CDC would place more value on self-reported information than on physiologic results.

Along the same lines, Treviño believed that for the CDC to promote a program that attempts to prevent cardiovascular disease and diabetes, but has *never* decreased blood pressure, cholesterol, or blood sugar is analogous to a pharmaceutical company selling an experimental drug to treat the same conditions, but which has never been shown to decrease blood pressure, cholesterol, or blood sugar. A drug without effects is called a placebo—and this is what the CDC was proposing to shove down the throats of children of color and those living in poverty.

EVERYONE PAYS

It is not only the families of children of color and those living in poverty that are being affected by such positions as that which the CDC was taking. Taxpayers everywhere are paying as a result of such opinions. Taxpayers end up paying unnecessarily for expensive medical treatments—treatments that could have been prevented, if the proper health awareness and educational programs were started at an early age in life.

The Diabetes Prevention Program was the largest National Institutes of Health funded research to study the effects of lifestyle changes and drug treatments to prevent type 2 diabetes among high-risk adults. The lifestyle program, when compared to drug treatment, was twice more effective in preventing type 2 diabetes and saved taxpayers $10,000 more for each case of type 2 diabetes that was prevented. So why doesn't society invest in prevention? Because the lobbying of the health care industry is too powerful! On October 28th, 2008, a Fox Network reported that according to the *Archives of Internal Medicine,* our spending on diabetes drugs nearly doubled from $6.7 billion to $12.5 billion between 2001 and 2007.

The Texas Health and Human Services Commission is an agency responsible for managing the state's Medicaid and Children Health Insurance Plan (CHIP) programs. The cost of providing medical care is so taxing that it is pulling the Texas Health and Human Services Commission into bankruptcy. To simply stay afloat, the agency had to pull an Enron-like accounting maneuver in 2002 (see letter that follows that briefly describes the plan) to pay off the huge medical costs that lay before it.

To point out the problems with such a maneuver, as well as the fact that there should not be a need for it, Treviño sent Don Gilbert, the Texas Health and Human Services Commissioner, the following letter in July 2002:

> The step proposed by [the] Health and Human Services Commission to restore the $200 million shortfall is to restructure administrators, hospital and pharmaceutical payments. These are short term-fixes that do nothing to the increasing rates of disease in low-income populations. In some Texas counties, diabetes is increasing at a rate of nine percent per year. Diabetes is the major cause for blindness, amputations, heart disease, strokes, and renal disease. In Texas, 2,000 patients are added every year to the large list of patients already on dialysis. The annual cost for treating a diabetic patient and a hemodialysis patient is $10,071 and $60,000, respectively. Our NIH-sponsored study shows that this problem will get worse. In Bexar County alone, there are an estimated 5,000 low-income children with undiagnosed (adult) type 2 diabetes. Once they enter the health care system, they will add another $50 million cost a year.
>
> Restructuring payments without decreasing disease is analogous to a business improving profits by shifting short-term costs to long-term debt without increasing revenue. This scheme has proven to be catastrophic for U.S. companies. The better solution is to decrease disease. This is being done in a school-based diabetes prevention program. The Bienestar has [been] shown to prevent diabetes risk in children and has [been] shown to reverse high blood glucose in diabetic children. Children in this program have learned to eat less fatty food, to eat more dietary fiber, and to be more active (physically). High [saturated] fat diet, low fiber diet and sedentary lifestyles are ninety-one percent of the cause for the $200 million shortfall (*N Eng J Med*, 2001;345:790).

This trend of focusing on the end effect and not addressing and preventing the cause would only continue. Of the $14 billion the Texas Health and Human Services Commission and Texas Department of Health would spend in 2007, a little over $13 billion was used to treat disease. Only $7 million (.0005%) would be spent on preventing it. It is distressing to promote health when profits are tied to disease.

INTERNAL INADEQUACIES, UNFAIR RESOLUTION

The CDC continued performing acts that appeared to hold back a physically-effective health care program from being disseminated throughout the Texas school system. In terms of scientific research, *efficacy* is the study that shows if a program can produce positive results in a controlled environment when implemented by research staff, and *effectiveness* is the study that shows if an efficacious program can reproduce its results in the "real world" when implemented by lay people. In April 2002, in response to a CDC grant announcement, staff from the SHRC, and many other agencies, submitted proposals to the CDC to study effectiveness of community-based prevention programs. SHRC wanted to study what school organizational factors (e.g. school district structure; school administrative staff commitment; teacher education, experience, and pay; and program effects and cost) predicted the possibility of the Bienestar program being sustained and institutionalized in the schools.

The grant was submitted by staff of the SHRC and afterwards Treviño received a letter from the CDC, on August 22, 2002, that surprised him. The letter was signed by a CDC staff named Elmira C. Benson, and her title was Team Leader, Section IV. Following is the first paragraph of the letter:

> Your application submitted in response to the Centers for Disease Control and Prevention "Grants for Community-based Participatory Prevention Research" (Announcement #02003) has been reviewed by the Special Emphasis Panel (SEP), a federally chartered study section. At that review meeting, the reviewers determined as part of a triage process that your application would not be competitive for possible funding with other applications reviewed at the meeting. Consequently, as stated under "Evaluation Criteria" in the announcement, we have withdrawn your application from further consideration. A priority score has not been voted for the

application and a formal Summary Statement will not be prepared. However, I am sending you the reviewers' comments, essentially unedited.

A panel of CDC reviewers had excluded the SHRC proposal from competing. Since the reasons provided were not clear, Treviño called Dr. Mary L. Lerchen, Scientific Review Administrator with the CDC.

"Hello, Dr. Lerchen, I'm Dr. Roberto Treviño with the Social and Health Research Center. We recently submitted a proposal in reply to a CDC grant announcement. We were surprised to hear that our grant was removed from the competition. I'm calling to get an explanation…?"

"Yes, Dr. Treviño, I have heard good things about your program," Lerchen responded cordially. "Can you tell me a little about your grant proposal, and what happened?"

"Our grant proposal is to implement a bilingual diabetes prevention program in the schools, and for no reason, we received notice that our grant was being pulled from the review process," Treviño said in a controlled and courteous manner. "We suspect that the reviewers did not read our grant well. Could you please review our grant, and the critiques given by the reviewers? We want to know if what was done was fair."

The following day, Lerchen called Treviño back.

"You are right! The concerns one reviewer had were really addressed in the grant. He must not have been thorough in his review."

At this news, Treviño wanted to leap out of his chair in frustration, but instead he forced himself to stay calm. He took a deep breath before he spoke.

"Dr. Lerchen, could you take this information to your superiors, and ask them if we can be given a chance to compete in this grant?"

"No, I'm afraid that is not possible," Lerchen objected.

"Why not?" Treviño reacted this time by raising his voice. "It's not fair that we get pulled out of the competition when our grant was not even read correctly."

It was a moment before Lerchen tried to offer an explanation.

"I can understand your concern, but you need to understand on that day we could not find a Scientific Review Administrator, and we selected someone who did not officially hold that position," Lerchen said, seemingly unaware that she was imparting the CDC's internal inadequacies to a non-staff member.

Treviño wanted to explode in frustration when he heard this news, but he held back so he could cull as much information from Lerchen as possible.

"We had a hard time getting a secretary and support staff to help us process the initial administrative steps of the grant," Lerchen naively informed him. "And to make it worse, we had a large number of grant submittals, and not enough qualified reviewers to help us score the new grants. Everything just went wrong," she confided.

"Dr. Lerchen, that is not acceptable," Treviño said, politely but firmly. He got up from his chair, and clenching the phone tightly in his hand, started pacing back and forth in his office. "It's upsetting to know that we have children who will go blind, lose limbs, and be on dialysis, and the CDC is muddling these grant applications. I need a better answer."

Treviño's words must have made an impact, because Lerchen's tone sounded somewhat nervous when she offered a response.

"Okay, Dr. Treviño, I will make sure that the reviewers who participated in the present grant announcement are not invited back to participate."

"How is that going to help the present situation?" Treviño demanded. That surely was a good solution for future grant processes, but certainly not for their current situation.

"I'm sorry, Dr. Treviño but there is nothing else I can do," was Lerchen's only response.

"Well, that is not fair. Not only will I be writing about what has happened here to Dr. James Marks, but I'll also be asking our congressmen to get in touch too."

With these words, Treviño hung up the phone. And as he had promised, he asked Congressman Charles A. Gonzalez to write to Marks, the Director of the CDC, and ask for a better explanation.

Gonzalez wrote Marks the following letter on October 3, 2002:

> I am writing this letter on behalf of the Social and Health Research Center in San Antonio, Texas to ask you reconsider their grant proposal for their Bienestar Program. Earlier this year, the Social and Health Research Center submitted a grant application to the Centers for Disease Control (CDC) for the Community-Based Participatory Prevention Research Program. Based on the reviewers' comments, their application was determined to be "non-competitive" for possible funding.
>
> The Bienestar Program is a school-based diabetes prevention program that has [been] shown to reverse

hyperglycemia in diabetic children. This program has been in operation for six years and is aimed at fourth-grade students from schools located in low-income neighborhoods. The Bienestar Program has been recognized by the World Health Organization and the American College of Nutrition for developing a cost-effective model for controlling diabetes in Bexar County.

Once again, I am writing on behalf of the Social and Health Research Center in efforts to persuade you to reconsider their grant proposal. If you have any questions regarding this letter, please do not hesitate to contact me.

Treviño also wrote to Marks and Dr. Frank Vinicor (CDC's former Diabetes Program Director) in October 2002, to protest the unfair review process. Neither responded to his letters.

CHRONIC UNFAIRNESS FROM THE CDC

The SHRC has two buildings, one for the creation and running of the programs, and one for the evaluation of the programs. These turn-of-the-century buildings are situated back to back, with one facing South Presa Street and the other facing South St. Mary's Street. They are located in an inner city, socially deprived neighborhood.

Across the street on South Presa is the Taco Haven restaurant, a site frequented by elected officials.

One day in December 2002, Treviño serendipitously spied U.S. congressman Ciro Rodriguez walking out of the restaurant. Both men had met before, and Rodriguez was aware of the work the SHRC was doing in the schools. The congressman was the best kind of politician: an individual who stayed close to the constituents he represented. He was known to not be influenced by special interest groups.

Treviño ran across the street to greet and invite Rodriguez to tour the SHRC buildings.

"Ciro, do you have time to come visit our center?" asked Treviño. He was breathing hard from chasing Rodriguez down.

"*Hey, Roberto, como estas?*" ("Hey, Roberto, how are you doing?") said Rodriguez with enthusiasm.

"*Muy bien. Tienes unos minutitos? Nada mas quiero presentarte a el personal que a hecho el Bienestar un exito.* (Very well. Do you have a few minutes? I just want to introduce you to the Bienestar staff that has made our program a success.) They would be very impressed to have a congressman come and visit them."

"*Claro que si, vamos*," ("Yes, of course, let's go,") Rodriguez replied as two men walked across the street to the Program building.

The staff of the SHRC was happy to meet the congressman, and showed him Bienestar's educational material. An educator himself, Rodriguez was especially appreciative of the children's colorful, bilingual health textbooks.

The two men then walked over to the Evaluation building, and the SHRC's statistician showed the congressman the program's most recent publications.

After introducing Rodriguez to more staff members and their work, Treviño invited him into his office.

"You have a great organization, and fabulous people working here. You must be thrilled," commented Rodriguez, as he surveyed the room, with its old dark pine floors and rustic orange cedar walls and ceiling.

At these words, Treviño grimaced slightly.

"Not everything is as great as it looks, Ciro."

Rodriguez's face changed drastically, and he asked, in obvious astonishment, "What do you mean?"

Treviño pulled out the letter the CDC Director had sent to Bell, and passed it along.

Rodriguez's face looked surprised, and then upset, as he read along. As soon as he finished reading the letter, he pulled out his cellular phone and called an aide at his office.

"Can you get me the phone number for Dr. James Marks? He's the Director of the CDC. I need it immediately."

Minutes later, someone called back with the number. Rodriguez asked if he could borrow Treviño's phone, and he dialed directly into the Director's office. Within a minute, Marks got on the phone.

Treviño listened carefully to the two men's conversation, as Rodriguez had put it on speaker phone.

"Good afternoon, Dr. Marks. How are you doing?"

"Fine," answered Marks warmly.

"I'm here with Dr. Roberto Treviño, the founder of the Bienestar health program. I'm sure you are aware of the new cases of Mexican-American children being diagnosed with type 2 diabetes. But I'm not sure if you are aware of Bienestar health program. This program is bilingual and has been shown to reduce blood sugars."

"Yes, sir, I'm aware of the program," Marks responded crisply.

"Well, I'm hoping your staff can look into this program with more detail."

"The CDC is always looking for effective and innovative health programs. We would be glad to look more into the Bienestar."

"I will have Dr. Treviño send you copies of their textbooks and their studies."

Rodriguez kept the conversation positive, and did not bring up the letter or the bad experience Treviño had had with the CDC grant reviewers.

"Yes, sir, please have him send them directly to me," Marks responded affirmatively.

Treviño immediately sent Marks a copy of the health textbooks and the publications. Yet he never heard back from him or anyone else at the CDC in response to the conversation or the program materials.

ENTER THE DRAGON

In October 2002, the Texas CATCH had just been selected as the only coordinated school health program approved by the TEA to operate in Texas public schools.

A month later, Treviño received a newsletter from the *Women's Policy, Inc* (Volume 8, No. 15) stating that, "The CDC will fund 20 state educational agencies through the Coordinated School Health Program, which reaches elementary and secondary school students and aims to increase physical activity and improve nutrition." Two-hundred million dollars had been appropriated for this operation, and in Texas, the CTN was the sole vendor.

When he heard about these funds, Treviño began writing letters, sending e-mails, and making requests at scientific meetings of the CDC's Diabetes Program Director, Frank Vinicor. Treviño continued this pursuit of Vinicor for two years because Vinicor was the CDC's highest authority on diabetes, and the CDC was supporting Texas youth at-risk for type 2 diabetes with a program—Texas CATCH—that had no evidence of lowering blood sugars. Lowering blood sugars is the only method known to stop blindness, amputations, and dialysis in youth at-risk for diabetes.

With each interaction, Treviño would make the same simple request of the CDC's Diabetes Program Director: "Please give us an opportunity to present Bienestar program's scientific results to high-level health officials at the CDC."

Finally, on January 20, 2005, Treviño received an e-mail from Mary Vernon-Smiley, MD, MPH. She was the Senior Medical Officer with the CDC's Division of Adolescent and School Health in Atlanta,

Georgia. The e-mail read as follow:

> Your article, *"Impact of the Bienestar School-Based Diabetes Mellitus Prevention Program on Fasting Capillary Glucose Levels"* has received a lot of recognition in our Division of Adolescent and School Health. We are very interested in your work and would love for you to come to the CDC and do a presentation regarding your research in schools. I am sending this e-mail to ask if you might be available in the near future to present your work at the CDC. Of course, we would be responsible for your travel expenses.
> If you are interested, please give me a call so we may discuss when you might be available. I look forward to hearing from you.

An ecstatic Treviño called Vernon-Smiley the following day.

"Is Dr. Vernon-Smiley in?" he inquired.

"This is she, how can I help you." The person at the other end of the phone responded.

"This is Dr. Treviño. I am responding to the e-mail you sent yesterday," he explained.

"Oh, Dr. Treviño, how happy we are to hear from you so soon." The voice changed completely, from an uninspired one to one with a more welcoming tone. "We have heard so much about your programs, and we want to invite you to speak to our staff here at the Centers for Disease Control and Prevention."

Treviño could not believe what he was hearing.

"Of course," he answered immediately. "It would be an honor to present results from our studies to the staff at the CDC."

"We can make the arrangements for your flight and hotel. You just need to tell us when you can come."

They exchanged some dates and topics for the presentation, and then Treviño made a second request of Vernon-Smiley.

"Dr. Vernon-Smiley, is it possible for the CDC to sponsor a researcher named Dr. Zenong Yin so that he can come and present his results for the FitKid study? He and Dr. Bernard Gutin, who at the time were both from the Medical College of Georgia, have developed an outstanding school health program that is showing to decrease body fat in children. I think the staff at the CDC can get a better understanding of school health interventions if we present two school health programs, both of which have evidence of either decreasing body fat or blood glucose in high-risk youth."

"That sounds like it would be a great presentation," Vernon-Smiley answered. "But let me check with my supervisors to see if we can cover the expenses for both of you to travel to Atlanta."

As soon as Treviño hung up with Vernon-Smiley, he called Yin. Yin was a professor of Health and Kinesiology at the University of Texas at San Antonio and a consultant with the SHRC. Prior to this position, Yin had been at the Medical College of Georgia in Augusta, Georgia, where he and Gutin had designed the successful FitKid school health program.

"Hey, Z, I just got off the phone with the CDC, and guess what?"

Without giving Yin a chance to answer, an enthusiastic Treviño rushed on. "They invited me to present the Bienestar program to high-level CDC health officials."

"That is so interesting," Yin said, surprised. "How did you get that invitation?"

"I had been on Frank Vinicor for years to let us go in and present to the CDC Directors of either Diabetes or School Health Departments," Treviño answered. "Remember? You were there at one of these meetings. It was in Washington, D.C., at the Translational Research meeting. I went up to him and requested that the CDC be more open to multiple programs. His response then was, 'It is beyond my control' but I didn't give up. And now the reason I called you," Treviño said, changing topics, "is because I also asked them to invite you to present."

"It took you two years to get you invited, and now you asked them to invite me too?" Yin laughed.

"You have a lot of experience and knowledge from implementing the FitKid school health program, Z. Plus, you have positive results, so they should know about your program too. What do you think? Can you go present with me?"

"If they sponsor it, I'll go."

"She sounded very positive," Treviño assured Yin.

Indeed, the CDC agreed to invite Yin, and the date for the presentation was set for Thursday, February 10, 2005 at eleven in the morning.

Right before 11:00 on that date, Treviño and Yin walked into the main lobby of the large CDC building located in a wooded suburb of Atlanta.

The two men walked over to the security desk to ask for Vernon-Smiley. She was called, and came down to the lobby to greet the two men. She was very friendly, and smiling. She was African-American, and on the way to the conference call, she started asking many questions about the work the SHRC was conducting with African-American children.

She led the two men down a floor to a small conference room. When the talk began, there were about twenty-two people in the audience. They heard the talk, they ate their lunch during the presentation, and when the talk was over, they simply got up and walked out the door. Treviño and Yin just looked at each other. They were hoping to meet with department directors but none showed up to the talk.

"Where are the high-level CDC health officials?" Yin asked, joking.

Treviño was determined to find an answer for that question. He went up to Vernon-Smiley, and after she praised him and he thanked her, he asked, "We know that the CDC is providing millions of dollars to the educational agencies of twenty states to implement coordinated school health programs. Do you know who we could talk to about being able to compete for those funds?"

Vernon-Smiley's smile faded. "I really…don't know, Dr. Treviño," she said in a serious tone of voice, a little surprised by the question. "I can provide you with the web site where the CDC makes their grants announcements. I know that the CDC has frequent announcements for school- and community-based health interventions. Yours would fit very well with those proposals."

Vernon-Smiley was well-intentioned and accommodating, but the responses to the questions must have been located on floors way above hers.

"Thank you," said Treviño as he reminded her that they also had an appointment with Li Yan Wang.

Yin had planned a visit with his friend, Li Yan Wang, at the CDC. She was a health economist with the Division of Adolescent and School Health.

Treviño and Yin walked up three floors to visit Wang. Wang stood nearly six feet tall, but her greater stature was in her scientific achievements. She had published a paper in the 2003 issue of *Obesity Research* journal showing that society could save $15,887 in medical care costs and $25,104 in loss of productivity costs (per child per year) if obesity was prevented at an early age in life. If left untreated, obese youth will suffer from higher rates of chronic disease and greater loss of time from work once they become adults.

After they greeted each other, Yin and Wang exchanged some phrases in Mandarin until they seemed to have come to some sort of an agreement. Then Wang turned to look at Treviño and said, "I will call Dr. Howell Wechsler to see if he can meet with you right now."

Treviño's eyes widened; his heart started to pound. Wechsler was the Acting Director of the Division of Adolescent and School Health. By meeting him, Treviño would be getting closer to the people who could open doors at the CDC.

Wang managed to get Treviño the appointment, and she walked him to Wechsler's office.

At Wechsler's office was a receptionist who brought Treviño through a conference room and into Wechsler's office. He was of tan skin and dark curly hair.

Wechsler immediately got off his chair, and stretched his hand out to greet Treviño.

"Dr. Treviño, it is an honor to have you here at the CDC. We have heard a lot about the work you are doing in the Mexican-American community. We would like to learn from you to see how we can work in those communities," said the Director.

"The honor is mine, Dr. Wechsler," Treviño responded before he went right at it. "I would love to work more closely with the CDC. We just presented downstairs the results from our new randomized control trial study. Briefly, this study showed that at the end of the school year, the 700 students who participated in the Bienestar program had lower blood glucose levels than a similar number of students who did not participate in the Bienestar program."

"That is amazing," Wechsler responded.

"The program is not perfect, but it is producing promising results," Treviño added. "How can we get the CDC to support it?"

Wechsler got off his chair, and invited Treviño into the conference room next door. There he pulled out a two-inch ringed notebook with the label, *School Health Index,* and put it on the conference table.

"Dr. Treviño, right now we are very busy trying to disseminate the *School Health Index*. This material is mostly questionnaires. If school staff and students invest a small amount of time filling them out, it could help them identify the weaknesses in their school health environment. And it could help them identify simple steps to create a healthier school."

"Questionnaires are important for self-assessment purposes," Treviño replied carefully, "but these alone are not going to lower blood glucose or stop people from going blind. These students need evidence-based programs."

"Well, I think the CDC is doing that too. It is following closely the implementation of the CATCH program in Texas. We hear that the diffusion of the CATCH program is going well."

"Well, it depends on who you hear it from," Treviño retorted. "Teachers at San Antonio's Northside School District say the Texas CATCH binders sit on the shelves, and teachers at El Paso's Ysleta School District have not even heard of the Texas CATCH."

Wechsler looked down at the notebook and then looked up at Treviño. "Well, there is no perfect program out there."

"Exactly!" said Treviño quickly. "Because there is no perfect program out there, the CDC should not be protecting the Texas CATCH program, and excluding other school health programs."

"The CDC does not protect any one program—"

"I have a letter that says it does!" Treviño interrupted. "In December 2000, the Texas Department of Health was willing to open up the door to other school health programs, but then Dr. James Marks sent Dr. Charles Bell, the Acting Commissioner of the Texas Department of Health, a letter (page 40) basically telling him to implement just the Texas CATCH program."

Wechsler made a frown, pursed his lips, and gave Treviño a long stare.

"I don't believe it," Wechsler finally responded.

"I'll fax you the letter as soon as I get back to San Antonio," Treviño said firmly.

Treviño faxed Wechsler the letter a week later.

Wechsler never contacted Treviño again after receipt of the letter and Treviño never heard from Vernon-Smiley about program adoptions.

POOR EXCUSE

In fact, it would take two years before Treviño would hear from anyone directly at the CDC. At this time, in April 2007, Dr. Holly Wethington, a research fellow with the CDC, called Treviño to inquire about the new study the SHRC had just published.

The study was about NEEMA, the program designed for African-American children. Dr. Mary Shaw-Ridley and other African-American researchers had translated the Bienestar program to the African American culture and experience. The study showed that African American children who participated in the NEEMA program decreased their blood sugars significantly between the start and the end of the school year.

"Hi, Dr. Treviño, I'm Holly Wethington with the CDC. I was doing a literature search and I ran across the NEEMA program. I read the NEEMA paper that came out this month in the *Journal of the National*

Medical Association. I was very impressed with the results. I would like to take this back to the CDC and see if we can do a pilot study with your program," she said sincerely.

"Of course," Treviño said, happy to hear the suggestion. "If it's okay with you, can we get Dr. Mary Shaw-Ridley and Charlotte Horner in on a conference call? They're the investigators behind this program."

"Sure," Wethington said, and both agreed on a date for the conference call.

When the time came, Shaw-Ridley and Horner joined in on the conference call. Both researchers presented the NEEMA with such vitality and convincing information that Wethington expressed her belief the CDC would surely support the program. This was, she said, because she was aware of no other school health program lowering blood sugars in African-American children.

Yet four months would pass without Treviño hearing again from Wethington.

One day, Shaw-Ridley phoned Treviño.

"Dr. T, have you heard from Dr. Wethington?" she inquired.

"Not a word," Treviño answered.

"She sounded real impressed with the NEEMA program," Shaw-Ridley said optimistically. "We need to plan for their visit. The school year is about to start."

"Mary, I hate to be negative, but I've had some bad experiences with people from the CDC," Treviño said, a little discouraged due to the CDC's unfair treatment of the SHRC in the past.

"I think Dr. Wethington is a good person, and she means right," Treviño went on. "But when she takes news of the study to her higher-ups at the CDC, and they find out that NEEMA is part of the Bienestar, they will send her back with a no-go signal. I can almost bet on it."

"How about if you send her an e-mail just to find out what's going on?" Shaw-Ridley asked tentatively, with still a ray of hope.

Treviño waited a bit longer before sending Wethington the following e-mail on July 6, 2007:

> We are following up on the CDC interest in conducting an evaluability assessment of the NEEMA program. We prepare for the next school year's intervention over the summer, and your decision will allow us to start preparations.

Wethington responded on July 11, 2007 with the following

e-mail:

> In June, the expert panel met and decided which programs will receive an evaluability assessment. Unfortunately, NEEMA was not selected. This was not because there were any shortcomings or concerns regarding the program. It was because the program did not meet one of four initial inclusion criterion: the program needs to be a stand alone after-school program. Since we were looking for programs that are purely after-school programs, NEEMA did not qualify because it is designated to take place during school hours and after school. On a side note, we excluded other programs for this exact same reason.
>
> Your name and program remain in our database. Should our inclusion criteria change next year to include programs that take place during the school day and after-school, NEEMA will be considered for the second round of this project.

It was apparent to Treviño that the state and federal bureaucrats would find no shortcomings in the SHRC programs but continued to make up loony criteria so that the programs could be excluded. And this kind of treatment from the CDC continued.

WHO IS IN CONTROL AT THE CENTER?
On May 31, 2007, the office of the Texas CATCH program coordinator, Deanna Hoelscher, sent the Texas Association of Local Health Districts members an e-mail unveiling the exclusive coverage the Texas CATCH program received from the CDC. Following is the information from the e-mail she sent:

> Thank you for…your efforts to create healthy school environments. These efforts have now been recognized by the Centers for Disease Control and Prevention (CDC). We are very proud to announce that on June 15, 2007 at 1 p.m. (CST) the CDC Public Health Grand Rounds featuring coordinated school health programs using the CATCH program will be broadcast live worldwide.
>
> This broadcast seeks to increase knowledge and

awareness of how the CATCH program gives schools and communities the tools they need to help children improve their diet and increase the amount of physical activity they engage in. A feature of the program will be videos from schools who are implementing CATCH as well as interviews with state, district, and school leaders in Texas. Additionally, background information about Senate Bill 19/1357 emphasizing how a coordinated approach and public policy in Texas can serve as a model for the nation will be described.

We wish you continued success in improving the health of children and their families in Texas. Attached is a flyer and fact sheet with more information on the program.

Sincerely, The Dell Center and CATCH Team

There is nothing wrong with helping children improve their diet and physical activity, but there is something wrong with one special interest group—the CTN—using the CDC to provide children at-risk for diabetes with a program never shown to decrease blood sugars. In addition, centrally planning school health curriculums may not take into account the importance of regional differences and culturally-appropriate learning material to change behaviors. Theory suggest that children from ethnic populations may improve their understanding of learning material if the curriculum uses examples and content from their own culture to illustrate key concepts, principles, and generalizations. Culturally relevant learning material provides opportunities for students to make connections from personal experience.

At the time, the highest-ranking CDC official whose name was listed as an organizer of the CDC Public Health Grand Rounds conference was Dr. Stephanie B. Coursey Bailey, the CDC's Chief of Public Health Practice. So Dr. Hector Gonzalez, Director of the City of Laredo Health Department, chose to send Bailey—rather than Hoelscher—an e-mail to criticize the Federal attempt to centrally control local school health programs. Following is the e-mail Gonzalez sent:

> Thank you for the information and congratulations for the effort to address school based programs to reduce obesity and diabetes. However in Laredo and many other Texas-Mexico Border Communities where the epidemic

is more accentuated, CATCH has never made an impact and I would entertain a meeting with you and others of the CDC, UTSPH, and Institute of Health Policy to inform you of a better program, the 'Bienestar'.

This program was developed by Dr. Roberto Treviño of the Social and Health Research Center from San Antonio, Texas for Mexican-American and Latino Children. In Laredo, we are using this program and are having wonderful results. We are committed to early intervention using this program in particular since initial data showed that four percent of third grade children in Laredo (almost 300) had abnormal glucose levels and thirty percent were overweight. With the support of the legislature which just ended, HB 3618 passed to provide this new and optimum early diabetes intervention from pre-k through 8th grade along the Texas-Mexico Border.

We cannot afford to give our children second best as they deserve better. Therefore, I am requesting a meeting to discuss Bienestar, because we cannot promote one program solely especially if it does not have the proven evidence-based diabetes results such as the Bienestar. Please contact me at your earliest convenience to discuss this. I am sharing this information with my colleagues Directors and Administrators of the Hidalgo, Cameron, and El Paso Health departments.

Gonzalez also asked Bailey in a phone conversation to visit the SHRC headquarters and learn more about the Bienestar program.

The e-mail evidently caused some kind of stir at the CDC because just two weeks later, Treviño received an e-mail from Mark Fussell, CDC's Senior Management Official in Texas, asking to visit the SHRC. A meeting was set for late June 2007.

When Fussell arrived at three p.m., Treviño showed him around the center and introduced him to the staff. Marketing consultants David Saldaña and Denise Jones showed Fussell the Bienestar and NEEMA health textbooks. They walked to Treviño's office, where Treviño pulled out seven publications showing evidence that the Bienestar and NEEMA programs had lowered blood sugars in children at-risk for diabetes.

While perusing through these studies, Fussell commented, "Dr. Treviño, I'm well aware of your studies, and I have nothing but praise for your programs."

"Mark, I'll be up front with you," Treviño said honestly. "We keep hearing from the CDC how good the Bienestar programs are, but then CDC turns around and supports only the Texas CATCH program."

Fussell stopped what he was doing, and looked up, a surprised look on his face. No doubt he was surprised at how forthright Treviño was being.

Not one to mince words, Treviño then summarized his perception of Bienestar's treatment by the CDC over the last several years: "We have been treated very unfairly by CDC."

Fussell's face contorted into something of a grimace before he nodded his head, signaling an unspoken consensus.

The rest of the meeting continued in a cordial fashion. Treviño had made his point, and while he knew, Fussell was well intentioned, Fussell currently was too low in CDC's bureaucracy to do anything about the issue at hand. Treviño recognized the staff member had just been sent to appease Treviño and Gonzalez.

CDC HAD NOT HEARD THE LAST

Several months later, in October 2007, Treviño received a call from Congressman Ciro Rodriguez's office.

"This is Meghan Riley from Congressman Rodriguez's office. He asked me to write a letter to the CDC and request that they support other health programs and not just the Texas CATCH program."

Treviño nodded his head at her words, and said, "Yes, I spoke with the congressman some weeks ago, and asked him to remove the horse blinders off the CDC. They need to see that there is no perfect program out there. Not the Bienestar, not the CATCH. Furthermore, for the CDC to support only one program that hasn't shown any evidence of improving physiologic measures is simply, and horrifyingly, unhealthy for children."

"What I'll do is draft a letter, but I want you to review it for scientific accuracy," she said.

Treviño agreed to this right away, but when the letter arrived via an e-mail attachment, he found it did not need much editing. Riley apparently knew the issue very well.

On September 10, 2007, Congressman Ciro Rodriguez officially sent the following letter to Dr. Julie Louise Gerberding, Director of the CDC at the present time:

> I am writing to request that the Centers for Disease Control and Prevention conduct a site visit at an important

medical facility in San Antonio, Texas. This non-profit facility, the Social and Health Research Center, is the principal investigator of the two largest NIH school-based health intervention initiatives, both of which are aimed at diabetes control and prevention. The programs are the Healthy Trial, which targets middle school children and Proyecto Bienestar Laredo, which targets elementary school children. In addition they operate the NEEMA program which targets African-American children. The Bienestar and NEEMA are the only two programs that have actually decreased blood sugar levels in high risk children.

I have been made aware, that at this time, the CDC is only promoting a program called Coordinated Approach to Child Health (CATCH) for diabetes control. However, research done through the CATCH program has not been shown to actually decrease glucose levels in children. Therefore, I believe that it is important that the CDC diversify the health programs that they support and consider endorsing the Bienestar and NEEMA programs.

I believe it is highly important that the CDC visit this facility and speak to the medical experts involved in implementing this program.

As of this book's writing, there has been no response from Director Gerberding.

WHO SHUT THE DOOR?

By 2007, Bell was the Deputy Executive Commissioner at the Health and Human Service Commission. The Health and Human Service Commission oversaw the TDH. Since Bell's superiors were those responsible for suppressing the Bienestar and NEEMA programs, Treviño had stayed away from approaching Bell for nearly five years so as not to compromise Bells' high-level job position at the state agency. Treviño believed any obvious relationship between the two men might jeopardize Bell's job.

But having always been curious about what had prompted the letter the CDC had sent Bell in 2001 (page 40; the letter in which the CDC director requested Bell to switch his support back to the Texas CATCH program), Treviño finally called Bell's secretary to set up an appointment with a man sympathetic to his cause.

It was February 2007 when Treviño and Saldaña met with Bell. The three men exchanged pleasantries. As usual, Bell was soft-spoken, courteous, and very knowledgeable when it came to health care policies.

Treviño started moving the conversation towards the issue he wanted to discuss by observing, "You have been a very good and fair person, Dr. Bell. When we at the SHRC were down, you threw us a lifesaver and kept us afloat. Thank you."

"You guys operate a good program, and it's making good changes in children. Why wouldn't I be there to help?"

"Well, I don't know if you knew this, but I got a copy of the letter Marks from the CDC sent you in January 2001."

At this comment, Bell's eyes and mouth opened wide.

"How did you get a hold of that letter?" he queried.

Treviño knew that Bell would not get anyone in trouble if he divulged this information to him.

"Dr. Philip Huang and Dr. Maria Alen were copied, and Dr. Alen faxed me a copy," he replied.

Bell then leaned forward to say in a whisper, "It's amazing how the big guys operate."

In as soft a tone as Bell's, Treviño responded, "I sensed you were under a lot of pressure to stay away from us, so I did not bother to call or visit you after that point. You've been a good man to our programs. I didn't want our friendship to cause you any problems."

"Thank you, Dr. Treviño," Bell responded, a glint in his eyes. "I admire you for the work you do for poor and underserved children. They need a champion like you."

Treviño felt it was important to applaud one of the men who had been so important to their cause.

"Dr. Bell, no one person or institution can do it alone. If it wasn't for you opening up the door for us in 2000, we would have folded."

"If it was up to me, yours and other school health programs would be operating in Texas," Bell said quietly and thoughtfully. "But there are lots of other forces more powerful than me that decide what is implemented in our schools."

"Talking about 'other forces', did the President and the CDC write that letter to try to keep us away from high-risk children?" Treviño asked, getting to the heart of the matter.

Bell paused. He stared at Saldaña and Treviño for a moment before he put his hands up in a clapping position. But instead of swinging them together, he swung them closed, as it to signify the closing of a gate.

After watching this gesture, Treviño simply queried in a quiet tone, "They tried to keep the Bienestar away from high-risk children?"

Bell nodded his head in agreement.

POLITICIAN CONTROL SURFACES

That the President interferes with health policies is not surprising. In July 2007, the *New York Times* reported that the former Surgeon General Richard Carmona told a congressional panel that top Bush administration staff repeatedly tried to suppress important public health reports because of political considerations.

Carmona said the Bush administration would not let him release reports on stem cell, sex education, contraception, and global health issues. In another instance, top officials had Carmona delay for years the release of a landmark study on second-hand smoking.

On the other hand, in reports that had favorable political considerations for the Bush administration, Carmona said he was ordered to mention President Bush at least three times in every page.

In October 2007, a similar article came out from The Associated Press, when it reported that the White House had "watered down" a health report produced by Gerberding, the CDC's Director. The Associated Press obtained documents that showed White House staff removed six pages from a testimony Gerderding had prepared for a Senate hearing on the impact of climate change on health outcomes. The six pages listed disease and other unhealthy outcomes that might flourish if the earth warmed.

Gerberding later downplayed the changes that had been made in her prepared text.

• DR. ROBERTO P. TREVIÑO •

Chapter 4

TEXAS "BURROCRATS" CENTRALLY PLANNING CHILDREN'S HEALTH

Located just outside downtown Houston and boasting forty-two institutions within its complex, The Texas Medical Center is the largest concentration of medical facilities in the world. In 2001, it had 5.4 million patients filling hospital beds to pay for the Center's $6 billion annual operating cost. Located in the middle of this luxurious medical complex is Houston's UTSPH office tower.

Houston's UTSPH, which operates the Texas CATCH program, has no shortage of power. Under two Texas governors, bureaucrats set up the CTN as the sole vendor of coordinated school health programs thereby giving it a potential for $17 million in revenue a year. And when Rick Perry took over as Governor of Texas in December 2000 after George W. Bush, the policies of Texas CATCH protectionism continued. The Texas Council on Cardiovascular Disease and Stroke; the Texas Diabetes Council (TDC); the School Health Program; and the Bureau of Chronic Disease and Tobacco Prevention were the four departments within the TDH that were used to stifle competitors of the Texas CATCH program.

TEXAS COUNCIL ON CARDIOVASCULAR DISEASE AND STROKE

At the June 2000 meeting of the Texas Council on Cardiovascular Disease and Stroke, Deanna Hoelscher was introduced as the newest member of the council. This was the first inclusion of a CTN member to the Texas Council on Cardiovascular Disease and Stroke. At the meeting she spoke about her background and affiliation with Houston's UTSPH.

After this introduction, the CTN members started moving fast to exert influence on the council. In July, the council's board members heard John Krampitz from Houston's UTSPH speak about the Texas CATCH program. He asked the board members to support the Texas CATCH. He also informed the board members that the Texas Diabetes Council has been supporting the dissemination of CATCH in Texas schools.

In September, Hoelscher requested that Tommy Fleming, Director of Health Education at the Texas Education Agency, make a presentation on coordinated school health programs so that they could worked in conjunction with one another. (A description of the content of Fleming's presentation, which occurred at the Council's October meeting, follow shortly.)

In October, Hoelscher asked if the name Texas CATCH program could be printed on the council's newsletter. She also requested that some of the American Heart Association money donated to the Council be used for the Texas CATCH material.

At that same meeting, Tommy Fleming and Peter Cribb presented the findings of the Texas CATCH program. They exaggerated these findings. For example, when they said the program was operating on 700 campuses, they were really referring to the fact that the TDH had funded travel expenses for Texas CATCH staff to make 700 school presentations of the program at different schools. Not all of these schools were to adopt the Texas CATCH program.

Fleming then asked the council to allocate $3,500 per school for the purchase of Texas CATCH materials, such as the PE, food service, and health education manuals. With 4,856 elementary schools in Texas, this would have meant $17 million a year in revenue for the CTN group.

The council members rolled their eyes at the suggestion, and did not swallow the 'pill' that was being offered. So, although the CTN people did not get to ransack the Texas Council on Cardiovascular Disease and Stroke's budget at the time, they ultimately were able to use the Council to promote their program on their web site, and in their brochures and pamphlets.

TEXAS DIABETES COUNCIL

The TDC is also a department within the TDH, and it too has its own board of directors. These persons are appointed by politicians and influenced by bureaucrats. The two bureaucrats who sat on the board in 2000 were Philip Huang, TDH's Chief of the Chronic Disease Prevention and Control Bureau, and Jan Ozias, Director of the TDC.

Even though it had been over a year since Archer had resigned, the TDC still had the Texas CATCH on their web site. Believing this might have been an oversight, Treviño called Ozias to have her either add other school health programs to their web site or remove the Texas CATCH program.

Ozias was short, with a round moon face and a hairdo reminiscent of the fifties. She usually spoke in a weary-sounding voice, her tone unflatteringly monotonous. She was right under Huang in terms of the TDH bureaucracy.

Treviño called her one day in March 2001, at nine o'clock in the morning. She had not yet arrived in the office, so Treviño left a message to return his call. When, by the afternoon, she had not returned it, Treviño called her again.

A female voice answered the phone.

"Good afternoon, this is Dr. Treviño. Is Ms. Ozias in?"

A pause.

"Good afternoon... Yes, this is Jan."

"Oh, hi Jan. How are you doing?"

"Very good. Running around from meeting to meeting."

"I just wanted to keep you in the loop and give you an update on the Bienestar program."

Treviño started slow and then sped up to his concern—why was only Texas CATCH on the TDC web site? Treviño talked about the Bienestar abstract that was accepted for presentation at the June 2001 American Diabetes Association meeting. The abstract would show that children who had participated in the Bienestar program had decreased their blood sugars between August and May of a school year. He reiterated that the Bienestar was the only program actually decreasing blood sugars in children in Texas.

"Dr. Treviño, you have a marvelous program, and I'm glad to hear it's showing good results. You must be commended for the work you do."

"Jan, it's not me who is doing the work. It's the children who are doing the work," Treviño reminded her in a gentle tone. "They're the ones changing, and they're making great efforts to change their families' lifestyles too. They're the one to be commended."

"You know what I mean," she said with a slow twang. "It's everyone working together."

"Well, that's the reason I'm calling. How can we get the Texas Diabetes Council to include other school health programs in their web site? Don't you think that the children and the schools would benefit more if the Texas Diabetes Council was more inclusive and allow several school health programs to compete?"

"Oh, Dr. Treviño, the Texas Diabetes Council believes strongly in working with other programs. You're welcome to come and make a presentation to the Texas Diabetes Council board. They would love to hear about your recent studies."

These were the words she spoke, but Treviño didn't trust them. Often it seemed her outward stance was to praise other programs and agree with their investigators, while her actual marching orders were to protect the Texas CATCH. While other programs heads were invited to make presentations to the TDC board, no one got passed this smoke screen.

Time continued to pass, and in August 2001, the TDH Office of Communication released their *Speaking of Health* newsletter. Following is an excerpt from that newsletter:

> TDH is working on the problem [diabetes] in a number of ways. Huang says the coordinated approach to child health or "CATCH" program stresses prevention. CATCH offers health classes and physical activity in elementary schools. Parents can learn along with their children.
>
> One element of the CATCH program is the parent involvement component and that's where the parents are involved in the homework that the kids bring home and they learn some of those same skills that the kids are learning in schools.

"These guys think we're stupid," Treviño told Irene Hernandez in a show of anger after he read the newsletter. "They tell me, 'No we don't support only one program,' but then they turn around and post only the Texas CATCH program on their web site and newsletters. Do they think I won't notice?"

Treviño then handed Hernandez a pamphlet. "Just read this pamphlet. It says how they are going to prevent diabetes with the Texas CATCH program. I ask how?"

Hernandez kept quiet for a while to let Treviño vent out his anger. "Dr. Treviño, they are lying [in the newsletter]! The parent program was the weakest component of their [Texas CATCH] intervention, and I know for a fact that schools where the Texas CATCH operates don't even implement this component."

When, months later, the TDC, or the Council designed to control diabetes in Texas, continued to feature exclusively on their web site a "diabetes" program that had nothing to do with diabetes, Treviño decided to take it to the next level.

In December 2001 he called Huang. By background, Huang was a physician with a Masters in Public Health. But Treviño suspected the reason he was on the TDC board was because he was tied to the CTN group, and he was one they could easily manipulate to their advantage.

"Good afternoon, Dr. Huang. This is Dr. Treviño."

"Hi, Dr. Treviño, how're you doing?" Huang casually responded.

By now Treviño was done with pleasantries. They didn't mean a thing. "Dr. Huang, why is it that the Texas Diabetes Council gives special preference to the Texas CATCH?"

Huang briskly responded, "I disagree with the assessment, Dr. Treviño. The Diabetes Council does not promote any one program."

While Treviño's initial reaction was to snap out a rebuttal to Huang, he took a deep breath and stayed calm.

"Have you looked at your web site? The Texas CATCH is all over it. I do not see any other program mentioned on it."

"I didn't know that. I'll look into it," Huang assured him.

"Well, once you see for yourself, could you please either remove the mention of the Texas CATCH program from it, or consider putting other school health programs on there too to raise awareness of their existence?"

"I don't know, Dr. Treviño," he said in a vague tone of voice. "I don't decide what goes into the Council's web site."

"Well, who does?" Treviño inquired. "Can you give me a name and phone number so I can call him or her about this matter?"

"I'll check into it and get back to you."

Apparently, Huang never checked into it, for Treviño never got a call back, and the Texas CATCH name continued appearing exclusively on the TDC's web site, brochures, and pamphlets. Additionally, in further communications with Treviño, Ozias and Huang, continued to say one thing and do another. Ozias would always praise the Bienestar program and Huang would always deny special treatment for the Texas CATCH program.

In Treviño's view, the Texas Diabetes Council, and its staff members were acting like pre-programmed robots when it came to protecting, defending, and promoting the Texas CATCH program. That meant that despite Archer's resignation, there was somebody above them still pulling their strings.

• DR. ROBERTO P. TREVIÑO •

INSIDE THE SHARK'S JAWS

It was February of 2002 when Treviño had an opportunity to speak about the Bienestar to the TDC's board members. The meeting took place in the 7th floor conference room of the TDH. Hernandez and Vincent Ramos, Texas Director of the League of United Latin American Citizens (LULAC), accompanied Treviño.

The TDC board members present were Gene Bell, Belinda Bazan-Lara, Victor Gonzalez, Judith Haley, Jan Hamilton, Lenore Katz, Margaret Pacillas, Jeffery Ross, Philip Huang, and Lawrence Harkless. Harkless was the new TDC chairman.

The atmosphere in the room was pleasant and cordial when Treviño and Hernandez, the SHRC's Associate Director, entered. There they saw the board members seated on a raised platform at expensive-looking conference tables. Everyone hugged and/or shooked hands when they entered.

Ozias called the meeting to order. The first speaker was Treviño.

Treviño walked up to the podium with a folder in his hand.

"Good afternoon, Mr. Chairman and board members. I want to thank you for giving me this opportunity to come and talk to you."

Treviño paused, took a deep breath and looked around at the members before he bluntly said, "The Texas Diabetes Council has been so unfair to our center that I'm surprised I was even allowed to enter into this building."

The entire conference room got quiet, and everyone's eyes were fixed on Treviño.

"This is the Texas Diabetes Council," Treviño paused again to make eye contact with each board member, "and yet it funds a program that has nothing, absolutely nothing, to do with diabetes."

Treviño walked up to Ozias and gave her copies of the studies on the Bienestar program. These were distributed to the different members of the board.

"As you can see with these studies, the Bienestar program operates in schools located in the lowest income neighborhoods. And even though society often dismisses these children as being beyond saving, these wonderful kids have made great strides to change their health behaviors and decrease their blood sugars."

Treviño took a deep breath before he carefully articulated. "There is no other program in Texas that has made such changes in children's health. The program you support through the TDC has never even measured a blood sugar, something that is critical to assessing someone's risk for diabetes."

No one said a word for a moment, and then Dr. Victor Gonzalez spoke up. Gonzalez was another board member who spoke well about the Bienestar program but had never taken action to change the TDC's policy of exclusivity.

"These are very impressive results," he observed, looking at his fellow board members while holding the published studies in his hand. "Why haven't we supported the Bienestar health program?" he wondered out loud.

"Dr. Gonzalez, the Texas Department has not supported the Bienestar program because it's too expensive to implement," Huang commented from his leather chair. "Also, it's more of a medical intervention, and it requires too many measurements."

"Dr. Huang," Treviño responded, taking a deep breath to remain calm, "the original CATCH study cost $25 million and it had 3,297 students in its intervention arm. That's a cost of $7,582 per student. Now, that is expensive!"

"But that's not what we pay to implement the CATCH program here in Texas," Huang retorted.

At this point, the associate commissioner of the TDH, Debra Stabeno, stood up and rushed over to the podium.

"Dr. Treviño, the state presently pays only three dollars a student to disseminate the Texas CATCH program, and we don't require any measurements from the schools," she observed.

"For the state to go around and say that by spending three dollars per student they can cure diabetes is deceptive," Treviño responded, looking down contemptuously at the shorter woman standing next to him. "Yes, the Bienestar is more expensive initially, at twelve dollars a child. But look at the alternative—$13,000 to care for a patient with diabetes, or $80,000 to care for a patient on dialysis. And if we do not implement early age diabetes prevention programs with proven results, that is the amount we taxpayers will be paying in the near future."

"With regard to measuring," Treviño continued, looking again at Stabeno with a steady gaze, "I'm a physician by background, and so I know full well that starting and continuing treatment of a patient with diabetes on a glucose-lowering agent, without ever measuring the response, is sub-standard care. It is unacceptable. The science shows that we need to measure!"

By this point, Treviño's words had created such a commotion that he simply picked up his notes and walked out.

Hernandez and Ramos followed.

• DR. ROBERTO P. TREVIÑO •

THE LITTLE FISH

At the time, the other TDH departments and committee stacked with CTN people were the School Health Program, the Bureau of Chronic Disease and Tobacco Prevention, and the Texas Adolescent Health Advisory Committee. Specifically, Fleming and Stephen Barnett, a pediatrician who traveled with Fleming to give Texas CATCH presentations, served on the School Health Program board. Huang, as mentioned previously, was the Chief of the Bureau of Chronic Disease and Tobacco Prevention. And Hoelscher served on the Texas Adolescent Health Advisory Committee.

The aim of these bureaucracies was to promote and protect the Texas CATCH program. And they would work to find a way to legitimatize the transfer of the public's money that had been assigned to these associations into the CTN coffers.

Chapter 5

PERRY SETS MECHANISMS IN PLACE FOR WITHDRAWALS

Under Governor Rick Perry, the TDH converted four of its departments into banks for the CTN group. Now Perry's bureaucrats needed to formulate withdrawal slips to transfer money from public funds to CTN pockets.

The process would be legitimatized through Statewide Action Plans. "Statewide Action Plans" were meetings organized by staff members of the TDH. What happened is that members of the TDH invited health experts from around the state to give input on designing a TDH action plan to address a specific health problem. The health experts attended one- or two-day meetings where they talked big and exchanged business cards among themselves and with TDH staff.

Yet afterwards, the health problem—diabetes—and the affected population stayed unchanged. The health experts who had attended the 'meetings' didn't know that as a result of the 'meetings', the TDH staff formulated "consensus" papers. In the fine print of these papers they inserted wording approving the dispensing of public funds for the Texas CATCH program. What ended up changing was who controlled the power—and the public monies.

FIRST WITHDRAWAL SLIP

The first of these 'meetings' was called, "The Type 2 Diabetes in Children and Adolescent Statewide Action Plan." This meeting was organized by Huang, and scheduled for November 2000. Oralia Garcia went to represent the SHRC.

On the second day of the meeting, the attendees were asked to sign up for different committees. Garcia signed up for the School Health Program committee when she noticed Tommy Fleming from the TEA would be on the committee. Moreover, Ann Pauli, Director of Paso del

Norte Health Foundation, was named chair of the committee. Garcia knew Paso del Norte Health Foundation had funded and introduced the Texas CATCH program to El Paso schools as a diabetes prevention program.

Suspicious of these associations, Garcia walked up to Pauli, and made sure to introduce herself.

"Hi, Ms. Pauli, I'm Oralia Garcia. I'm the Director of Research and Evaluation at the Social and Health Research Center. I'm really looking forward to working with you on this project. Can you please keep me informed of any meetings this committee has?" Garcia said as she extended her arm to give Pauli one of her business cards.

Pauli looked at Garcia and, with a half-smile said, "Of course. We are happy you signed up for this committee."

But Pauli did not look too excited to have Garcia on her committee.

And indeed, the committee met at the time, formulated recommendations, and excluded Garcia from the process.

Garcia fumed to Treviño about this later.

"Dr. Treviño, I've called Dr. Huang and Ann Pauli, and they simply don't return my calls. I called them, sent them e-mails, and told them a hundred times I wanted to be part of the process. And they still excluded me. I can't believe they are doing that."

Treviño agreed. "These meetings and committees are a farce, Oralia. Everyone walks out feeling good, but at the end, the talk never impacts the people being affected."

"I know! My intention for joining was to keep the CTN people in check. They're always pulling something behind people's backs," Garcia said miserably.

Her prediction proved accurate. When the statewide action plan final document was produced, recommendations one and two were: 1) Implement the CATCH program in eight to ten schools in each education service center region and 2) Fund a full-time CATCH coordinator in each of the state's 20 education service centers.

According to some committee members Treviño contacted, the Texas CATCH program was never discussed at the meeting, but the name was still snuck in the "consensus" paper. The only person that had a suspicion this would happen, was pulled off.

SECOND AND THIRD WITHDRAWAL SLIPS

The next statewide action plan was "The Texas State Plan to Reduce Cardiovascular Disease and Stroke." This was organized in November

2001.

Its final recommendation would be, "Utilize the Texas School Health Network to provide training, support, and technical assistance for the implementation of the CATCH program."

The Governor's Advisory Council on Physical Fitness followed in November 2002. And what was its final recommendation?

"Promote the Texas CATCH to prevent diabetes".

WITHDRAWAL NUMBER FOUR MEETS RESISTANCE

They also promoted a similar strategy in December 2002, through "The Strategic Plan for the Prevention of Obesity in Texas." On this one, however, they would get more of a fight than they anticipated.

Connie Mobley, a member of the "Strategic Plan for the Prevention of Obesity in Texas" and a nutrition consultant with SHRC, faxed Treviño a copy of the draft document. In the draft, it stated, "Provide incentives to schools for joining the CATCH program." When Treviño read the word "CATCH" in the document, he immediately called Dr. Jose Gonzalez, a pediatric endocrinologist and professor at the University of Texas Medical Branch in Galveston.

Gonzalez was an important member of this Strategic Plan.

"Dr. Gonzalez, this is Dr. Treviño with the Social and Health Research Center in San Antonio. We implement the Bienestar school-based diabetes prevention program. This program has shown to decrease blood sugars in children at-risk for diabetes."

"Dr. Treviño, I'm aware of your program and the good work you're doing," Gonzalez answered in a dry tone of voice. "How can I help you?"

"I saw your name on the Strategic Plan for the Prevention of Obesity in Texas, and I wanted to share a concern. The draft document states, "Provide incentives to schools for joining the CATCH program." This document gives exclusive support to a program that cannot provide any evidence for having lowered blood glucose."

As a children's diabetes specialist, Gonzalez understood that the endpoint of an intervention is to stop a medical illness, and obesity was a risk factor explaining the increase in youth-onset type 2 diabetes.

"Could this document be left neutral instead of giving exclusive support to one program?" Treviño asked politely.

"I fully support your efforts, and will assist however possible. However, we exclusively supported the CATCH in this document because it satisfies Senate Bill 19 [a state legislative bill aimed at implementing a coordinated school health program to prevent childhood obesity and diabetes]," Gonzalez explained. "As you know, the bill requires a coordinated school health program." (Author's note: The legislative bill and the TEA's connection to it will be explained in full in chapters 8 through 12.)

"But what you're telling me then is that the committee members are making decisions based on political concerns rather than on scientific evidence!" Treviño retorted. He had lost his patience.

"I concur. Your program is well run and has shown good preliminary results," replied Gonzalez, in an attempt to appease Treviño. "But you should not view this as a battle between your program and the CATCH program. This is legislation that directs the TEA to implement a coordinated school health program, and the TEA has selected the CATCH program because it satisfies all the requirements. I would recommend that you approach the TEA in a non-confrontational manner," he advised sternly, "and discuss your program's specifics with them."

Treviño sighed heavily as he set the receiver down. There were many individuals like Gonzalez who were unaware that a recurring pattern was at play here. The CTN had an enormous power over state government agencies for a long time, yet individuals unaware of this seemed to always end up with a perception of Treviño as being the aggressor and a trouble-maker.

Treviño called Mobley afterwards, as she had been instrumental in designing the Bienestar health program during its formative years.

"Connie, how is it that the Texas CATCH people have managed to get the Strategic Plan for the Prevention of Obesity members to provide financial incentives to those schools that adopt their program?"

"We never agreed on that," she said, surprised and startled to hear this news. "At our meetings no one even mentioned the name 'CATCH.' I have no idea how they got their name in there."

"Well, it's happened. This is like the fourth statewide action plan where they round up experts to put committees together and, without their acknowledgement, bureaucrats sneak in wording that hands over public money to the CTN," Treviño explained.

Mobley tried reaching Claire Heiser and Phil Huang to ask who had approved financial incentives for implementing the Texas CATCH. Heiser, like Huang, was on the staff of the TDH and an organizer of the strategic plan for obesity prevention. Neither returned her calls.

Treviño called Dr. Tom Baranowski, a professor at Baylor University and a heavyweight in Texas in terms of children's health programs. Treviño explained to him his concerns that bureaucrats were organizing the strategic plan to benefit the Texas CATCH program.

Forgotten Children: A True Story of How Politicians Endanger Children

Baranowski was distressed to hear this, and told Kelder, Houston's UTSPH Texas CATCH coordinator, over lunch that the committee should make the document program-neutral and, instead, recommend setting high standards by which programs eligible for committee funding should be evaluated before any monies were to be expensed. Baranowski then tried to organize a meeting between Treviño and Kelder, but Kelder never agreed on a date.

Baranowski also e-mailed Dr. Kenneth Goodrick, professor at Baylor College of Medicine and the Strategic Plan for the Prevention of Obesity Vice-Chairman. He informed him in the e-mail that despite the huge amount of money invested in the CATCH program, it had not been shown to prevent obesity.

Goodrick agreed with him, and this ultimately triggered a movement among the Strategic Plan committee members to remove the CATCH name and the incentives promised to the program from their document.

NO LONGER SITTING PRETTY

It was the first week of January 2003, and Treviño was scheduled to present at the TDC quarterly meeting. He was going to request an investigation into why Ozias and Fleming, TDC board members who had ties to the Texas CATCH, were allowed to sit on the TEA's review panel that was responsible for approving school health programs. Clearly this should be considered a conflict of interest.

As a courtesy, Treviño called Fleming the week before, to inform him of his upcoming presentation. When told Fleming was not in the office, Treviño specified in his message that he would be bringing up Fleming's name in his presentation. Yet for the day of the meeting, Fleming chose to send Hellen Bedgood, TEA Assistant Curriculum Director, on his behalf.

Treviño did not leave a similar message for Ozias, for as the director of the TDC, her presence was mandatory at the meeting.

The day of the meeting approached. Treviño knew by this point in time, the TDC's staff and board members expected a stormy situation every time he presented to them. And he did not disappoint during this particular presentation.

"Good afternoon, ladies and gentlemen," Treviño started in a calm but stern voice. "In October 2002, we had the Bienestar program reviewed by the TEA. Among the panel of reviewers were Jan Ozias and Tommy Fleming."

Treviño stared at Ozias; the only clear expression on her face was that of a sneer.

"Both individuals have strong ties to the Texas CATCH school health program," Treviño continued. "As you know, Ms. Ozias is the Director of the Texas Diabetes Council, and the Council has the Texas CATCH program posted exclusively all over their web site and on their brochures. Mr. Fleming also goes around the state giving talks for the Texas CATCH program. That is a conflict of interest, so it should come as no surprise to anyone present that their preferred program was the only program approved for the schools by the TEA."

Treviño walked toward the board members and distributed a Conflict of Interest Disclosure form.

"Any time a person sits in state or federal panels to review programs or grants, they must sign this form. After a bit of research, I have discovered that the TEA did not request this form from the panel of reviewers, and Ozias and Fleming did not disclose their ties to the Texas CATCH program. This was a mistake by both them and the TEA."

Paul Cruz, the TEA Deputy Commissioner, had provided Treviño with this information.

A great deal of whispering started among the TDC board members, and it became somewhat difficult to hear because they sat in tables on a platform above and set back from the general audience. While the TDC's meetings were open to the general public, usually the audience consisted only of twenty to thirty people who had a special interest in diabetes.

When the whispering finally ceased, Dr. Victor Hugo Gonzalez looked past Ozias to stare noticeably at Bedgood. Bedgood was African-American, slightly heavy-set and unfamiliar with the surrounding politics.

"I'm sorry, what is your name?" Gonzalez asked her.

"Hellen Bedgood," she responded.

"Are you with the TEA?"

"Yes sir, I'm here on behalf of Tommy Fleming."

"Why would the Texas Education Agency form a panel of reviewers without requesting the members to sign a conflict of interest form?"

"I'm not sure. I was not involved with the review process," she answered.

"Ms. Bedgood, what is your position at the TEA?" Gonzalez said, raising his voice and looking angry.

"I'm the Assistant Curriculum Director," she responded somewhat hesitantly.

"You're the Curriculum Director, and you don't know the procedures at the TEA?" Gonzalez drilled down on her.

"I was not involved," she said, starting to fidget. "Health curriculums is another department, and it's handled by Tommy Fleming."

"Well, why isn't Mr. Fleming here?"

"I don't know. He didn't give me a reason. He only asked me to attend on his behalf," she said in a nervous tone.

Treviño, who was still standing at the podium, knew he was watching an innocent person being hammered. So he interrupted by saying, "Dr. Gonzalez, thank you for your efforts on my behalf, but I do believe your questions are being aimed at the wrong person.

Ms. Bedgood was not a member of that review panel. It was comprised of, among others, Jan Ozias and Tommy Fleming."

Treviño then deliberately looked at Ozias again.

Gonzalez's voice took on a friendlier tone when he inquired,

"Ms. Ozias, were you a member of that review panel?"

"Yes, Dr. Gonzalez," Ozias said. "I was asked by the TEA to participate," she answered as an explanation for the presence on the committee.

"Well, the TEA should've done their homework before selecting the panel of reviewers," Gonzalez said.

Unfortunately, his words worked to shift the blame away from Ozias, and place it on the staff of the TEA.

"Dr. Gonzalez," Treviño interjected, trying to get him back to focusing on the culprits, "what I'm requesting is an investigation of two Texas Diabetes Council board members who sat on a state committee to review programs while knowing they had a conflict of interest."

Gonzalez paused and stared at the other board members hoping someone else would respond to Treviño's request. When no one else responded, Gonzalez turned to face Ozias and politely asked, "Ms. Ozias, could your staff please conduct an investigation into this matter, and provide us with a report by the next meeting in April?"

"Yes, sir," responded Ozias, and she lowered her head to jot some notes in a pad.

After this contentious meeting, Treviño was concerned that Bedgood would blame Treviño for the heat she had taken. He did not need another enemy at the TEA, and he sent her a letter to convey his regrets that she had been caught in the middle of something she knew nothing about.

With respect to Treviño's request, when April's TDC board meeting came around, there was no mention of any investigation.

Ironically, Treviño's request for an investigation, as well as the removal of the Texas CATCH from the Strategic Plan for the Prevention of Obesity, would actually end up backfiring on the SHRC.

FIRING SQUADS
The CTN people were not happy that the Texas CATCH name and incentives had been removed from the Strategic Plan for the Prevention of Obesity in December 2002, and that an investigation into two Texas CATCH loyalists had been requested in January 2003. And so they either retaliated with full force or the next serious of events were purely coincidental.

Tommy Thompson, the Secretary of the U.S. Department of Health and Human Services, would speak in Austin on January 23, 2003 to push the Texas CATCH program. Eduardo Sanchez, the Texas Health Commissioner, would speak in San Antonio in February to an audience of school staff and health experts about the Texas CATCH program. The Texas Medical Association would provide funds to a group of San Antonio physicians' wives in March to promote the Texas CATCH in San Antonio schools. And Kathy Shields, from the TDH Region 8 office, would promise the Edgewood Independent School District in April new CDC money if they would remove the Bienestar program from their campuses.

At the time, Tinker Murray, a professor at Texas State University, and a good friend of Treviño, had a friend within the TDH who provided him with this information about the doings of the CTN people. This was the same person who had informed Murray about the upcoming Thompson and Sanchez meetings.

When he started hearing of these plans, Treviño told Oralia Garcia glumly one day, "I guess we shouldn't have pissed them off."

"Hell, yeah, we should've pissed them off!" Garcia rebutted. "And we should do it every time they try to keep our programs away from children who need it," she reminded angrily. "We're in the middle of an obesity and diabetes epidemic. There's enough diabetes in this state for CATCH, Bienestar, and ten other programs!"

"Well, how do we remove these gun barrels they are pointing at our heads?" Treviño queried, his spirits low.

"We need to go to the meetings where Thompson and Sanchez are presenting, and stand up to them," Garcia responded quickly. "We need to let them hear us say, in front of the public, that one model doesn't fit all."

"I so admire your commitment, Oralia. I don't know how you do it," Treviño responded with gratitude. She was just the lift he needed this day.

"If we don't do it for these children, no one else will," Oralia sagely observed.

"Well, then, let's put your plan into action. Who goes to what meeting?"

"I know you have clinic on Thursday, so I will drive to Austin and attend the U.S. Department of Health and Human Services town hall meeting," Garcia replied. "And don't worry a bit about it. I can do it alone."

"If it wasn't for you, I would've already collapsed," Treviño laughed ruefully as he looked at his busy schedule. "Now, what do we do about Sanchez?"

"I know that Dr. Sanchez is speaking at the Adam's Mark hotel at eight o'clock in morning. Maybe you and I can catch him before his talk and fluster him enough to knock him a bit off track," Garcia suggested thoughtfully.

"I have clinic at nine, so that'll work for me," Treviño noted. "I'll meet you at the Adams Mark at seven-thirty that day."

BUSH'S SECRETARY OF HEALTH

Oralia's solo meeting was the first that came up. She traveled to Austin on a cold and rainy day to hear the talk being given by the Secretary of Health.

When she arrived, she looked around the room and noted the audience consisted of mostly politicians and the media. Dot Richardson, Vice Chairman of the President's Council on Physical Fitness and Sports, and Mark McClellan, Commissioner of the Food and Drug Administration, were in attendance. Sitting in the midst of these dignitaries was Peter Cribb, the CTN's salesman.

"It is with great honor that we present the U.S. Secretary of Health, Dr. Tommy Thompson," a man announced.

Thompson came out wearing a conservative dark blue suit and a large smile on his face. He stared at the audience until everyone quieted, and the voices that could be heard in the background faded out. Then he spoke extensively about the problem of childhood obesity and its complications, and spoke of the increasing new cases of type 2 diabetes among Mexican-American children.

Toward the end of his lecture he endorsed the Texas CATCH program as an outstanding diabetes and obesity prevention program.

Garcia's temperature started to rise when she heard him endorse a program that hadn't been shown to affect diabetes in children at all. Still at the same time, she was a bit overwhelmed by the Secretary of Health's presence; he was an impressive individual with many noteworthy accomplishments. So it wasn't until Peter Cribb came out to parade overweight Mexican-American children in front of the audience, in an attempt to give the meeting an emotional overtone, that Garcia—fully aware that his program did not take the ethnicity of these children into account—raised her hand.

The moderator came and stood next to her.

"You will be next," he advised her quietly.

When it was her turn, she spoke these words, words that she knew would get a reaction.

"Secretary of Health, my name is Oralia Garcia, and I'm an NIH pre-doctoral student conducting diabetes and obesity research among children at the Social and Health Research Center in San Antonio, Texas. I thank you for visiting our state and for your efforts towards helping us with the diabetes and obesity problem, particularly among minority youth.

"While I applaud your efforts to help us combat the obesity and diabetes epidemic in our state, I strongly encourage you to recognize that one program does not fit all. My question to you is, why must we only endorse one program? Why only the Texas CATCH program to meet the daunting needs of Texas children? There is an evidence-based, school-based program that has lowered abnormal blood glucose in children, particularly in Mexican-American children. It is the Bienestar program. I encourage you to also endorse that program and others as well. As you well know, Texas is a diverse state in terms of the population it sports, and diabetes is affecting Mexican Americans at a disproportionate rate. I hope you can help us provide the children with more culturally appropriate and evidence-based school health programs."

Oralia paused, took a deep breath and, looking right at Tommy Thompson and Peter Cribb continued. "Furthermore, while it's nice to see Mexican-American children in the audience, these children need to be in school."

At these words, the audience got quiet. Garcia noted that it was so silent, you could have heard a pin drop.

The Secretary of Health's countenance changed from happy to serious. He held on to the podium and answered, "Actually, the Native Indians have it the worst, and we will work with the Texas Education Agency and the Texas Department of Health to help them prevent obesity too."

Obviously caught by surprise, he had ended up providing a response irrelevant to the population at hand.

Oralia knew she had delivered a loud and clear message, but as she sat down, she was not convinced that the people on the center stage had truly listened.

It was Cribb's turn to speak next. Obviously thrown by Garcia's words, he talked about Senate Bill 19 in a voice that trembled. Then he stated that the Texas CATCH program was the only TEA-approved program, and if other organizations wanted their program included, they had to go to the TEA to get its approval.

Garcia returned to San Antonio quite disappointed. Although others in the audience had spoken up, echoing her perspective that one program does not fit all, the issue did not seem to be a priority for those who seemed to have most of the power in the government and schools.

PERRY'S HEALTH COMMISSIONER

As planned, Treviño and Garcia met up at the Adams Mark hotel early morning on February 13, 2003 hoping they would have a chance to encounter Sanchez. By the time it was 8:50, there was still no sign of Sanchez. As the two had been cooling their heels for well over an hour, Garcia went up to the registration table and asked if Sanchez was still scheduled to talk.

When the woman replied that Sanchez's 8 a.m. talk had been moved to 10:00, Treviño and Garcia looked at each other in shock and disappointment.

"Oralia," Treviño said in a subdued tone, "you know I'll have to leave to get to the clinic! But you stay here to listen to what he has to say."

With those words, Treviño walked away, visibly upset he would be unable to meet up with Sanchez at all.

Around half past ten, when Treviño's office at the clinic was filled with patients, Treviño got a call from Garcia. Garcia explained she was in the side aisle of the conference room walking towards the back door exit. Treviño could hear the murmur of a still-talking Sanchez in the background.

"Dr. Treviño, Sanchez came right out and said that the Texas Department of Health will be pushing the Texas CATCH program to all Texas schools," Garcia angrily whispered. "He is also saying a lot of stuff that doesn't make sense."

"Like what, Oralia?" Treviño asked quickly.

"One moment he's talking about forming partnerships with different agencies to operate programs in the schools, and in the next breath he's talking about the Texas CATCH being the only program to be implemented in schools. That's not a partnership! That's totalitarian rule at work."

Treviño, stuck in his clinic with fourteen patients left to see, anxiously paced up and down the hallway at the medical clinic on Barlite Boulevard.

"Goodness, Oralia! Your news makes me want to drop everything and rush over to the Adam's Mark."

"You won't make it, Dr. Treviño," Oralia advised firmly. "By the time you get here he'll be gone."

In his heart, Treviño knew she was right. So instead he asked, "What else is he saying?"

"He also mentioned that a new study was published showing that the Texas CATCH program had prevented obesity in children. Can that be true?"

"Oralia, no, it's not true," answered Treviño. He had been scouring the literature for months now, and there was no such publication showing that the Texas CATCH program prevented obesity in children. "You go back and question that finding. Drill down on him about that, okay?"

"Okay," said Oralia, and hung up.

As soon as Sanchez finished his presentation, Garcia's hand was the first to go up. She felt good about the audience in attendance, a group of university, school, and community health experts. However, she also knew they would be unaware of years of secret machinations by the CTN people, and that the speakers at the meeting were high-ranking TDH and CDC officials. And she had noted that next to Sanchez on the stage was Hoelscher, the Texas CATCH representative.

When the moderator called on her, Garcia spoke the following words.

"Dr. Sanchez, I would like to thank you for visiting our city, and I applaud your efforts in helping us to combat the obesity epidemic, particularly your efforts to combat childhood obesity in Texas."

Garcia's voice was calm but stern, and she stared right at Sanchez, looking directly into his eyes.

"As you can see, we're all here to help you reverse these trends. But while we in the audience are extending to you our helping hands, what we would like to ask is that you not tie them by endorsing just one school-based program."

Garcia raised both hands in the air as she made this comment.

"Please look around at the audience and notice the diversity in terms of ethnicities, ages, and genders that is present in just this room! The population of the state of Texas is as diverse as the audience in this room, so to come tell us that one program is appropriate for all the different children in the state of Texas is unrealistic."

Another representative from the SHRC was present in the audience. This was Maria Caballero, a Registered Nurse responsible for coordinating the Bienestar program testing of blood sugar in the schools. She was sitting right next to Garcia. After the words from Garcia, she overheard attendees nearby making the following comments to one another:

"What is wrong with her (Garcia)? How can she talk like that to the Commissioner of Health?"

And, "It is embarrassing for our city to have such an honored guest get harassed by this lady."

Garcia, though, was completely deaf to the surrounding voices. Her mind was focused on the Commissioner; her heart, on the children of the state of Texas. So she continued questioning Sanchez's intentions.

"Dr. Sanchez, you also mentioned that a study was published showing the Texas CATCH program had prevented obesity in children. Can you give us a reference on that paper, because to my knowledge, there are no publications from the Texas CATCH showing it prevented obesity?"

Sanchez's facial expression transformed from one of self-assurance to one of insecurity, and his voice trembled noticeably as he responded hesitantly, "I, I agree with you… One size does not fit all. We need to be open to other programs."

Sanchez then stopped all further questions and went on to introduce the next speaker, Deanna Hoelscher, without providing a reference for the 'study' that supposedly showed the prevention of obesity in children by the Texas CATCH program.

PARTNER'S AT WORK

That evening, there was a reception at the Adams Mark hotel in San Antonio for the conference speakers and attendees. Treviño and Oralia had decided earlier to attend this event, and walked in the beautiful ballroom together.

The first individuals Treviño's eyes settled on were Dr. Karen Coleman and Peter Cribb, who were together conversing. Coleman, then a professor at the University of Texas at El Paso, was tall, slim and always friendly. At the time, she was a consultant being paid to evaluate the effectiveness of the Texas CATCH program in El Paso schools.

Treviño went up to Coleman and Cribb, and stretched out his hand to shake their hands. Coleman greeted him, but Cribb's face simply got red, and he deliberately walked away without stretching out his hand.

Treviño watched his retreating back, and when he turned around to face Coleman, she noted, "Roberto, they hate you. I don't understand why."

"Karen," Treviño sighed heavily, "I know why. I've advocated an open and competitive system in terms of school program adoption, one where many programs have the opportunity to participate. I'm looking for opportunities for not only the Bienestar program, but for all the other programs out there that have some scientific evidence to support their results, as well as any new programs that don't, but have potential.

"Who knows; maybe a graduate student will develop a new school health program that produces better results than the Texas CATCH and the Bienestar! Let's find out! That's what I, and every other parent and citizen should want, but how will we ever discover the worthwhile programs available to us if the door is shut because of politics?

"The politicians want one program, and one program for all. And that's just not right. Because I don't keep quiet about this, I keep getting shunned by those who support the Texas CATCH exclusively—and that's what you've just seen happen here, with Cribb."

Coleman carefully and forthrightly responded, "Even though I'm a consultant for the Texas CATCH program, I agree with your perspective. It shouldn't just be one program for all."

Coleman paused, got close to Treviño, and whispered, "Roberto, I am going to e-mail the first draft of a manuscript on the CATCH El Paso evaluation results. I will be submitting it to the *Journal of the American Medical Association*. Let's see what happens. Please review it and give me your comments afterwards."

Treviño's eyes welled up at her kindness. "Thank you, Karen. You are a very fair person, and I value you for your openness."

"Let me tell you who is not fair. These guys from the Texas CATCH," Coleman barked out suddenly.

Treviño could not keep silent upon hearing these words. "Why?" he inquired.

"The fact of the matter is that, in El Paso, sixty-one percent of the teachers didn't even implement the Texas CATCH program because they felt it was culturally inappropriate for their children! The Texas CATCH program is not bilingual like yours."

"Can you tell me why the Texas CATCH people are being unfair?" Treviño wondered out loud.

"They want me to exclude those findings I just mentioned from the manuscript," Coleman answered directly. "But, I cannot, and I will not.

Those are the findings, and they need to be mentioned."

Treviño nodded his head, further words being unnecessary between the two. His pleasure at her honesty was reflected in his facial expression.

In another area of the reception, Garcia was confronting Ann Pauli from the Paso Del Norte Foundation. It was a chance meeting, and Garcia could not pass it up. This was the first opportunity she had had to speak directly with Pauli since being cut by the Chairwoman from sitting in on the "Type 2 Diabetes in Children and Adolescent" Statewide Action Plan (see page 71), and she let her justifiable frustration and fury show.

"Why was I removed from that committee?" Garcia asked deliberately, without exchanging pleasantries. "You didn't even give me the courtesy of returning my calls. What were you trying to hide?"

Incensed at her unfair treatment, Garcia continued barking out questions without giving Pauli even a chance to respond.

"Who was involved in that committee? Who gave y'all the authority to use public money to fund the Texas CATCH program? And how can you say that the Texas CATCH program is a diabetes prevention program?"

It was around this point that Treviño, on the other side of the room, happened to glance over. When he saw Garcia's body language, he noted that she was being too overtly aggressive, almost pushing her finger into Pauli's chest. Concerned that nearby guests might get the wrong impression of Garcia as being the troublemaker, he strode over quickly to interrupt the interaction.

Looking into Pauli's eyes, he said softly but furiously. "It was unfair what y'all did. We're not going to sit back and let the children in our state get screwed. They deserve health care and education that is appropriate for them!"

With these words, he took Garcia by the arm and led her away, to give her an opportunity to calm down.

FOOT SOLDIERS IN THE SKIRMISH

Although the Bienestar program was not a TEA-approved program in 2003, it had been adopted by some schools. The San Antonio, the South San Antonio, and the Edgewood Independent School Districts (ISD) were the school districts in Texas operating the Bienestar program on their campuses.

The SHRC was operating through a large NIH grant to prevent

type 2 diabetes, and to detect and treat children being diagnosed with type 2 diabetes. Without the SHRC having schools in which to conduct their studies, the NIH would not have funded the SHRC. So the small non-profit needed these schools to keep its funding—just as the schools needed the SHRC to detect and treat the five to seven percent of their children being diagnosed with diabetes! The SHRC then used its arrangement with Dr. Daniel Hale, a pediatric endocrinologist, to provide these children with free medical care.

The fact that the SHRC was getting this kind of support and funding was something the CTN must not have been pleased about. To cut off the SHRC from the schools, and in the process, the children from their medical care, the CTN sent in foot soldiers.

The Bexar County Medical Society is the association that represents San Antonio physicians; the Bexar County Medical Society Alliance is the affiliate of this association that represents the physicians' wives. The physicians' wives, who were not aware of the skirmish and the reasons for it, were used to push the Texas CATCH program to San Antonio area schools. When the Texas Medical Association (TMA) funded them with $10,000 for this purpose, the Alliance planned the *CATCH a Star Family Wellness Fiesta* event for March 8, 2003. It was poorly attended, and fortunately had no impact on the school districts where the Bienestar program operated, because those schools were already pleased with their students' responses to the Bienestar.

The following month, Treviño made sure to present the Bienestar health program to the Bexar County Medical Society's Public Health Committee to make them aware of the program and its results. After hearing about the program's effectiveness, the chairman, and the committee members agreed to support the Bienestar program in the present schools.

The CTN continued to push its agenda through foot soldiers. A woman named Kathy Shields, who was with the TDH Region 8 office, was sent to extirpate the Bienestar program out of Edgewood ISD. They had attempted something similar, with the San Antonio ISD before, but as Roger Rodriguez, SAISD Director of Health Curriculums, had chased them out, they were now approaching Edgewood ISD. The Edgewood ISD was the second largest school district which had the Bienestar program in operation, and any kind of pull-out here would have been harmful to SHRC present grants.

Treviño found out about this latest attempt when Julia Garcia, Edgewood ISD Director of Nursing, called him early one morning in

May 2003. She was aware of the unfair treatment the Bienestar program had received from state agencies.

Treviño was in New Orleans for a conference, but quickly returned Julia's call.

"I didn't want to bother you while you were away, but I thought you would find this important," Garcia started in a serious tone. "It's about an attempt to get the Texas CATCH program adopted by our schools, and get the Bienestar program out."

Treviño was used to hearing unscrupulous acts by the CTN people, so he responded with these words: "At this point, nothing surprises me, Julia. What are they up to now?"

"Do you know a Kathy Shields?"

Treviño racked his brain. "Is she a short, blond, anglo girl?"

"Yes."

"I met her with Dr. Chip Riggins," Treviño remembered. "Dr. Riggins is the director of the regional Texas Department of Health office. I had invited him to a diabetes screening at Hawthorne Elementary School in SAISD. It took two letters and two phone calls to get him to visit the schools where children are being diagnosed with diabetes. But I wanted him to hear firsthand how painful it is when we must call mothers to inform them that their children have tested positive for diabetes.

"Shields accompanied Dr. Riggins. At the time, there were two children who had tested positive. When I called the parents, I made sure Riggins heard me talking to the parents. But while it tore me apart to hear the mothers' responses, I don't think the reactions impacted him at all."

"You're right, Dr. Treviño," Julia responded immediately. "I don't think the reactions even touched them—because Kathy Shields called the office of Dr. Luis Gonzales, the Edgewood ISD superintendent, and introduced herself as a grant writer with the San Antonio Metropolitan Health District."

"What did she want?"

"She offered Dr. Gonzalez a lot of money if he would remove the Bienestar program, and bring in the Texas CATCH program."

"Money from where?" Treviño said, raising his voice at this new information.

"Apparently, she is writing a CDC grant for the City of San Antonio Metropolitan Health Department, and if it is funded, he would be offered part of that money. But I wonder why, with twelve school districts in San Antonio, they chose to approach us," Julia wondered.

Treviño immediately understood what was at work here.

"I can't believe they are doing that. They want to bring in a program that has never lowered a blood sugar into neighborhoods where diabetes has made pharmacies and dialysis centers a vital part of the business district. We're not good for the dialysis business," Treviño analyzed, "and so they must want to erase us from the face of this earth."

"I know for a fact that families living in the Edgewood area have the highest rates of poverty and diabetes in the state," Garcia said, confirming Treviño's assessment.

Treviño gave a bitter laugh, and shook his head in utter frustration.

As soon as he returned to San Antonio, Treviño called Gonzalez and Kathy Shields to set up some meetings. He was hoping he could convince both parties to include the Bienestar program in the CDC grant. But he knew he had to move fast, because SHRC's NIH grants depended on a successful relationship in the schools.

When the meeting with Gonzalez came about, Gonzalez was cordial, and afterwards, Treviño got a letter of support from Dr. Gonzalez in preparation for the CDC grant.

The following morning, Shields arrived at the SHRC with another co-worker. The Associate Director of the SHRC, Irene Hernandez, joined Treviño for the meeting.

Treviño and Hernandez were extremely gracious in the meeting as they hoped to persuade Shields to include their program in the CDC grant. Together the two carefully presented the program, its measurements, and its results.

Treviño concluded the presentation by stating, "I want to thank you for taking time to listen to our presentation. I know you're writing a CDC grant, and we want to be part of your proposal. I think we have some good scientific evidence that can strengthen your proposal."

Shields and her colleague looked impressed both during and after the SHRC presentation. Then Sheilds spoke up to say, "It's true that we're writing a CDC Healthier Steps grant. But we're looking into bringing in new programs to the schools. We'd rather work directly with the schools, and provide them with money so they can develop their own programs, rather than granting money to a program already at work."

"The Bienestar program took eight years of hard work and adjustments before it could show evidence of decreasing blood sugars," Treviño said forcefully as he leaned forward in his chair. "Children in the Edgewood ISD cannot wait another eight years for another program to work effectively. They are walking around with undiagnosed type 2 diabetes, and they need effective programs right now."

"Well, we are open to ideas, and you have a good idea," Shields observed with a smile.

"Ms. Shields, we're more than just an idea," Hernandez reminded Shields politely. "We have results."

"Can you give us an opportunity to write what would be our section of the grant so you can consider incorporating it into the main narrative?" Treviño asked, toning down the volume of his voice.

Shields agreed to Treviño's suggestion, and he felt pleased with the meeting. Perhaps things might work out after all.

But it went downhill from there.

Later during the same week, Treviño would receive a call from Gonzalez's secretary.

"Hello, Dr. Treviño," the female voice on the other end of the phone said. "Dr. Gonzalez wanted me to let you know that he wishes to rescind the letter of support he gave you."

Treviño could not believe what he had just heard.

"I'm sorry," he said in disbelief. "Can you repeat what you said?"

"Dr. Gonzalez wants you to destroy the letter of support he gave you," she said again, but this time sounding nervous.

"Why?" Treviño demanded, his forehead furrowing in surprise.

"Ms. Shields has convinced him to pull your program out of our schools, and bring in a new program instead," she forthrightly responded.

Treviño could not believe this news.

"But the Bienestar is working very well in your school system, and has shown to decrease blood sugars in your children there!" Treviño bluntly informed the woman while he heard his name being paged at the center.

When he heard Julia Garcia was on the other line, he hung up with Gonzalez's secretary to talk to Garcia. He wanted to let her know what was going on, as she was a strong supporter of the Bienestar program and saw daily the reality of its positive impact on schoolchildren.

"Julia, I just got off the phone with a staff member from Dr. Gonzalez's office! She basically told me to flush his letter of support for the Bienestar program down the toilet!"

"That's why I called you, Dr. Treviño," Garcia said. "I heard the news, and I wanted to make sure that you had been informed."

"Julia, thank you for being so considerate and open. But let me call Gonzalez directly, and I will call you back once I've had a chance to converse with him," Treviño promised, and hung up.

Gonzalez's staff answered the phone, and passed the call through.

"Hello, Dr. Gonzalez," Treviño politely said, taking a deep breath to stay calm. "I spoke to a member of your staff, and she told me you wanted our letter of support to be rescinded. May I ask why?"

"Well, I've just spoken with Kathy Shields. She convinced me that it doesn't make sense to give you the CDC money when we can keep it for our own programs."

"First of all," Treviño reminded, "she cannot promise anything if she hasn't even written a grant. And, if she ultimately does have the money to grant, what are you going to do with it? You may have to let eight years pass before you can develop a program that has the outcomes of the Bienestar, if you are that lucky! Don't overlook the fact that there are children in your schools right now walking around with diabetes who cannot wait. They need medical treatment now!"

Gonzalez was quiet for a moment, no doubt reflecting on all the services the SHRC provided his district. At the time, SHRC grants were giving Edgewood ISD health textbooks for the children, food service staff, and parents. In addition, the program was screening the schoolchildren for type 2 diabetes, and providing those who screened positive with free medical care.

Treviño knew that Gonzalez was a fair man, and an asset to his school system. And sure enough, Gonzalez reconsidered his position, assuring Treviño that the Bienestar would not be removed from his district.

The story did not end here. The following school year (2003-2004), the Bienestar program would extend its reach to even more schools in the Edgewood ISD.

But Gonzalez would find his contract not renewed by the school board for other reasons, and Shields would come to discover that her grant proposal did not receive funding in the submission.

Shields resubmitted the grant the following year, and on the second time around, she was successful getting funded. This time, however, Shields included the Bienestar program in the award. The staff members of the SHRC never questioned her about why she tried to exclude the Bienestar program or what made her change her mind. They were just happy to be part of the San Antonio Metropolitan Health Department team.

BANKROLLING THE TEXAS CATCH

The CTN people did not need to retaliate with such force. Money was still pouring into their coffers. Over the years, Perry oversaw state policies laid out to provide CTN with large amounts of public money so they could give children at-risk for diabetes with a diabetes prevention program that was, in reality, an illusion. Perry and the CTN had arranged a system where politicians, not health professionals, controlled the money, and were essentially the ones determining the medical treatment of children with pre-diabetes and type 2 diabetes.

It is unknown why they did this; but the consequences might have been: endanger children living in poverty and profits for the health industry. Nothing wrong with the latter, when ethical!

Specifically, the money that flowed from the state of Texas to the CTN each year was as follows:

YEAR	MONEY
1998	$ 173,351
2000	$ 350,154
2001	$ 836,063
2002	$ 609,000
2003	$ 749,954
2004	$1,186,073
2005	$ 299,983
Total	$4,204,578

TAKING IT TO THE BORDER

The multi-state lawsuit, over the marketing of the George Foreman Grills, won by Texas Attorney General Greg Abbott is an example of how they passed money over to the CTN. The attorney general's office announced in a press release on September 13, 2004:

> "...Texas's share of a multi-state $8 million antitrust settlement with Salton Inc. over its marketing of George Foreman Grill, will provide $585,000 to the Texas Department of Health Services for its renowned child diabetes prevention program."

The program being referred to was the Texas CATCH, and Treviño found it particularly ironic that a program which itself was forming a monopoly in terms of the all-out protection afforded it by the government was going to receive money from an antitrust lawsuit.

With this new money the CTN people began flashing it in the faces of school staff from Laredo, Texas school districts. Fortunately, school districts in the state of Texas acted differently than one another. When the staffs at schools in Laredo, Texas, were approached by CTN promoters, they decided to learn more about both programs, the Bienestar and the Texas CATCH, to determine which had more benefits for their children. They did not act impulsively and make an unwise decision when state monies were dangled in front of them.

Before making a decision on what course to pursue, Patricia Keck, Laredo ISD Director of Nursing; Linda Flores, United ISD Director of Nursing; and Dolores Medrano, United ISD Assistant Superintendent made a visit to the SHRC in October 2004. Also present at the meeting were Roger Rodriguez, Director of Health Curriculum for the San Antonio Independent School District (SAISD); Janice Fox, SAISD Director of Food Services, and Irene Hernandez of the SHRC.

When Keck, Flores, and Medrano arrived at the SHRC building, Hernandez gave them a tour of the facility, and then took them to a conference room for the meeting. There, Treviño and Hernandez presented research which showed the Bienestar program's success in decreasing blood sugars in children. Rodriguez and Fox then talked about the SAISD experience implementing the Bienestar program, explaining how easy it was for the district to adapt the program into their Scope and Sequence instructional policy.

For these presentations, the staff members of the SHRC stayed with the science and avoided any mention of CTN politics. While the staff members wanted to complain out loud about the unfair treatment the SHRC had received, they avoided doing so. They knew that if their small and fledgling non-profit center was pitched against the large and credible Houston's UTSPH and TDH, the Laredo entourage would probably favor the large organizations. So the SHRC staff decided to stay with the program's results, since these vouched best for the effectiveness of the Bienestar.

"We are very impressed with the results of the program, and more important, that it is bilingual," Keck commented afterwards. Keck had short hair, was short in stature, but she was long in asking questions and analyzing every data presented.

"We are aware of the increasing number of children being diagnosed with type 2 diabetes," she continued, "and many of these children are Spanish-speaking. Your program fits well in South Texas."

But it seemed that Keck and Flores wanted to know more than just the science. Flores looked straight at Treviño, and she leaned forward to put her arms on the conference table.

"We know there have been some differences between the Bienestar and the Texas CATCH programs," Flores said. "Can you tell us about these differences?"

These words surprised everyone in the room, and it got quiet for a moment. The tension broke when Treviño cracked a smile.

"The Texas CATCH is an education intervention, and the Bienestar is a medical intervention," he clarified. "The Texas CATCH program has modified behaviors, and the Bienestar program has modified biological markers. Children in South Texas are beyond an education intervention. They are walking around with a serious illness, and they need a more intense program that can restore blood sugars back to normal."

Treviño tried to keep his words neutral, and to not disparage the Texas CATCH program in any way despite the continued battles he had had with its proponents.

"Have you tried meeting with the CATCH people?" Flores asked Treviño. "I think there is enough room in Texas for more than one program."

"Yes, but the Texas CATCH people don't want any other program playing in Texas," Treviño responded. "We have tried to convince them that both programs can exist, and that both programs can even complement each other, but they are not about sharing. They want it all."

"Dr. Treviño, we are also aware that the Texas Education Agency has refrained from approving your program for many years," Keck queried further. "Why wouldn't they?"

Treviño knew why Keck had asked this question. Many school district staffs were intimidated by the TEA, and shied away from any controversy that might incite an investigation from the agency.

To Treviño's surprise, Rodriguez moved in to respond to the question, answering in a serious and measured tone.

"Because they've been unfair. We have spent three years operating the Bienestar successfully in our schools, and I have been at TEA meetings where TEA staff members have actually threatened me if I didn't replace the Bienestar with the CATCH program."

Flores and Keck looked somewhat bewildered at Rodriguez words.

He continued, "On another occasion, the Texas CATCH people approached me and offered money to me personally if I implemented their program in our schools. I told them no. Not only is it illegal to receive money during work hours, it's unethical to be paid money to implement a program."

Everyone looked appalled when they heard this news, and as the meeting came to a close, Medrano whispered to Treviño, "In our school district, I'll make sure that only the Bienestar plays."

Three weeks later, Flores and Keck called Treviño to inform him that their schools districts would be adopting the Bienestar program. They had done their review, and found another major difference between the Bienestar and the Texas CATCH programs: when the programs were introduced into a new school, the Bienestar measured outcomes and the Texas CATCH did not.

When the CTN promoters failed in Laredo, they next targeted the Brownsville, Texas school district. The Brownsville ISD staff were swept away by the money the state was providing for the Texas CATCH training, books, and publicity, and unfortunately chose a program for their students that did not help prevent or treat type 2 diabetes and its complications.

Forgotten Children: A True Story of How Politicians Endanger Children

Chapter 6

THE BROWN ONE TURNS HIS BACK

TRAITOR OR FRIEND?
When Governor Rick Perry approved Dr. Eduardo Sanchez as the new Commissioner of Health in November 2001, it meant that the first Mexican-American would be serving as Commissioner of Health for the state of Texas.

Sanchez hailed from Corpus Christi, Texas, and had come out of the public school system to become a physician, with a specialty in Family Medicine. He was tall, with dark brown wavy hair and a naturally tan skin.

The south Texas community was proud that one of their own was to be the first Commissioner. Would things finally be changing for the better for the children of Texas?

Soon after Sanchez's appointment was announced — on November 27, 2001—Treviño sent Sanchez a letter inviting him to visit San Antonio to observe the schools where the Bienestar program was being implemented. In the letter, Treviño detailed for Sanchez the results of a study which reported that nearly five percent of Texas children living in poverty were being diagnosed with type 2 diabetes, and that these children, by participating in the Bienestar program, had decreased their blood sugars by a whopping twenty percent.

The message to Sanchez could not be clearer. Texas children living in poverty were being diagnosed with type 2 diabetes, and the Bienestar program was restoring their blood sugars back to normal. These children were being put on a path that could lead to a healthy future for them.

The lack of response to Treviño's communication indicated the path Sanchez would go down in the future.

BROWN VERSUS BROWN

Vincent Ramos, Texas Director of the League of United Latin American Councils (LULAC), had heard of the Bienestar program and its positive results. He invited Treviño to be part of the health symposium he was planning, where investigators would present their studies about the health problems affecting the Hispanic community. Ramos also set a meeting with Sanchez, and invited Treviño, hoping to get the TDH to provide funding for the symposium.

The meeting with Sanchez was set for January 2002. During the meeting, Ramos explained the plan and expectations of the symposium. Sanchez agreed to support the symposium, and asked that the TDH have a strong presence there, and input on final recommendations. Ramos agreed to this, and then he reintroduced Treviño and the good work the SHRC was doing in south Texas.

Treviño smiled at this praise, and in turn praised Sanchez.

"First I want to congratulate you on your appointment, and let you know that many in the Hispanic community are very proud of you," Treviño told Sanchez. "I'm sure you have been extremely busy in your new position, and you're being pulled in many directions."

Sanchez nodded his head to signal his agreement.

"But the reason I'm here is this: to inform you of the high number of children being diagnosed with type 2 diabetes in our state. Nearly five percent of the children we tested for diabetes this year had high blood glucose levels. These kids are only nine years old and they will go blind, lose limbs, or be on dialysis before they reach adolescence if their blood glucose is not corrected to normal levels. This is not right, Dr. Sanchez, and there is much we can do."

"I see your concern, but my priority right now has to be bioterrorism," Sanchez informed Treviño, lifting his head and putting his hands on the desk in front of him. "Our country is under a major threat from terrorists, and protecting our borders comes first."

The attack on the World Trade Center towers had happened only four months before, and American citizens, and the nation, were still reeling from the attack and the implications it held for America's future.

"I wake up in the middle of the night thinking about the attack on the twin towers," Treviño sympathized. "About a year ago, my family and I were on the roof of one of the towers. And now it's gone. I can't believe anyone would go to that extreme and harm innocent people. So indeed I see your point, but I am hoping you can also see the point of view of the parents in this state whose children are being diagnosed with diabetes. It doesn't have to be like this! We can do something about it

Forgotten Children: A True Story of How Politicians Endanger Children

while we are also protecting ourselves from terrorism."

"Dr. Treviño, I am the Commissioner, and I will decide what health issues will be addressed by the Texas Department of Health," Sanchez informed Treviño, a slight tone of arrogance coating his voice.

"Yes sir, you are the Commissioner," Treviño said with a smile. "But can you also make time to visit our center and the schools where the Bienestar program operates? You need to see first-hand the impact the program is having on the children and school staff! There is no graph or statistics that can replace the emotional impact it makes to observe our schoolchildren participating with enthusiasm in the components of our program."

"As I told you, I'm extremely busy and have other priorities. I'm sorry I don't have the time to visit San Antonio soon."

Treviño left the TDH disappointed at the Commissioner's reluctance to make time for the children. But at the same time, he understood the very real threat bioterrorism posed his state and nation.

SANCHEZ'S 'HEALTH' POLICIES

With Sanchez not too interested about the needs of south Texas children, Treviño started wondering about what health policies Sanchez would implement to address the growing problem of youth-onset type 2 diabetes.

One day in early February 2002, Treviño's phone rang.

When Treviño picked it up, a weary-sounding voice at the other end of the phone greeted him with the words, "Hi, Dr. Treviño."

"Who is this?" Treviño queried politely, since the caller had not identified herself.

"Oh, I'm sorry! This is Jan Ozias."

"Jan, how you doing? What can I do for you?"

"We at the Texas Department of Health are real impressed with the Bienestar program. I just want to keep the Texas Diabetes Council board up to date on all the good things your program is doing. Can you tell me how many children in the Bienestar program who had high blood sugars were started on medicines?"

On the surface, the question was innocent enough. But Treviño believed that Ozias was really checking to see if diabetes drugs rather than implementation of the Bienestar program were correcting the children's abnormal blood sugars. In Treviño's experience, Ozias was often used by the CTN to collect information from the SHRC, and pass it along, so that the CTN people could use it to their program's advantage.

"None," Treviño answered proudly. "You should've received a

copy of an abstract that was published and presented at the Diabetes Translation conference in Boston."

"Oh! When did you send it?"

"Last week."

"And what did the study show?" Ozias asked.

"It showed that children participating in the Bienestar program decreased blood sugars, and it did so without the need of drugs to treat diabetes."

"Thank you, I will look for the study in my mail. Can you also tell me the cost of the Bienestar health program?"

"The health education textbook on its own costs $4.50 per student. If the schools implement the health education, plus the food service, the parent, and the P.E. components, the total cost is $12 per student."

Two weeks later, the TDH circulated an internal document. Not only did it not mention the successful Bienestar program outcomes—although it mentioned the Bienestar program—it misrepresented the cost of the program. Among other things, the document stated that Bienestar's books cost $100 per pupil, and the Texas CATCH books cost $1 per pupil.

So Treviño called Ozias as soon as Rosario Hamilton, a nutritionist employed by the TDH, e-mailed him a copy of the document. He was incensed about the current misrepresentation of the program, especially in light of the fact that he had articulated the correct program cost to Ozias in their phone conversation just two weeks earlier.

When Ozias picked up the phone, Treviño bypassed introductions and pleasantries.

"Jan," he said, raising his voice, "the annual cost for treating diabetes with drugs and other medical interventions is $13,000 a patient, and if the Texas CATCH program can treat the condition for $1, they should bottle it and sell it over the counter. Also when you called some weeks ago I clearly told you that the cost for all the Bienestar components was $12. But an internal memo from the Texas Department of Health quoted the cost as $100. That is a lie!"

Ozias kept quiet so Treviño continued.

"Jan, please put me on the Texas Diabetes Council board agenda so I can have an opportunity to clarify this misrepresentation."

Jan responded with a soft and trembling voice, "Dr. Treviño, the agenda is already full."

Treviño knew he was not going to get anywhere with this little fish, so he went up the stream.

He targeted Huang, the TDH's Chief of the Bureau of Chronic

Disease Prevention and Control, and Ozias immediate boss. Treviño sent him a letter in late February 2002 to complain about the staff at the TDH misrepresenting the Bienestar program in their report, as well as the TDH's exclusive support of the Texas CATCH program. He also sent a copy of this letter to the Commissioner of Health Sanchez.

Huang responded with a letter of his own in March 2002. It said in part:

> ...Please be assured that the entire Bureau, including the Diabetes Council, is committed to learning about, supporting and assisting all projects and promising programs that addressed health promotion and chronic disease prevention and control. We seek to develop partnerships and lend support to programs in many ways not just through contractual awards and co-sponsored functions.

As Treviño was reading the letter, he paused and turned to his computer, then went into the TDC web site. Sure enough, the Texas CATCH was all over the TDH's home page, and the site even featured a link to Houston's UTSPH. No other school health programs were named on the site.

Treviño shook his head, dispirited. This was characteristic of Ozias and Huang: to talk one way, but walk another way. Treviño felt stuck. He was getting nowhere with Ozias and Huang.

Treviño finally decided to pursue the tactic of re-appraoching the Health Commissioner. On July 10, 2002, he sent the Commissioner a second letter inviting him to visit San Antonio. This letter included a table that showed the Bienestar program as being more cost-effective, than current medical treatment for diabetes. The prior year, the annual cost of the Bienestar's four components was $12 per student, and it had decreased blood sugars by thirty-two percent. In comparison, the current annual cost to care for an individual with diabetes was $13,000, and the most potent drug treatment available to individuals at the time only decreased blood sugars by twenty-eight percent, or four percentage points less than the Bienestar program.

Sanchez failed to respond to Treviño's invitation. Once again, Treviño felt stuck—as it would be unwise to accuse Sanchez, the first Mexican-American Health Commissioner, of possessing the same kind of narrow-mindedness as Huang and Ozias.

BECOMING UNGLUED

Treviño's "stickiness" became unglued when the Texas Board of Health, which serves as the governing body of the TDH, received the following reports.

First, in October 2002, Sanchez reported to the Board of Health members that Houston's UTSPH was assigned to direct the implementation of school health programs as required by Senate Bill 19. Treviño knew that since Senate Bill 19's purpose was to implement coordinated school health programs, this would be a conflict of interest, because Houston's UTSPH was already promoting its own program: the Texas CATCH program.

Then in his November 2002 report to the Board of Health, Sanchez featured the Texas CATCH program as a model school health program and announced that the Division of Child Wellness at the TDH was changing its name to the School Health Program.

It was apparent to Treviño that Sanchez was changing his departments around to set the CTN up with a system to peddle the Texas CATCH program into the schools. This must mean Perry had hand-picked Sanchez for one purpose: to centrally plan the Texas CATCH program operations. They had put a badge on his chest—and sent him out to suppress his own.

Treviño was enraged. His fury erupted at home, when he informed his wife Maria del Carmen and his son, Robert Emerick of how upset he was at having to deal with politicians and bureaucrats when it came to matters of public health. [At the time of the conversation, Treviño's son Robert Emerick (Robby) was sixteen years of age.]

TREVIÑO: *"Pinches bolillos me ponen a este Mexicano pendejo en frente pa' pararme. Si fuera bolillo ya me lo hubiera llevado de encuentro."* ("Damn white guys put this dumb Mexican in front of me to hold me back. If he [Sanchez] would have been a white guy, I would have confronted him a long time ago.")

MARIA DEL CARMEN: "Robert, stop talking like that! What is wrong with you?"

TREVIÑO: "Maria, you don't know all the crap I go through with these guys."

MARIA DEL CARMEN: "It doesn't matter. You still shouldn't be talking like that."

TREVIÑO: "*Los bolillos* (the white guys) do it on purpose, Maria. They put these Mexicans in charge to shut us up. This is the first Mexican American Commissioner, and here I am going to have to bring him down."

ROBBY: "Aggression will get you nowhere, Dad."
TREVIÑO: "Aggression got Malcolm X a lot."
ROBBY: "Peace got Martin Luther King a lot more."
TREVIÑO: "Martin Luther King's peace prolonged the civil rights movement. Malcolm X's aggression shortened it."
ROBBY: "Yes, by telling blacks to get sticks and beat the white man!"
TREVIÑO: "Well, if the white man was slaughtering blacks in the south, then hell yeah!"
ROBBY: "So is that what you would do now, Dad?"
TREVIÑO: "I'll start on my knees, but if that doesn't work, I'll get up and get a stick."
ROBBY: "Martin Luther King's peace movement did a lot more for civil rights than sticks."
TREVIÑO: "Martin Luther King had too much patience."
ROBBY: "But his patience paid off. Look at how society has rewarded him by naming schools, buildings, and a holiday after him."
TREVIÑO: "Martin Luther King tried to work the heart, but *they* don't have a heart!"
ROBBY: "And what did Malcolm X work? Shoot'em in the head!"
TREVIÑO: "Malcolm X scared the shit out of them!"
MARIA DEL CARMEN: "Robert, stop cussing!"
TREVIÑO: "I'm sorry, Maria, but I'm pissed off!"
MARIA DEL CARMEN: "They are doing bad things, I know. But if you wish bad things on them, that makes you no different than them."
TREVIÑO: "I don't care about myself. I care about the poor children these son of a guns are gonna kill!"

As the weeks passed, Treviño continued to endure similar mistreatments, bias, and stalemates, and his family at home continued to hear about these actions. The stress at home was building up, so Treviño decided to take his family on a vacation trip to Dallas, Texas. In Dallas, they were driving along a wide boulevard which led right into the museum that was exhibiting the Tutankhamen collection. Treviño's children, Robby and Bianca, were on the back seat when Robby turned his head to stare at a street sign. Whatever it said so provoked Robby's interest that he almost got off his seat to get a good look at the street sign.

Robby turned his head back to the front and asked, "Dad, can we stop here to lunch in one of these restaurants? This looks like a nice neighborhood, and there are lots of nice restaurants."

Treviño looked over at the street sign to see where they were. The boulevard they were on was the Malcolm X Boulevard.

THE WHITE GUY KICKS BUTT

Treviño walked in the SHRC one afternoon and noticed a man working with Melissa Romero, an SHRC evaluation staff member. The man was white, with a slim face, glasses, and neatly-groomed graying hair.

"*Quien es el bolillo?*" ("Who is the white guy?") Treviño asked Albert Salinas, the financial director.

"His name is Dave Dawson. He's an IT guy Melissa met at the University of Texas Health Science Center at San Antonio," Salinas responded. "Melissa has been having a hard time accessing our study data, and he offered to help her."

Treviño nodded his head. He was well aware that the SHRC, as a small non-profit center, had information technology and systems that were outdated.

"Does he work for the health science center?" Treviño queried

"No, he's a retired colonel from the air force."

"*Y de donde es?*" ("And where is he from?")

"He's from east Texas," Salinas answered, shrugging.

"East Texas? That's where they tie blacks from the ankles and drag 'em in the streets!" Treviño responded sharply and suspiciously. [In 1998, in Jasper, Texas, James Byrd, a black man, was hunted down by three white supremacists, tied to the back of a truck, and dragged until he died.]

Salinas winced, surprised at this prejudicial comment coming from Treviño's mouth.

Treviño deliberately walked into his office without going up to Dawson to introduce himself and say hello. Because of the story in east Texas and the hardships Treviño had been experiencing—often from those of other ethnicities—he had formed what turn out to be an unfair judgment on a good man.

Despite Treviño's standoffishness, Dawson kept coming to the office to work with Melissa, and soon Melissa's data output was increasing remarkably.

After two weeks, Treviño went into Melissa's office and introduced himself to Dawson. It was a short exchange, but Treviño thanked the man for helping with the data management. He then walked over to Salinas' office.

"How much has he been charging us?" Treviño asked Salinas.

"Nothing, Dr. Treviño. I've asked him to give us an invoice, and he just shakes his head 'no'."

"Wow," Treviño said, lifting his brows in surprise.

Days later, Melissa Romero gave the SHRC a two-week notice of resignation. She had taken a new position with the UTHSCSA.

On hearing the news, Treviño became concerned about her departure, since no other staff member knew the data base.

"Irene," Treviño said to the Center's Associate Director, "with Melissa leaving, I am worried about how to locate the data sets for our projects."

"No one else in SHRC has any sort of statistical background," Hernandez replied. "So I've asked Dave if he knew where all the data was located, and he said yes. He's reorganized the data base, and made the information more accessible."

"Did you ask him if he could show the new statistician we'll be hiring where the data sets are located?"

"I did, and he said, 'Of course.'"

When six weeks had passed since Dawson had started coming to SHRC to work on the data base, Treviño went to Salinas's office and asked if he had compensated Dawson for his work yet.

Salinas responded, "No."

"Albert, we need to pay him," Treviño said, upset. Dawson had helped them immeasurably by simplifying the storage and management of the SHRC's data. "Have you even been tracking his time?"

"No," Salinas confessed, lowering his head.

"We shouldn't expect people to do work for free. Please make a check for $1,000, and I'll hand it over to him."

When Treviño spied Dawson the following afternoon in a corner working quietly on the data base, he greeted Dawson and stretched out his hand. In it was the envelope.

"What is this?" Dawson asked.

"Compensation for your work, Dave," Treviño responded with a smile. "You have turned us onto a topnotch IT system. The quality and number of progress reports produced by the evaluation staff has increased significantly since you've been here. We need to compensate you for that."

Dawson stretched his hand out and pushed Treviño's hand and envelope away.

"No, thank you, its okay."

Smiling, Dawson walked downstairs and out the door.

The pattern continued. For years, Dawson continued coming to the SHRC nearly every day to work without requesting any sort of compensation.

During that time, Dawson helped the SHRC's acquire a powerful server that handles large amounts of data at a fast speed. He developed software for the teachers and program staff so that they could enter the number of lesson plans taught and the number of students in attendance at the lesson. In addition, he saw to it that SHRC data could be entered through the web from anywhere in the U.S. and Mexico. This was important, since the SHRC had two major projects operating in Mexico, and entering lesson plans taught and attendance rates were important to monitor the fidelity of the Bienestar program implementation. The success of the program depended on all components of the program being implemented as planned.

Dawson also programmed the SHRC's laptops so that the evaluation staff could collect data in the field from thousands of children expeditiously. The laptops were programmed so that if outlier data was entered, the system prompted the evaluation staff to question the validity of the information. If there was any doubt, the data could be recollected right there and then, rather than the evaluation staff having to come back another day.

With their new technology, the evaluation staff could synchronize their computers in the afternoon so that in the morning, the biological data was ready for analysis. Thus, by the following day, school nurses were able to receive the name and blood sugar values of those students who had abnormal levels. This allowed the staff of the SHRC to refer students with abnormal blood sugar levels to physicians without delay.

Dawson also designed a scanning system where behavioral and demographic data could be entered faster with fewer errors. In sum, Dawson had completely reconfigured the SHRC's Evaluation Department's ability to collect data with higher accuracy and efficiency. The information technology he built prepared the SHRC to compete for national awards.

For example, in 2004, the NIH announced a nationwide grant to develop and test a middle-school diabetes prevention program—The Healthy Study. It was the largest grant ever funded for school health interventions. It was a multi-center trial and it was going to be very competitive.

Many universities from around the country applied, and only seven sites with the highest merit scores were selected. Oregon Health and Science University, the University of North Carolina at Chapel Hill, the University of California at Irvine, Baylor College of Medicine, the

University of Pittsburg, Temple University, and the SHRC were the seven sites. George Washington University was the coordinating center for the Healthy Study; and the National Institute of Diabetes, Digestive and Kidney Disease, the NIH arm located in Bethesda, Maryland, was the operating center.

It was the second largest NIH grant ever awarded to the SHRC.

"Dr. Treviño, Dave is amazing," Hernandez commented to Treviño one day. "Thanks to him, we're now the little train that can."

Treviño looked at Hernandez and gave a smile.

"Irene, I don't think Dave is human. I think he's an angel."

BACK TO THE BROWN ONE

In March 2003, Treviño continued his pursuit of Sanchez, sending him the following letter:

> Attached are letters from Edgewood Independent School District students, coaches, principals and cafeteria staff showing their support for the Bienestar [program]. The EISD is among the poorest school districts in Texas, and we estimate that 1,500 of their children have undiagnosed diabetes. This is a medical illness that needs aggressive detection, prevention and treatment. Without an intense medical intervention these children will lose their eyesight, will lose an extremity or will lose kidney function before they reach adolescence. The approach by the Texas Department of Health to target only students' health beliefs and behaviors without targeting blood glucose levels will not be enough. It is high blood glucose that will cause blindness, amputations, and dialysis, and it is lowering their high blood glucose that will prevent blindness, amputations and dialysis. We urge you to consider supporting the Bienestar program because it is based on best practices and has successfully lowered blood glucose in children participating in the program.

This letter was copied to Governor Perry, state senators Frank Madla, Jane Nelson, Leticia Van de Putte, and Jeff Wentworth; and state representatives Pete Gallego, Garnett Coleman, and Mike Villarreal.

There would be no response from Sanchez or any of the politicians.

• DR. ROBERTO P. TREVIÑO •

And when Texas Attorney General Greg Abbott's office sent out its press release in September 2004 about how the funds from the George Foreman Grill lawsuit would be used to fund the Texas CATCH program (see page 91), Treviño sent Sanchez the following e-mail (with an excerpt from the web site of the grill lawsuit announcement) cited below:

> The web below shows an example of how our state agencies make decisions on children's health based on politics and not on science. The Texas Department of Health gave the CATCH program $585,000 for their 'renowned children's diabetes prevention program'. The CATCH has never measured a blood sugar, nonetheless lowered one. How can anyone play politics with the health of children? It is science that should drive the decisions that determine what are the best health interventions for Texas children. The Bienestar is the only renowned children diabetes prevention program (attached was a study on the Bienestar program published in the *Archives of Pediatrics and Adolescent Medicine* was attached). I hope you reconsider your giveaway.

Copies were sent to Charles Bell, Greg Abbott, and the following state senators and representatives: Frank Madla, Leticia Van de Putte, Elizabeth Jones, Ruth McClendon, Carlos Uresti, Jose Menendez, Trey Martinez, Joaquin Castro, Judith Zaffirini, Jeff Wentworth, Robert Puente, Frank Corte, Michael Villarreal, Ken Mercer, Pete Gallego, Garnett Coleman, Eddie Lucio, Juan Hinojosa, Kenneth Armbrister, John Shields, and Eliot Shapleigh.

Again, no one responded to the information, so Treviño followed up with an e-mail to the politicians representing Bexar County (Madla, Van de Putte, Jones, McClendon, Uresti, Menendez, Martinez, Castro, Zaffirini, Wentworth, Puente, Corte, Villarreal, and Mercer). He asked them to help ensure that Sanchez be brought to the table so he could explain why the Texas CATCH program was called a "renowned child diabetes prevention program" in the press release without there being any evidence on which to base this claim.

This time, someone took action. Van de Putte (D-San Antonio), a heavy-set, light-skinned, Mexican-American senator and practicing pharmacist, sent Sanchez the following letter on November 30, 2004:

We are writing to request an audience with you to discuss the matter of the Bienestar program. Currently, Bienestar is the only program effectively decreasing blood glucose levels in high risk children, yet the Texas Department of Health gives funding only to one program known as Coordinated Approach to Child Health (CATCH). It is my understanding that the TDH calls CATCH a "renowned children's diabetes prevention program" when it has never lowered the level of blood glucose in any child. We must place programs shown to restore normoglycemia within our children's reach.

The needs of constituents are better met when lawmakers unite to support health policy models that are most effective. Children's health issues are uniquely critical in nature because the lack of child health care will eventually translate into higher number of adults with chronic disease and larger medical expenses that affect all legislative districts.

While I am a strong proponent of innovation, any proposal involving disease prevention programs should be reviewed for best practices. We should move cautiously. Doing it right is far more important than doing it quickly. As state legislators we must consider new solutions that benefit South Texas, which has one of the highest rates of child-onset type 2 diabetes. Thank you for your consideration. I look forward to our meeting.

When Sanchez did not give Van de Putte the courtesy of a timely response, Treviño called the Senator's office, and spoke with David Yañez, her legislative aide.

"Hey David, this is Dr. Treviño. I am calling to get an update on the letter the Senator sent Dr. Sanchez."

"We have not heard back from him," Yañez replied in a rush.

"Could you or the Senator call his office to get a response?" Treviño queried.

"The Senator sent a pretty strong letter, and that is as far as we can go," Yañez claimed.

Treviño didn't appreciate this response when the health of children was at stake.

"And what about the children? Do we let them go blind and lose limbs just because the Commissioner doesn't feel like giving us a response?"

"Dr. Treviño, what proof do you have that the children will go blind and lose limbs?" Yañez pushed back.

"The proof is on Southwest Military Drive [south San Antonio]," Treviño retorted. "Go up and down the boulevard, and you should be able to gauge how sick this community is. CVS and Walgreens pharmacies are sprouting out like wild weeds in every major intersection because of the increasing rates of diabetes and its complications."

Unfortunately, Treviño was to end his conversation with the senator's aide knowing he had hit a dead end.

It took two months before Sanchez responded to Senator Van de Putte's letter. In it he justified the TDH's support for the Texas CATCH program with legislative mandates and law codes rather than scientific evidence. He also informed Van de Putte that his staff would be contacting her office to schedule a date for the meeting. But his staff never called Van de Putte's office.

Sanchez had sent Treviño a copy of his response to Van de Putte. Treviño responded to this letter immediately. In it, Treviño again described the health outcomes of the Bienestar and the Texas CATCH programs. He also referenced nine studies published on the Bienestar program's health outcomes. He ended the letter with the following paragraph.

> ...Although the Bienestar is the only program shown to improve children's physiology and biology, we [at the SRHC] still believe there is no perfect program out there. The science of school health interventions is in its early phase, and to prune other programs and protect one from competition is a disservice to the children of Texas. Our request is to let programs compete for best practices and let schools at the local level decide what program best fits their student population. We look forward to our meeting.

Sanchez wrote back to Treviño informing him that schools with students at-risk for diabetes can use their own funds to contract with the SHRC, and that the TDH will be using their funds to implement the Texas CATCH in the other schools. In other words, schools with students at-risk for diabetes were left to the Bienestar program and were getting no funding, while schools with healthier children were receiving the Texas CATCH program with funding from the TDH.

Forgotten Children: A True Story of How Politicians Endanger Children

Treviño was getting nowhere with Sanchez and Van de Putte.

Robert Puente (D-San Antonio) was a state representative from the Southside of San Antonio. The Southside of San Antonio residents were mostly Mexican-American and poor.

Puente was tall and handsome, and also known for having cozy relationships with lobbyists. The *San Antonio Express-News* wrote an editorial on June 21, 2007 about Puente and a real estate partnership he had with Marc Rodriguez, a lobbyist. The editorial said that Puente and Rodriguez were returning favors back in forth. Puente carried legislative bills for and sold personal property to Rodriguez for a hefty price. Eventually Puente had to resign because of these allegations. But before the resignation occurred, Puente who had been getting the copies of the letters between Treviño and Sanchez, sent Treviño this short letter on October 12, 2004:

> As much as I would like to help you with the TX Department of Health, I am unable to assist you without knowing more about Bienestar and your competitor CATCH. Although you have provided me with an article published by the Journal of the National Medical Association, I do not have the expertise to critique it.

Treviño shook his head in amazement at the letter in his hands. Over the years, he had sent Puente piles of both lay and scientific information on the Bienestar program. How could it be that Puente seemed to always come back with the same response of, "Send me more information"? It seemed to Treviño that Puente was reluctant to question any unfairness displayed by those who were in power.

As fate would have it, Treviño would get his chance to challenge Puente about his stance. At a San Antonio Spurs championship game, in May 2005, Treviño was standing in line for a beer. The crowd around him was screaming in excitement as the tense game progressed.

Treviño had been waiting to order for about ten minutes when he looked to the right and saw Puente. Puente was standing next to a cocktail table surrounded by five sharply dressed men, and appeared to be having a great time. Their conversation looked animated.

Despite knowing he would be losing his place in the long line, Treviño got out of line to approached Puente. He could not pass up on the opportunity to question Puente's commitment to his constituents.

When he moved through the men to stand right in front of Puente, the representative's eyes opened wide in surprise.

"Dr. Treviño, isn't this a great game?" Puente shouted loudly.

It was difficult to hear in the noisy AT&T arena, so Treviño raised his voice to shout back in return.

"Robert, I've been mailing you letters, I've been sending you e-mails, and I've been leaving you phone messages, and all I get from you is 'Send me more information,'" Treviño complained. "Every year we are diagnosing children who are younger and younger with type 2 diabetes. Most of them are poor black and Latino kids, and they live in your neighborhood. These children are screaming out loud about their hurts, but no one is listening to their cries. You need to listen to them, Robert," Treviño shouted with an angry facial expression.

After Treviño uttered these words, Puente grabbed him by the arm and pulled him aside so that the other men could not hear their conversation. He was obviously somewhat stunned and embarrassed.

"Dr. Treviño," he stated, before he paused for a while, "they're scared of a successful program!"

And that is all he would say.

Treviño walked away wondering exactly who were *they*, and why *they* would be scared of a successful program.

THE CHILDREN'S CRIES REMAIN UNHEARD

Treviño called Albert Eng in November 2004, who was state representative Mike Villarreal's (D-San Antonio) aide. Treviño called Eng to set up a meeting with Villarreal. He had noticed that Villarreal's staff members were prone to calling to get more and more information about the Bienestar program, but nothing ever seemed to come out of this.

Eng set up a breakfast meeting with between Treviño and Villarreal at Taco Heaven in San Antonio for breakfast the following in morning.

When Treviño walked in for the morning meeting, Villarreal was already there. An Ivy League graduate with a degree in finance, Villarreal was young, with a squared chin and cheerful smile. He was a man who looked great on camera.

"Representative, I really want to thank you for taking time to meet with me," Treviño said courteously.

"You're doing great work," Villarreal commented, "We're proud of you."

"It's not just me. It's lot of people working together. But more important, it's the children. They're the ones making the changes, and they are the reason why I'm here."

"I've received your e-mails and copies of the letters you've sent Dr. Sanchez. You have been treated unfairly," the representative said in a forthright manner.

"Not me, Representative, the children," Treviño quietly corrected him. "I managed to leave the projects behind me, get a medical degree, and now have a beautiful family. So I'm doing great. It's the children in the barrios who are being treated unfairly."

"Well, that's what I meant, the children," Villarreal responded.

"I really appreciate your staff calling my office to get information about the Bienestar program," Treviño said. "But what is it that you want to do with that information?"

"We're just trying to understand the program better," Villarreal answered politely.

"But we need to act," Treviño pointed out. He was tired of waiting and waiting and having nothing happening!

"Well, I think what you are doing is the right thing," Villarreal counseled Treviño. "Keep writing letters to the Commissioner of Health, with copies to us and the Governor."

"I have spent four years writing letters to commissioners and elected officials, to no avail," Treviño responded despondently. "It's not working."

Villarreal suggested another idea here. "You need to hire a lobbyist. I know a good firm, and they're very reasonable with their fees."

"I can see a big conglomerate affording a lobbyist, but the children we represent have no means to hire a lobbyist. And we're a non-profit center without funds to do that either."

Treviño shook his head. His hope dissipated as a result of this meeting as well.

Afterwards, Treviño walked back to the SHRC. The first person he encountered there was Hernandez.

With a big smile she asked, "How was your meeting with Representative Villarreal?"

"I don't understand politics, Irene," Treviño said simply as he lowered his head. "He gets elected by voters to represent them, but then he asks voters to hire a lobbyist to do his job! From where are these children who are poor and need diabetes education programs going to get money to hire a lobbyist?"

Treviño raised both hands in the air, totally frustrated. Nothing new had come out of this meeting. He was right back where he had started.

In the same month, Senator Madla called Treviño to inform him about a phone call he had with Albert Hawkins, the Commissioner of the Department of the Health and Human Services. In the state health hierarchy, Hawkins was one level above Sanchez, and one level below Perry.

"Roberto, I talked to Hawkins this morning about the Bienestar program. He had been briefed on the program by staff members of the TDH who told him that the program was too expensive and did not have the outcomes CATCH had."

"Senator, that is not true," Treviño responded desperately. "Look who is briefing him: the staff at the TDH. They have tried to tie our hands so they can give South Texas children a placebo program."

Treviño then promised to fax Madla three peer review publications showing that the Bienestar had improved the behavioral and biological outcomes of children. He did so the very same day.

Madla called Treviño back the following day. "I sent Hawkins the studies you forwarded to me. But he has said he could not help us."

"Why, senator? As part of his role, Hawkins operates the Medicaid program. Doesn't he see we are bleeding public money by having to spend it all on diabetes complications? Why not prevent diabetes in our children in the first place?"

Madla responded in a serious tone. "Hawkins said this decision was way above him, and that he had no power to reverse it."

Treviño could not help but grit his teeth at this news, but made sure he did not take out his frustration on someone who had helped before, and was trying to help now.

"Thank you, sir," Treviño said when he hung up.

Madla's information proved of extreme interest to Treviño. Through it he had found out who was halting medical progress for the children of Texas.

In the state political hierarchy, the next person in power above Hawkins was Rick Perry. It was time for Treviño to start putting pressure on the Governor himself.

Chapter 7

PERRY AND SANCHEZ ARE UNMASKED

The bureaucrats in Texas continued to repeatedly deny that they were providing special preference for any one program. Huang even wrote to Treviño stating that the TDH was committed to supporting and assisting all promising programs that addressed health promotion (see page 99). But on October 8, 2004, Kimberly Sasser, Program Coordinator for the Obesity Prevention and Public Health Nutrition and Physical Activity Division of the Texas Department of State Health Services (DSHS formerly TDH), circulated an internal memo to high level administrative staff. The memo was not meant for the general public, but in early 2005, a former DSHS employee sent Treviño a copy. The memo stated the following:

- The DSHS and TEA will purchase Texas CATCH materials and fund demonstration projects for CATCH.
- They also will pay to develop a diabetes unit for the Texas CATCH.
- Those parts of the DSHS responsible for funding the Texas CATCH program will be: the Texas Diabetes Council, the Cardiovascular Health & Wellness Program, and the Public Health Nutrition and Physical Activity Council.
- The Texas CATCH program is operated by the CATCH Texas Network (CTN).
- The CATCH Texas Network is Houston's UTSPH, Flaghouse, Inc. and *others*.

What all this meant was that the Governor and Commissioner of Health for Texas were using public money to fund a 'children's diabetes program'—when the program itself did not even have a lesson plan on diabetes.

• DR. ROBERTO P. TREVIÑO •

Treviño wrote Governor Perry a letter on April 6, 2005 and sent a copy to Senators Leticia Van de Putte, Frank Madla, Jeff Wentworth, and Judith Zaffirini; Representatives Joaquin Castro, Frank Corte, Ruth McClendon, Jose Menendez, Trey Martinez-Fisher, Robert Puente, Michael Villarreal, Carlos Uresti, and John Shields. He knew it was critical that others be aware of what was going on, so not only did he send a copy of the letter to the media (via Don Finley at the *San Antonio Express-News*), he also sent it to Albert Hawkins and Charles Bell at the Texas Department of Health and Human Services and to Joe Bernal at the State Board of Education.

In the letter, Treviño told the Governor that Latino children would go blind, lose limbs, and be on dialysis if effective treatments for their diabetes, and their high-risk conditions, were not instituted immediately. He also informed him that the TDH had discounted and treated unfairly the Bienestar program, which had shown compelling evidence of decreasing blood sugars. The last paragraph of Treviño's letter read:

> ...The Department of State Health Services [formerly TDH] supports only the UT Houston School of Publics Health's CATCH program. The CATCH program has never decreased blood sugars and is not bicultural. Since 1997, when Dr. William Archer was Health Commissioner, we estimate that the DSHS has funded the UT Houston School of Public Health nearly $4 million. More recently, Commissioner Dr. Eduardo Sanchez gave the CATCH program $585,000 and sent us a letter confirming his exclusive support for the CATCH program (see attachment). In this communication, he appears to say that it is the responsibility of the Bienestar and not of the DSHS to care for high risk children. We ask that you request the DSHS to let other programs compete [for DSHS funding] and let local schools decide which program shows positive effects and best fits their student's needs.

Dede Keith from the Office of the Governor responded to Treviño's letter with this one dated April 18, 2005:

> Thank you for contacting the Office of the Governor.
> Obesity certainly is a problem in Texas. Governor

Perry is very concerned about health problems that arise from poor nutrition and inactivity. As a strong advocate for physical fitness, during the 2001 legislative session, the governor signed legislation to improve health education and require daily physical activity for elementary school students. Governor Perry also established the Governor's Advisory Council on Physical Fitness to improve healthy eating and physical fitness, and he has challenged all Texans to become physically active as part of the *Texas Round-Up*.

As the correspondence from the Texas Department of State Health Services (DSHS) indicated, the department offers a small amount of grant money to the CATCH program. You may consider continuing to work with DSHS and the Texas Diabetes Council, as I am sure Dr. Sanchez and Dr. Lawrence B. Harkless of the Diabetes Council greatly appreciate input on this issue.

In addition, if you believe additional funds are needed for groups coordinating school health plans, you may consider contacting state legislators as well, as they are in the process of developing the budget for the coming biennium. For your convenience, their contact information is enclosed.

Treviño shook his head when he received this letter. He knew full well that the legislation Perry had signed, the Advisory Council he had established, and the DSHS he oversaw were set up to funnel money to the CTN. His letter had not done the trick, so Treviño had to keep the pressure on Perry.

The next thing he did was organize a bombardment of letters from community leaders and organizations. The number and caliber of individuals and organizations that sent letters to Perry, in support of the Bienestar program, were impressive. Among its supporters were: the American Diabetes Association (South Texas branch); the Mexican American Physicians Association; the San Antonio Hispanic Chamber of Commerce; the Intercultural Development Research Association; and the American Heart Association (San Antonio Division), as well as a plethora of Texas medical school professors and physicians in private practice.

Perry used Sanchez to respond to this heavy artillery of letters. Sanchez sent the following letter in June 2005 to the backers of the

• DR. ROBERTO P. TREVIÑO •

Bienestar program:

The Texas Department of State Health Services (DSHS) is pleased to provide information in response to your letter of April 19, 2005, to the Office of the Governor. You expressed concern for evidence-based and culturally appropriate interventions for Latino children to address overweight and the resulting risk for serious health conditions. DSHS agrees that approaches selected by communities and supported by this department should support healthy lifestyles.

Each school district is required to have a coordinated health program by 2007 that can help reduce childhood obesity. The Texas Education Agency (TEA) invites programs to be considered as a coordinated program. Schools choose from among these TEA-approved programs or may submit their own program for approval. Both the Bienestar and the Coordinated Approach to Child Health (CATCH) are on the approved TEA list. School districts may choose to implement Bienestar if they feel it is best suited for their needs.

Currently, DSHS contracts with the University of Texas-Houston, School of Public Health to do coordinated school health program training in the schools. The UT School of Public Health specializes in training the CATCH program as their area of expertise and thus they train at schools that have already chosen the CATCH program. The availability of the UT training does not preclude schools from choosing among the other approved coordinated school health programs.

DSHS shares your conviction that, to be effective, coordinated school health programs should be culturally appropriate. The DSHS Office for the Elimination of Health Disparities reviewed the CATCH and determined that it was culturally appropriate. Schools report that they adapt materials and activities to the needs of their students and families. Also our reviews of CATCH show evidence that it is effective in changing risk behaviors associated with diabetes and other chronic diseases. It is not, however, our intent to imply that it is the only coordinated school health program that is evidence-based and effective. We support the development of a variety of effective interventions from which schools may choose.

Unfortunately, this letter generated more questions than answers. Sanchez had mentioned in this letter that the contract the DSHS had with Houston's UTSPH was to provide training on the Texas CATCH program. The question then became, why does the DSHS have a contract for Texas CATCH training **but not for any other state-approved programs?** *If the DSHS is funding training on only one of the approved programs, then is this not showing the DSHS's special preference for that program?*

Because of the children, and the fact that their very lives were at stake, Treviño had no choice. He had to keep going.

BRING IN THE CHILDREN TROOPS

Edgewood ISD, which supports the Bienestar program (page 86), is located on the west side of San Antonio. Neighborhoods in this area are among the ten poorest in the state. This area alone has more patients on dialysis than there are in the seven counties surrounding San Antonio. So Julia Garcia, Edgewood ISD Director of Nursing, and the school district's Bienestar program coordinator, asked her school district's students, teachers, and parents to write letters to the governor in support of the Bienestar program.

In response to this call for action, fifty-eight fourth-grade students, parents, and teachers, wrote letters to Perry in June 2005 describing their positive experiences with the Bienestar program.

The children wrote about what they learned in terms of health, and how they changed their behaviors as a result of that knowledge. The teachers wrote about the easy adaptability of the Bienestar components into their instructional guides. The parents wrote of their children coming home to demand cereals with higher dietary fiber, and asking to take more family walks on the weekends.

Did the letters from these children have an impression on the Governor? You decide.

In response, Perry sent the SHRC a paper award with a gold shining seal and his signature. The award was sent in July 2005, and it was titled, "The Shining Stars of The Bienestar Health Program."

So the SHRC had received a pretty, legal-sized paper award, while the CTN was receiving millions of dollars in public money.

Treviño decided to test the governor's sincerity. In January 2006, the DSHS released the announcement for the Nutrition and Physical Activity Best Practices grant. The SHRC submitted a proposal to compete. On March 14, 2006, Brett Spencer from the DSHS sent out the list of awardees. SHRC had competed for the grant, and did not get awarded; instead, Houston's UTSPH, **which did not even compete**, was one of the awardees.

Quickly Treviño composed the following letter on March 15, 2006, and e-mailed it to these legislators: Frank Madla, Leticia Van de Putte, Elizabeth Jones, Ruth McClendon, Carlos Uresti, Jose Menendez, Trey Martinez, Joaquin Castro, Judith Zaffirini, Jeff Wentworth, Robert Puente, Frank Corte, Michael Villarreal, and Ken Mercer. It said:

> I estimate 40% of South Texas youth are at risk for diabetes and the Bienestar is the only school health program reported to decrease blood sugars in children (*Archives of Pediatrics and Adolescent Medicine,* Sept., 2004). Despite this large risk to South Texas Children, the DSHS has exclusive arrangements with a health program that has never lowered a blood sugar and is not culturally appropriate for South Texas children (the CATCH program).
>
> We [the SHRC] competed for a grant and did not get awarded and the CATCH, which did not compete, was awarded. Although nationally we have competed and received three National Institute of Health grants, we get no support at the state level.
>
> For three years I have tried to set up a meeting with Dr. Eduardo Sanchez and he has refused. For two years I have asked legislators to facilitate this meeting and no one has been able to do it. You need to know if we are addressing the health care of children appropriately. I hope you can help facilitate this meeting among us.

Treviño was fed up with politicians and bureaucrats lying, so he also rolled up the "Shinning Stars…" award and sent it back to Perry on June 13, 2006 with the following letter:

> A large study we are associated with showed that 40% of middle school students, mostly minority, have undiagnosed high blood sugar levels and we have concerns that the state is inappropriately addressing

this problem (see attached study). The state, instead of implementing evidenced-based diabetes prevention programs, is providing these children with a placebo program that has never lowered a blood sugar (the CATCH school health program). If evidence-based interventions are not implemented, these children will go blind, lose limbs or be on dialysis before they reach adulthood. Following are some examples of unethical practices by state agencies:
- The Texas Department of Health, in August 1998, released a grant application designed for the CATCH program. Only the CATCH got funded.
- The Texas Education Agency, in March 2002, formed a committee with 8 members associated with the CATCH program to select school health programs for SB 19. Only the CATCH got TEA approval.
- The Department of State Health Services, from 2000 to 2006, gave the CATCH program $4 million without allowing other programs to bid or compete.
- We sent a letter to your office in April 2005 expressing these concerns and your office decides to do nothing.

The state supporting a culturally and medically inappropriate school health program will have harmful consequences for millions of Texas children. Again we request that the state reverse these unethical practices and consider the Bienestar and NEEMA school health programs which are the only programs shown to decrease blood sugar levels in high risk children (see attached study). I await your response on this matter.

After this strong letter, Dede Keith from the Office of the Governor wrote back informing Treviño that the TDH would stop funding the Texas CATCH.

ONE MAN DOES STAND UP

A month after Treviño had sent his March 2006 e-mail, which chastised Texas politicians for not being able to set up a meeting with Sanchez, one politician did stand up. He was State Representative Joaquin Castro, who was a dark-skinned, attractive, Mexican-American man in his mid-twenties. He had a twin brother who was a Councilman and a Mayoral prospect in San Antonio. The media could not distinguish one from the other, and there were jokes that the twins were substituting for each other at meetings.

In April 2006 Treviño received a phone call from Castro's aide, Jorge Urby.

"Hi, Dr. Treviño," said Urby. "Representative Castro had received an e-mail from you weeks ago, and I'm sorry I'm just getting back to you. Representative Castro asked me to arrange a meeting with Dr. Sanchez."

Treviño could not believe his ears. His call for help had been heard, and someone in politics was actually going to do something about it! Somewhat shocked, Treviño settled back into his chair to listen to what Urby had to say.

"I read the e-mail from Brett Spencer. It's hard to believe that the Department of State Health Services awarded an organization that did not even apply, while it did not award yours, which is a nationally recognized program. But it happens, Dr. Treviño. I've been in the Texas Capitol for over a year, and I must admit, I've seen many things that don't make sense around here."

"Jorge, I don't sleep at night just thinking about children going blind, losing limbs and being on dialysis. In terms of the programs that Texas legislators and bureaucrats are choosing to fund, I just want someone to show me scientific evidence that the children who are at risk for diabetes will be taken care of appropriately via these programs. Maybe those responsible for the selections do have a good explanation, but as of right now, all I get is a run-around and double-speak."

Urby cut to the chase. "I want to learn more about your program. Could I make an appointment to visit your center?"

The meeting was set up, and Urby met with Denise Jones and David Saldaña from the Marketing Department at the SHRC. He was able to walk out with more information than what he needed.

Urby then e-mailed Becky Brownlee, in Sanchez's office, to inquire as to why the Texas CATCH program got funded although it did not even apply for the grant. She did not answer the question, but instead she responded with a reason of why the Bienestar was not selected. The reason was that the Bienestar was too 'medical' because it had to measure blood sugars [by finger prick and glucose monitors] in the schools. Urby then sent her the following e-mail:

> Good Morning! I want to thank you for sending me an e-mail detailing the situation with Bienestar.

It gave me great insight on why the program was not chosen. I would like to still go ahead and schedule a meeting between Dr. Sanchez and Dr. Treviño, along with Representative Castro. The reason would be to talk about the big picture and the best ways to attack the growing problem of diabetes in children. If we can make this meeting happen and answer all the questions necessary then everyone can go home happy. Dr. Treviño has informed that all he wants to do is help. Please let me know when a good time would be for Dr. Sanchez and I will see what we can do about scheduling the meeting.

Two weeks went by with no response from Brownlee. Urby sent her another e-mail reminding her about setting up the meeting. She responded with the following e-mail:

> Thanks for checking in…it has been fairly crazy w/the Legislature coming back in session, b/c there are several committee hearings that he [Sanchez] has either already attended or is scheduled to attend.
> I would like to ask that you provide us with a little more time to develop our proposal for continued funding of coordinated school health services. As I mentioned in the previous e-mail, we're looking at the possibility of a competitive process for the dollars. No decisions have been made yet, but I know our staff is trying to schedule a meeting with Dr. Sanchez to get his approval. I think it would be a much more productive discussion for everybody if we can come to the table knowing exactly what our future funding plans are. My assumption is that this is what Dr. Trevino is most interested in.

Another month went by, and Urby had to send Brownlee a third reminder. She responded by saying that it would be impossible for Dr. Sanchez to meet personally with Dr. Treviño, but he would be glad to set up a phone conference. Urby was disappointed at this news, but Treviño was ecstatic that there was any type of scheduled dialogue with Sanchez at all.

The meeting was set for Friday, June 2, 2006 at four o'clock in the afternoon. Roger Rodriguez and David Saldaña were with Treviño. An aide was with Sanchez, and Castro was alone on his end of the line.

"Good afternoon, gentlemen," Castro said in his soft-spoken voice. "I want to thank everyone for making time from their busy schedule to discuss the adult type of diabetes affecting children. I hope we can come to an agreement that favors the children."

"Thank you, Representative," said Sanchez. "I'm hoping we do not go into the past, and we move forward from here to address this problem."

"The time we have now to do something for these children is too short to take time discussing the past," Treviño snapped out, expressing his frustration over the delays he had encountered with Sanchez's office so far.

"I believe many reports have been written about the problem of type 2 diabetes in youth," Castro interjected quickly in a calming manner. "What we need is solutions. My hope for this meeting is to understand what prevention programs the state is implementing, and how these are being evaluated."

Sanchez started out first. "The Department of State Health Services has organized several statewide action plans to address the problem of diabetes and obesity in children, and we have come out with specific recommendations. I have also rearranged my departments to address better school health programs. We have the departments of Physical Activity and Nutrition, School Health, and of course, the Texas Diabetes Council."

It was hard for Treviño not to be contentious here. He had chased Sanchez for three years, and this was the only opportunity he had to question him.

"Dr. Sanchez, the statewide plans and departments you set up were meant to fund the Texas CATCH program. I have no problems with this if you can demonstrate to us that the Texas CATCH program has decreased blood sugars. Can you tell us if the Texas CATCH program has any evidence of decreasing blood sugars?"

Silence from the other end of the phone.

"Dr. Sanchez, can you tell us if the Texas CATCH program has been shown to decrease blood sugars in children?" Treviño repeated slowly and deliberately.

"I don't know," Sanchez finally muttered.

"It hasn't, Dr. Sanchez," Treviño answered for him.

"It has prevented obesity in children," Sanchez objected, raising his voice. "A study out of El Paso showed that children in the CATCH program were able to prevent obesity."

"First of all, it did not prevent obesity. Second, the program was

Forgotten Children: A True Story of How Politicians Endanger Children

tested by a research design of poor quality. And third, the number of schools and students in the study was not enough to make sense of it," Treviño contested. "Karen Coleman, the principal author, sent me the first draft of that study. According to her, sixty-one percent of the teachers did not even use the Texas CATCH program because it was not culturally appropriate."

Sanchez tried to change the focus of the discussion away from science and hard facts. "I admit I'm not as knowledgeable as you are about youth-onset type 2 diabetes, and its prevention. So I'm not going to sit here and discuss studies with you."

"Dr. Sanchez, you are the Commissioner of Health, and to make decisions regarding children's health without having the appropriate knowledge does children a disservice," Treviño reprimanded.

"Dr. Treviño, what is it that you want from the Department of State Health Services?" Sanchez said with a stern and angry voice.

"Money," Treviño answered immediately.

"No," Sanchez responded without hesitation.

"The Department of State Health Services has given the CATCH over $4 million dollars," Treviño pressured Sanchez. "How can we get the Bienestar program in that loop?"

"The Department of State Health Services is going to stop funding all school health programs," Sanchez responded.

"Does that include the CATCH program?" Treviño drilled down.

"Well…we have a contract with them, and it extends into this year and part of the following. We need to honor our agreement. But after that, the Department of State Health Services has no more plans for funding school health programs."

"Not investing in children's health is the worst policy the Department of State Health Services could ever have," Treviño said forcefully. "If we do not stop unhealthy behaviors in people at an early age, we will not have enough money in all our state government buildings to pay for the health care cost which will be coming at us!"

"Funding school health programs has brought on too much controversy for the DSHS," Sanchez clarified.

"Well, the controversy wouldn't have happened if the Department of State Health Services concentrated on program evaluation rather than program protection!" Treviño hammered his point home.

"Dr. Sanchez, this is Roger Rodriguez. I'm the Director of Health Curriculums with the San Antonio Independent School District. If you decide to put panels together to evaluate school health programs, I'd be glad to serve."

At this point, Sanchez stopped the conference call short to excuse himself stating he had other commitments. The conference call was on a Friday, and by the Thursday of the following week Sanchez announced his resignation. In an e-mail he wrote to DSHS employees he stated: "First and foremost, I want to make clear that this has been a difficult decision to make. However, it's made with the responsibilities to my family as my first priority. I have to give more of my time and of myself to my wife and children."

The news of his resignation spread fast among the SHRC staff. It ignited a hopeful fire in the hearts of everyone in the SHRC's two buildings.

THE SNAKE GROWS NEW HEADS

Camille Miller, Director of the Texas Health Institute in Austin, frequently featured Sanchez and the Texas CATCH program in the Institute's newsletter. Six months after Sanchez resigned; the Institute's newsletter had two striking announcements. The first announcement was that Sanchez was now working for Houston's UTSPH. The SHRC's staff members were surprised, but not dispirited. They were just glad he was gone from public office.

The second announcement was that Perry had approved Dr. David Lakey to replace Sanchez as Commissioner of Health.

The first thing Lakey did was convene a workgroup to address the problem of childhood obesity. What was disheartening to the SHRC was that he named, as co-chairs of the committee, Deanna Hoelscher and Camille Miller, the coordinator and a supporter, respectively, of the Texas CATCH. Clearly, the vicious cycle of unfair favoritism, with its conflict of interest, remained in full force.

Chapter 8

A FOE MORE FORMIDABLE THAN THE TDH

The reality that the TDH was exclusively funneling money to a program that had no proven medical value for diabetes, without bidding or competing, was unprincipled. Yet while this cut state funds for the SHRC, it did not limit their programs from operating in the schools. In fact, the SHRC's programs were in place because the SHRC was competing for, and winning, grants on a national level, and receiving the awards.

So what would truly be disastrous for the success of the SHRC, and its programs would be if the Texas Education Agency (TEA) interfered with the health curriculums used in the schools. The TEA was the 'Texas state police' in terms of approving school textbooks and overseeing operations that were allowed in the school districts. This meant the TEA had the power to cut or eliminate the SHRC's programs from operating in the schools. Without having schools in which to conduct their studies, the SHRC would no longer receive research grants on any level—city, county, or national.

A CATCH 22

Tommy Fleming was the TEA's Director of Health and Physical Education. He looked the part; at six-foot two, he was slim, always nicely groomed, and had a natural tan. He had a gregarious personality, and in his powerful position, it was easy for him to influence people so that they became his followers. But his talk was heavy, and his science light.

On January 8, 1999, Fleming presented the Texas CATCH program—a program without even a lesson plan—as a 'diabetes education program' to the State Board of Education (SBOE) Committee on Instruction. The SBOE is the governing board of the TEA, and their role is to establish policy, not approve textbooks or curriculums. Yet due to Fleming's presentation, the TEA gave the Texas CATCH program their exclusive approval in the schools. Fleming excluded other school health programs from his presentation.

Fleming then sent letters to school districts and traveled the state promoting the Texas CATCH program as the only TEA-approved diabetes prevention program. In early January 2001, he sent an e-mail to the Texas Association for Health, Physical Education, Recreation and Dance (TAPHERD) explaining why the TEA endorsed the Texas CATCH as a diabetes prevention program. (TAPHERD is the association that represents physical education teachers and coaches.) The three reasons he provided were the following: the SBOE approved it; the legislators mandated it; and the TEA's legal counsel required it (forget medical experts!). A legislative bill was written exclusively for the Texas CATCH (see next chapter), and the TEA legal counsel was prepared to enforce it.

The Texas CATCH was well-protected against competitors. No other state in the union or federal law gave a school health program such a powerful position. In the state of Texas, politicians and lawyers were deciding the medical treatment of children with type 2 diabetes.

As all this was going on, Treviño received a call from Roger Rodriguez about a professor at Texas State University who was upset about the TEA's practice of promoting a sole vendor in terms of school programs.

"Robert, there is a person I want you to meet," said Rodriguez. "His name is Tinker Murray. He has written health textbooks, and also has a school health program that is showing good results with children."

"What is the name of the program?" Treviño inquired.

"It's the TAKE 10! program."

"Yes, I've heard of it. It's out of Atlanta, right?" Treviño recalled. "I will give him a call. Maybe he has some insight as to why TEA supports only the Texas CATCH program."

Treviño called Murray, a member of TAPHERD who also happened to know Fleming well, the same day.

"Dr. Murray, this is Dr. Treviño with the Bienestar health program. How are you doing?"

"Good," Murray responded. "I am glad you called. I'm having problems with the fact that the TEA is endorsing only one program."

"My problem is bigger," Treviño said, somewhat desperately. "We've been bullied by the Texas Department of Health, and now we've got the TEA on our butts!"

Murray laughed and responded with, "Have you read the e-mails Tommy is sending around?"

"Are those the ones to the members of TAPHERD?" Treviño wondered.

"Yes," Murray answered simply.

"Yes, I have. Roger Rodriguez sent me a copy. Have you asked Tommy why the TEA supports only one program?"

"I called him two weeks ago."

Here Murray paused, before he continued, "We had a big disagreement."

"What happened?"

"Well, he gave me this bull about the State Board of Education approving only the Texas CATCH program," Murray responded indignantly. "So I asked him to recommend the TAKE 10! program to the State Board of Education."

"What did he say?"

"He told me that the TAKE 10! program was a good program but that he had to run it by Peter."

"Which Peter?" Treviño asked.

"Peter Cribb," Murray answered.

"Peter Cribb!" Treviño erupted. "He's with the Texas CATCH program, so he has no business telling the TEA what programs to run in the schools! That's crazy!"

"Fleming then called me again last week," Murray continued in the same vein. "In that conversation he told me that he had approached Peter, and Peter felt it would be best to get the Texas CATCH program off the ground, and to not waste energy on getting other programs in."

That's all Treviño needed to hear. It seemed like the CTN was literally controlling the TEA now!

Deciding to target the source of the problem, Treviño sent Fleming a letter on January 18, 2001, showing the rates of type 2 diabetes among Texas children, as well as a description of the Bienestar program and the success it had had decreasing blood sugars. The letter ended with the following paragraph:

> ...Although the Texas CATCH school-based program may be an extraordinary program, it may not be appropriate for South Texas children or for African American children. We ask, therefore, that TEA consider recommending other curriculums that demonstrate positive results and more culturally appropriate

materials.

Treviño also attached two studies to the letter showing that African-American children in the original CATCH program, compared with children in control schools, were more likely to drop out, and increase their body fat and blood pressures.

Fleming did not respond to this important news.

Treviño sent him a second letter on February 21, 2001. This time he sent copies of the letter to State Senators Frank Madla and Judith Zaffirini—and this time Fleming responded.

Fleming's letter, dated March 7, 2001, was this:

> This is in response to your letter dated February 21, 2001, regarding an update of the Bienestar program, and your request to know the Agency's position regarding the [Texas] CATCH program. I regret to say that your original letter dated January 18, 2001, was either misfiled or never reached my office. I apologize for the delay in answering your concerns.
>
> One of the biggest problems we face in prevention education is the fragmentary nature of curricular interventions, and the lack of coordination within school health programs and communities. There are many prevention programs related to the priority health-risk behaviors that exist among youth and young adults. Some of these school-based prevention programs operate in isolation from one another with little effort to coordinate program activities. It was with this in mind that the CATCH program was adopted by the State Board of Education as the diabetes education program that a school district may use in the health curriculum required under Texas Education Code, Section 28.002 (a)(2)(B).
>
> Bienestar and [Texas] CATCH are examples of school-based prevention programs and both, in my opinion, are excellent programs. However, the decision to adopt [Texas] CATCH was made because the Board recognized the value of the program's coordination of four components—health education, physical education, nutrition services, and parent involvement. It allows the physical education teacher to work hand-in-hand with the food service division of a school. It encourages parents

> to assist in the overall effort to develop good habits early in life. It provides classroom health instruction. In other words, the health promotion message comes from multiple directions rather than just from the classroom or the gym.
>
> [The Texas] CATCH is but one avenue to improve the health status of adolescents. I would be most happy to meet with you and explore ways in which Bienestar can become a part of our efforts to advance the cause of children's health.

Fleming copied Ann Smisko, the TEA's Associate Commissioner, Curriculum, Assessment, and Technology and Adams Jones, the TEA's Assistant Commissioner, Governmental Relations, on his letter.

Treviño responded to Fleming's letter with this one within two days:

> The Bienestar school-based diabetes prevention program was developed six years ago and initially piloted in parochial schools located in low-income neighborhoods with predominately Mexican American residents. Although parochial school fourth-grade Mexican American students residing in poor neighborhoods were mostly English-speaking, and understood fourth-grade level learning material, fourth-grade Mexican American students residing in the same neighborhoods, but attending public schools and residing in nearby public housing, were not. The Bienestar health curriculum has since been translated to English and Spanish and been rewritten at the third-grade level. Experience has taught us that variability in learning exists even within the same ethnic population and that programs need to be tailored around the specific needs of their targeted population. In behavior modification programs, one size does not fit all.
>
> The Bienestar is aimed at fourth-grade students from schools located in low-income neighborhoods because low-income populations have higher rates of diabetes and diabetes complications than more affluent populations. Four programs were developed to modify the social systems that have the most influence on children's health

behaviors—home, classroom, school cafeteria, and after-school care. The Bienestar, therefore, consists of a parent, a health class, a school cafeteria, and an after-school program. In the Bienestar program, the health promotion message comes from multiple directions rather than just from the classroom or the gym.

Bienestar students, when compared to non-participating students, have significantly decreased fatty food intake, have increased their fruit and vegetable intake, and have increased their physical fitness levels (see attached studies). The diabetes-related health behaviors have, in turn, demonstrated a favorable impact on biological markers. In those with impaired glucose levels at baseline, the Bienestar decreased their mean fasting glucose levels from 117 mg/dl to 93 mg/dl ($p<.05$) without medications. The NIH just awarded the Bienestar $2 million dollars, and the national American Diabetes Association officials credit Bienestar's success to its early age intervention (see article). We invite you to visit the schools where the four Bienestar components are being implemented.

Treviño made sure to copy both Ann Smisko and Adams Jones on this letter.

Yet not only would Fleming lie about not receiving Treviño's letter dated January 18, 2001, he had passed copies on to the CTN people. Treviño knew this because of an incident that occurred in late March 2001, when both he and Hoelscher, coordinator of the Texas CATCH program, were invited by the Texas Medical Association to present their programs at one of their general meetings in Austin. Treviño was already sitting in the hotel restaurant having breakfast when Hoelscher walked in. She sat down two tables away from Treviño, and her back was towards him. It was pretty obvious to Treviño that she hadn't noticed him during her arrival.

Treviño kept his eyes on her, and noted that when she opened up her briefcase, she pulled out three letters with the SHRC's logo on them. This made Treviño curious. He hadn't written any letters to Hoelscher, and was pretty sure that none of the SHRC's staff members had been in touch with her.

Treviño got up closer behind her to view the dates on the letters. When he did so, he noted they were copies of the three letters he had sent Fleming—including the one Fleming had claimed never reached him!

Treviño sat down to finish his breakfast, and then walked over to greet Hoelscher. He wanted to make sure she knew he had seen what she had pulled out of the briefcase.

At his approach, Hoelscher immediately scrambled to put the letters back in the briefcase.

"Good morning," said Treviño, his face sporting a nervous smile. He was a bit off balance from having seen for himself just now how much control the CTN people had on state government agencies and their representatives.

Hoelscher did not verbally greet Treviño, and just stared back at him, showing a facial expression of surprise and anger.

"How are you doing?" Treviño persisted, still keeping his smile.

"Good," she finally muttered, and turned her face back down.

Because Hoelscher was unwilling to converse with him, Treviño dismissed himself and strode away.

The situation was worse than what he had realized. Based on what he had seen with his own eyes, he had a foe more formidable than the TDH—the TEA.

A BOXER IS RECRUITED TO FIGHT THE FOE

Over the next few months, Fleming would be under unrelenting pressure from Treviño, Tinker Murray, Roger Rodriguez and Joe Bernal to change his unfair stance.

Bernal, a member of the SBOE, was in his late sixties. He had grown up in a poor and rough San Antonio neighborhood, and had picked up boxing as a youth to fight himself out of that neighborhood. He went on to get a Ph. D. in education, and became a state senator.

Short in stature and feisty in temperament, Bernal would prove an important ally in terms of cracking down on the TEA. In fact, it was Bernal who would pressure the staff members of TEA to bring in health experts and get their opinion on coordinated school health programs.

At the request of Bernal, David D. Anderson, Fleming's boss and Director of Curriculum and Professional Development, convened a group of physicians, educators and other health experts in October 2001 to advise the TEA on the rules for the legislative requirements of Senate Bill 19 (see next chapter). SB 19 was passed by the 77th Legislature for the purpose of getting schools to adopt a coordinated school health program to prevent obesity, cardio vascular disease, and type 2 diabetes. The four components were physical activity, health class, parents, and food service.

The group, who convened, provided input and recommendations to the TEA staff so they could draft the language for the rule. Many medical and academic experts were in attendance, and when they provided recommendations, the name "Texas CATCH" was never mentioned. The proposed rule language then was taken to the SBOE members for their final approval.

At the end, the TEA ignored the experts and the SBOE members. In fact, Fleming sent out an e-mail to school district administrators to tell them the TEA had selected the Texas CATCH program, and why. His reasons were the same as they had been before the group of medical and health experts convened: legislature mandated it, SBOE approved it, and legal counsel required it. Never mind what the physicians had to recommend!

Since Treviño was getting nowhere with Fleming, he shot off the next volley at Fleming's boss, Anderson. He wrote him a letter on November 19, 2001 where he stated the increasing rates of type 2 diabetes among Texas children, and ended with the following two paragraphs:

> ...Diabetes is an expanding problem that not even our government, our medical centers, or our universities have been able to control. To claim that a health curriculum can be used to prevent diabetes is a strong statement. The health of Texas children is at stake, and we cannot assume anything at this point. Instead, children's health curriculums that have proven results in decreasing abnormal glucose levels should be the ones to be recommended. The Bienestar is the only health curriculum shown to reverse hyperglycemia in Texas children. The National Institutes of Health is so convinced that they funded the Bienestar $2 million.
>
> I will never forget your words at the TEA SB 19 meeting, 'we do not expect one program to fit all'. That statement is so true, and it is another reason why Bienestar is the most appropriate for South Texas Children. We thank you for including us in TEA health agendas and are still interested in inviting you to visit the four Bienestar programs (parent, school cafeteria, classroom, and after school health club). We have enclosed a potential date and agenda for your visit. Let us know if this is okay.

Forgotten Children: A True Story of How Politicians Endanger Children

Treviño sent copies of this letter to Bernal and Fleming. Anderson never responded.

Bernal continued to assist the SHRC in its efforts to get the TEA to approve the Bienestar program. He called the Commissioner of Education Jim Nelson, as well as Anderson and Fleming, to inform them about visiting schools where the Bienestar operates. After Bernal's call, Anderson and Fleming were pressured into attending the SHRC's San Antonio's headquarters on December 13, 2001. (Note: Bernal did not expect Nelson to attend because as Commissioner, he was extremely busy.)

Present at the SHRC for the meeting were Anderson, Fleming, Janice Fox (SAISD Food Service Director), Roger Rodriguez, Senator Frank Madla, Omega Arteaga (Senator Van de Putte's aide), Buzz Pruitt (professor of health at Texas A&M), Bernal, and Treviño.

After Treviño asked everyone to introduce themselves, he made an introductory statement.

"I want to thank David Anderson, Tommy Fleming and everyone else for taking time off from their busy schedules to visit our center and schools. We have a tight schedule, so after this introduction we will be visiting two schools to observe P.E., health class, food service, and parent components.

"We have a serious medical problem affecting children as young as eight years of age, and most of these children are minority children living in low-income households. These children will go blind, lose limbs, and be on dialysis before adolescence if we do not intervene.

"We are concerned about the approach the TEA has taken to control diabetes in youth. The TEA supports the Texas CATCH program, which has no evidence of having lowered, or even measured a blood sugar."

As Treviño let his eyes roam around the room, he could not help but notice that both Anderson and Fleming looked somewhat uncomfortable, their bodies repositioning on, and fidgeting in, their seats.

The room remained quiet as Treviño continued.

"David, you organized the focus group meeting to get input on the language for SB 19, and even though the words 'Texas CATCH' were never mentioned, Tommy sent this e-mail after the meeting telling school district administrators and TAPHERD members that TEA supports the CATCH only."

Treviño placed the e-mail in question (page 132) on the table. Anderson picked it up, read it, and gave it to Fleming.

"Tommy, where in SB 19 does it say that only the Texas CATCH program can be adopted?" Bernal asked out loud.

• DR. ROBERTO P. TREVIÑO •

At these words, Treviño pulled out another letter from Senator Jane Nelson, the author of SB 19. It showed that the name 'CATCH' had been removed from the bill, although the first draft did have the name CATCH on it. Fleming picked up the letter and, as he read it, he frowned, then tilted his head backwards to gaze up at the ceiling.

"I must have read the bill wrong," Fleming ultimately said, looking somewhat perplexed.

"How could you?" Bernal drilled down on him. Not one to hold back, he kept going at it. "You have a Ph.D., and you work at the education agency!"

"Gentleman," Anderson interrupted to get the heat off of Fleming, "the Agency has no special preference to any one program. And if there has been a misperception, we want to rectify it."

"I don't think it's a 'misperception,'" Rodriguez qualified as he picked up the e-mail Fleming had sent out to school districts and TAPHERD members. "I'm a member of TAPHERD, and this is not the only 'misperception' Tommy has sent out. There've been many."

Fleming stayed quiet during this time, obviously intending for Anderson to do most of the talking.

"I think I understand the concern very well," Anderson diplomatically interjected, "and we need to be open to other programs. Is everyone okay with this approach?"

"It's not enough," Bernal forcefully said as he looked at Fleming.

At this point, Fleming was not meeting Bernal's eyes.

"Tommy needs to send a letter signed by the Commissioner to all the school districts informing them that TEA does not support only one program. And it needs to be done soon," Bernal demanded.

Fleming finally looked up at Bernal when he promised, "I will send it out this week."

As it was getting close to noon, Treviño asked everyone to start moving out to the schools. The group visited Rodriguez Elementary School, where they observed the food service staff being trained and educated in the Bienestar program. They also watched the children walk through the cafeteria line to get their food. Both Fleming and Anderson verbally indicated they were impressed by the number of children choosing and eating fruits and vegetables.

They next visited Briscoe Elementary School to observe a P.E. class. There were close to sixty fourth-grade children present, and the two P.E. teachers had the children doing moderate to vigorous physical activities taken from the Bienestar P.E. Manual. It was obvious the children were having fun, and Fleming and Anderson noted out loud the palpable excitement exhibited by the children as they were doing their exercises.

A little girl with wavy black hair, chocolate-colored skin, and a faded blue dress came up to Treviño and said, "*A mi me gusta mucho el Bienestar.*" ("I like the Bienestar a lot.")

She said it with such excitement that Treviño got down on his knees so he could make eye contact with her.

"*Como te llamas,*" ("What is your name,") he asked her.

"*Me llamo Gloria,*" ("my name is Gloria,") she answered with a big smile and sparkling brown eyes.

"*Dile al señor alto que esta alla lo que me digistes,*" ("Tell the tall man over there what you just told me,") Treviño said as he pointed to Fleming.

The child walked over to Fleming, and after looking at his face, returned back to Treviño.

"*Pero no hablo ingles.*" ("But I don't speak English.")

"*Dile,* ("Tell him") 'I love the Bienestar,'" Treviño told her.

The little girl then walked over to Fleming and pulled on his pants.

"I *lof* the Bienestar," she said in a warm tone as the much-taller Fleming gazed down at her.

A PROMISE BROKEN

By the following Tuesday, or four days after the SHRC meeting on December 13, 2001, Fleming sent out the following e-mail to the school districts:

> Attached you will find the nomination/application material for CATCH trainer candidates. As mentioned to you in earlier correspondence, the selected candidates will be trained during the CATCH Institute to be held in Austin on June 12-14. The nomination/application packet attached contains a cover letter that explains the process.
>
> I will be out of the office beginning Wednesday, December 19 and will return to the office on December 28. Should you have questions about this packet, please call the CATCH office in Austin and speak with Peter Cribb.

Treviño faxed Fleming a copy of the e-mail with the following note.

Simply worded, direct and honest in its approach, it differed markedly from the type of treatment Treviño and the supporters of the Bienestar program had received from Fleming:

> What you say and what you do differs, and this is getting very confusing. You sent this e-mail to all the school districts in Texas. I will forward this to Dr. Joe Bernal.

Bernal then called Treviño to discuss the copy of Fleming's e-mail he had just received from Treviño.

"I can't believe these guys told us one thing and did another," Bernal complained, completely bewildered.

"Dr. Bernal, I have spent two years dealing with these kinds of guys, and that is their standard treatment," Treviño observed.

"*Que cabrones*," ("Bastards,") Bernal uttered.

"What is the next step, Dr. Bernal?" Treviño asked.

"Go to the board," Bernal answered quickly. "At some point you need to let the State Board of Education know about the unscrupulous behaviors of members of the TEA staff."

But the next board meeting was months away, and Treviño could not wait. Instead, Treviño went up the TEA hierarchy ladder, and decided to target both Jim Nelson and the members of the SBOE.

Written on December 26, 2001, Treviño's letter first explained, in two paragraphs, the problem of youth-onset type 2 diabetes, and the results of the Bienestar program. The last three paragraphs of the letter were:

> ...After presenting Bienestar's positive results to David Anderson (Managing Director, Curriculum and Professional Development) and to Thomas Fleming (Director of Physical and Health Education), it was agreed that they would work on a letter from you to school administrators explaining that no one health education program would get TEA preferential treatment. The agreement was that TEA would support the intent of this year's enacted Senate Bill 19 (see Senator Jane Nelson's attached letter), which clearly removes TEA's past practice of giving preferential treatment to one program.
>
> The TEA is presently supporting a health education

program that is culturally and medically irrelevant to south Texas children. South Texas children are bilingual and are suffering from diabetes, and TEA's preferred program has no Spanish translation, has no lesson plans on diabetes, and has never lowered a blood sugar. As stipulated by SB 19 (sec. 28.04) (c) (A-E), all programs designed to prevent obesity, cardiovascular disease, and type 2 diabetes through coordination of the following should be acceptable:
   (A) health education,
   (B) physical education,
   (C) nutritional services,
   (D) parental involvement, and
   (E) instruction to prevent the use of tobacco.
Maybe TEA should set these criteria as minimal standards for health education programs and leave the choice to individual school districts. Leaving the choice to school districts will promote two favorable outcomes: a) competition among school-based health curriculums and b) adaptation of the program that best fits the school's needs. Competition and adaptation of the fittest are two foundations of this great country.

Treviño sent copies to these SBOE members: Grace Shore, Joe Bernal, Cynthia Thornton, Alma Allen, Mary Berlanga, David Bradley, Don McLeroy, Geraldine Miller, Dan Montgomery, Richard Neill, Rene Nuñez, Rosie Sorrells, Judy Strickland, Chase Untermeyer, and Richard Watson.

Commissioner Jim Nelson, who was a lawyer from Odessa, Texas, and a good personal friend of George W. Bush, never responded. So with his letters getting nowhere, Treviño called Fleming to question why he promised one thing but did another.

"Hey Tommy, this is Roberto," Treviño said, jumping past superfluous greetings and formalities on the phone. In an angry tone he accused, "You met with us and told us that the TEA would be sending out a letter to inform school districts that the TEA does not give special treatment to any one program. But what about that e-mail you sent out to the school districts?"

"Wait, Dr. Treviño, wait!" Fleming tried to interrupt.

"No! I won't wait because our children can't wait!" Treviño said furiously. "You're playing a political game with the lives of children."

"That is an insult, and I will not take that from you," Fleming responded, raising his voice. "How could you say that I don't care about the health of children? I've dedicated almost a lifetime to school health and physical education, so for you to come and tell me that I don't care about children is an insult."

"Well then, listen to what you say, and think about what you have done," Treviño continued, not letting Fleming's anger intimidate him. "At that meeting, you and David told us that the TEA gave no special preference to any one program, and that you would send out a letter to all school districts. Did you do it?"

"You don't under—" Fleming tried to say.

"Did you do it, Tommy?" Treviño articulated with emphasis, raising his voice.

"Are you going to let me talk?" Fleming asked.

Treviño paused at this point to let Fleming respond.

"I spoke with our legal counsel, and he ruled that the TEA had to stay with the CATCH program because the SBOE had approved it back in 1999."

(Note: The legal counsel for the TEA was a man named David A. Anderson, not be confused with David D. Anderson, the TEA's Director of Curriculum and Professional Development.)

"Tommy, he's an attorney! You're the health expert! You, not the attorney, should be deciding what the best health intervention is for children with type 2 diabetes."

At these words, Fleming slammed the phone down.

Treviño looked up towards the ceiling and locked his hands behind his head in frustration. Lawyers and bureaucrats deciding the kind of medical treatment of children with type 2 diabetes would receive had become pretty standard practice in Texas.

It was unfortunate that this had been set into motion by Senator Jane Nelson's Senate Bill 19. Fundamentally, this bill was good for the health of Texas children, but the politicians and bureaucrats, who were motivated by self-interest would mess it all up.

Chapter 9

THE BULLDOZER LEGISLATIVE BILL

Jane Nelson, the Republican Party State Senator from Grapevine, Texas, was a powerful woman in the Senate. Being a former teacher and a SBOE board member made her passionate about education, and her campaigns often focused on reducing the size of the government and containing health care costs. Her intentions usually seemed good, and so it was that on November 13, 2000, she filled Senate Bill 19 (SB 19).

The bill proposed that the public schools dedicate themselves to the improvement of children's health by offering a program to prevent obesity, cardiovascular disease, and type 2 diabetes. The bill's coauthors were Senators Eliot Shapleigh, Leticia Van de Putte, Jeff Wentworth, and Judith Zaffirini, and Representative Manny Najera.

A portion of the first draft of the bill read:

> ...COODINATED HEALTH PROGRAM FOR ELEMENTARY SCHOOL STUDENTS.
>
> (a) The agency [TEA] shall make available to each school district a coordinated health program, such as the Coordinated Approach to Child Health program (CATCH), designed to prevent obesity, cardiovascular disease, and Type II diabetes in elementary school students. The program must provide for coordinating:
>
> (1) health education;
> (2) physical education;
> (3) nutrition services; and
> (4) parental involvement.
>
> (b) The agency shall notify each school district of the availability of the program and provide technical assistance in implementing the program...

Nelson generally embraced local control, but in SB 19 she was embracing state control. For example, when Senator Eddie Lucio (D-Brownsville), Chair of the Joint Interim Committee on Nutrition and Health in Public Schools, had recommended expansion of breakfast programs, Nelson had written him back in December 2004 stating in part, "...I am troubled by recommendations that could encroach on local control, such as expansion of breakfast programs at no cost to children." Yet through the SB 19 draft, Nelson would be using a *state* bulldozer to move the Texas CATCH program forward.

Her change in stance shocked many people. When Roger Rodriguez had walked into Treviño's office with a copy of the bill, and when Treviño read it for the first time, Treviño's eyes flew open, and he involuntarily took a step back, the shock being so great.

"They're not going to give us any choice on health programs. It's the Texas CATCH, and that's it," Rodriguez commented with a solemn facial expression.

Treviño remained speechless, his only response being to purse his lips together to blow out air.

"Roberto, I don't like this at all. With this bill the state is going to shove the Texas CATCH program down our throats! Yet SAISD has eighteen percent Spanish-speaking children as its students, and the Texas CATCH program is not even bilingual. What good is it going to do those kids?"

"Forget the bilingual aspect." Treviño responded dryly, regaining a bit of his equilibrium. "The program could be in ten languages, but if it doesn't have any medical value, it will be useless to the children whose bodies need it."

"What do you think we should do?"

"I don't know, Roger. Right now I feel like a boot is pressing on my throat, cutting off my air supply. For if this bill is being driven by Senator Nelson, we don't have a chance. She is a powerful lady in the Capitol, and no doubt it will pass."

"I don't like it at all," Roger kept repeating, but by now Treviño's mind had moved on to something else.

"Who got her to add in the wording about CATCH?" Treviño wondered out loud. "And what does she know about diabetes prevention and treatment?"

"I'm sure the Texas CATCH people got her to do this for the money," Roger said speculatively. "Can you imagine all the school districts having to buy their health textbooks from a sole vendor?"

"Money," Treviño questioned, somewhat puzzled by Rodriguez's suggestion. "The Texas CATCH people are university professors. They get paid the same regardless of how much money they bring in. What you've said doesn't make sense to me."

"What I meant is that the Texas CATCH program is also licensed by Flaghouse," Rodriguez elaborated.

"What is Flaghouse?"

"Flaghouse is a major distributor of physical education equipment to schools," Roger explained. "They're currently based in New Jersey."

A light clicked on in Treviño's head.

"In a November 2000 letter, the Texas CATCH people requested $3,500 per school from the Texas Department of Health," Trevino said, with a thoughtful look.

"And there are 4,900 elementary schools in Texas," Rodriguez added, quickly.

Treviño took out his calculator and started punching keys furiously. "That's $17 million dollars for the CTN people!" he gasped.

INTERRUPTING THE MONEY STREAM

Treviño and company would not be the only ones trying to stop a monopoly in the making. Murray, the Take 10! Trainer, faxed Treviño a copy of a letter drafted by Dr. James Morrow.

Morrow, a professor at University of North Texas, had written Nelson the following letter:

> I am concerned about an upcoming decision regarding the implementation of the CATCH program as the ONLY program to be used in public schools for diabetes and obesity prevention. There are a number of other nationally and state developed programs that address these issues.
>
> It seems inappropriate to have a single program identified for all districts across the state. The CATCH program is quite good but there ought to be other programs that schools can choose from rather than a single program. Identification of a single program is much akin to choosing a single textbook that MUST be used statewide. I suspect that this would not be appropriate or approved.
>
> Please consider other well-established, effective programs that might accomplish the same goals as the

• DR. ROBERTO P. TREVIÑO •

CATCH program. I will be happy to identify some of these programs (e.g. The Fitnessgram program was developed by the Cooper Institute in Dallas) should the need arise.

Treviño also wrote Nelson a letter on December 20, 2000, to commend her for her initiative in recommending starting diabetes prevention programs for children at an early age, and also to inform her of the Bienestar program and its results. The letter ended with the following paragraph:

>...Although the CATCH school-based program may be an extraordinary program, it may not be appropriate for South Texas children or for African American children (see study). We ask, therefore, instead of specifying the CATCH program in your bill, could you open the door to other programs that demonstrate culturally appropriate curriculums and positive results.

Treviño sent copies to Senators Frank Madla, Judith Zaffirini, and Leticia Van de Putte.

Knowing that Madla was the most daring and concerned when it came to taking on the group or groups blocking the Bienestar program, Treviño then called him again for help.

"Have you seen Senator Nelson's Senate Bill 19?" he inquired of Madla.

"No."

"It's a good-intentioned bill aimed at increasing physical activity, and preventing disease in children," Treviño explained. "But what I don't like is that it has the name CATCH in it."

"These guys keep popping up," Madla agreed. "I will talk to Senator Nelson, and ask her to please remove the name 'CATCH', and to add 'culturally appropriate' programs to the bill instead."

On January 4, 2001, Madla wrote Treviño a letter; the last paragraph stated:

>...Additionally, Victoria [Madla's aide] has been working with Senator Jane Nelson's office staff and they have reported that Senator Nelson has graciously agreed to accept the proposed amendments to SB 19. The amendments will remove from SB 19 the reference

to the CATCH program and require that the programs established by school districts in compliance with SB 19 be 'culturally appropriate' for the schools' population.

On January 9, 2001, Nelson wrote Treviño the following letter:

> Thank you for your letter regarding my efforts to help curb childhood obesity. My intent with Senate Bill 19 is to ensure that all school districts are able to provide successful programs such as the Bienestar to their students. Please know that it was not my intent to exclude any program that helps us reach our goal of improved children's health. In fact, I have already asked for a committee substitute bill that will remove the mention of the CATCH program to clarify that other model programs are eligible, rather than only this specific program. In addition, I have requested language that will insure that programs be culturally sensitive and appropriate.
>
> I appreciate you taking the time to contact me and my office. I hope that you will continue to be involved in this process as I work to get SB 19 passed. Many thanks for all that you do to protect the health of our children.

A grateful Treviño wrote Nelson back. In his letter he thanked her for removing exclusivity and promoting competition.

APRIL FOOL

What Treviño didn't know was that they had a backup plan to secure Texas CATCH exclusivity in SB 19. In fact, they had left wording in there that put Fleming at the helm—and as the captain, Fleming would be putting the Texas CATCH right back where it had been before. The new revision came out in April 2001, and it read as follows (Note: bold emphasis added to indicate the wording that would allow for slipping the CATCH back in):

> **COORDINATED HEALTH PROGRAM FOR ELEMENTARY SCHOOL STUDENTS.**
> (a) The **agency [TEA]** shall make available to each school district **a** coordinated health program designed to prevent obesity, cardiovascular disease, and type II

diabetes in elementary school students. **The** program must provide for coordinating:
(1) health education;
(2) physical education and physical activity;
(3) nutrition services; and (4) parental involvement.
(b) The **agency [TEA]** shall notify each school district of the availability of **the** program.

The "agency" meant Tommy Fleming, and the words "a" and "the" meant one program—the Texas CATCH. You see, as Fleming had snuck in the Texas CATCH program for SBOE approval back in 1999, it remained the only TEA-approved coordinated health program. Unfortunately, the SHRC staff did not pick up on this technicality at the time, and they and the Bienestar program would suffer for it.

These meanings of "agency", "a" and "the" were confirmed when Dianne Everett, Director of TAPHERD and a follower of Fleming, would interpret this section of the bill as follows:

> This section directs the Texas Education Agency to 'make available' to schools a coordinated health program for elementary grades K-6. The Texas Education Agency has identified the program for training will be the CATCH (Coordinated Approach to Child Health) program.
> CATCH is a commercially available curriculum, which means that schools will need to purchase the program and student materials. The Texas Education Agency will provide the training for free but has not been funded to provide the curriculum to schools.

So the real effect of SB 19 was that *not only did it take away the choice of a health education program from the schools, but it left them with a fiscal responsibility.* John Keel, Director of the Texas Legislative Budget Board, pointed this out when he wrote the following memo to Bill Ratliff, the Lieutenant Governor, on May 24, 2001:

> School districts that have not already purchased the CATCH program would incur costs associated with purchasing the program in order to meet the bill's requirement that the program be implemented in each school district beginning with the 2001-2002 school year. The Texas Education Agency does not maintain

data by which to predict the number of school districts that would need to obtain the CATCH program.

Despite the fact that the Legislative Budget Board estimated a cost of approximately $55 million to the schools to adopt the Texas CATCH, the bill was signed into effect by Governor Perry on June 14, 2001.

In December 2001, the Texas CATCH institute sent a letter that started with the following two paragraphs:

> I [Cribb] am pleased to inform you that the Texas Education Agency, the Center for Educational Development in Health and Physical Education and the Coordinated Approach to Child Health (CATCH) Program has made a commitment to establish a CATCH Institute to occur in June of 2001.
>
> This institute is a logical follow-up to the passing and enactment of Senate Bill 19:
> - SB 19 states that ESCs [Education Service Centers] are to 'provide necessary training' to comply with SB 19; and
> - The training is for the 'implementation of the program approved by the agency'; and
> - The only program approved by the agency [TEA] is the CATCH program.
> - SB 19 also states that each school district shall 'implement the program approved by the agency in each elementary school district'...

The bulldozer Nelson created cleared away all competition from the Texas CATCH program path—and she must have known it. SB 19 was her baby, and she was aware of every act taken on it.

UNFAIRNESS UNVEILED

Because SB 19 sat the TEA on the driver's seat, the SHRC staff went to the governing body of the TEA: the SBOE—to protest the exclusive promotion of the Texas CATCH.

On January 10, 2002, Treviño and Roger Rodriguez drove into Austin to testify at a meeting of the SBOE. The CTN people were informed that Treviño and Rodriguez were coming up to testify, and so they prepared Dr. Stephen Barnett to testify on behalf of the Texas

CATCH program at the same meeting.

Barnet was a retired pediatrician and chair of the Texas Medical Association (TMA) Committee on Children and Adolescent Health. What was confusing was that only a year ago before, Barnett had sent Chase Untermeyer, former Chair of the SBOE, a letter saying that the TEA should avoid imposing any opinions on the medical treatment of schoolchildren, while at the present meeting, he would be telling non-medical experts at the TEA to make decisions on the medical treatment of schoolchildren. Clearly he would be contradicting himself.

In attendance at the meeting, there must have been approximately a hundred people (between TEA staff members and guests). David D. Anderson and Fleming were present, as was SBOE Chairwoman Geraldine Miller, a Republican who believed in local control and free enterprise.

Barnett spoke first at the meeting.

"Good afternoon, Ms. Chair and board members," Barnett started, reading from a note pad. "I represent the Texas Medical Association, and I am here to speak about childhood obesity." He presented statistics on the increasing rates of obesity among children, and the association between obesity and type 2 diabetes in children.

"Schools need to do a better job to improve the health of Texas children," he continued. "Only two percent of Texas schools have daily P.E. classes, and school cafeterias do not meet the desired five-a-day servings of fruits and vegetables. We have a great program called the Texas CATCH program. The Texas CATCH program was approved by the State Board of Education in 1999 as a diabetes education program. We thank you for your support of this program," he said, looking at the board members. "This program has reached students in over 800 schools in Texas. We need your continued support."

Barnett was walking away from the podium when Bernal called him back. "Who is the Texas CATCH program?" Bernal asked in a serious tone and with a frown. "Where are they from?"

Barnett seemed startled by Bernal's firm tone and demeanor.

"The Texas CATCH is out of Houston," he responded carefully.

"Was it written by Houston professors for Texas children?" Bernal asked.

"No sir, I believe the first curriculums were written by investigators in Minnesota."

"Well, that is completely opposite to the saying, 'You cannot expect something made in Minnesota to work here in Texas.' Why would you go all the way to Minnesota when we have good programs here in

Texas?"

Barnett's face got red, and he began fidgeting behind the podium. "Because of the results, sir," Barnett responded in a shaky voice. "The CATCH program was a national study conducted by some of the best investigators in the country. It produced more than 26 publications, and it has made some positive changes in children's health behaviors."

"Has it ever decreased blood sugars, something that is necessary to control diabetes?" Bernal asked simply.

Barnett looked around the audience to see if someone else could answer that question.

"I'm not sure," he finally conceded.

"You're a physician; is that correct?" Bernal queried.

"Yes, sir."

"So you are promoting this program as a diabetes prevention program, and you don't know if this program has lowered blood sugars? That is indeed surprising. And what do you mean when you say that this program is being implemented in 800 schools?"

Barnett looked around, perhaps hoping Fleming would jump in, but instead Fleming slouched down in his chair.

"It means they conducted training in 800 schools," Barnett answered.

Bernal did not ask what he meant by "trainings", but Treviño knew that "training" here really meant that Texas CATCH staff members were using public's money to travel to make presentations to the schools about the program. It did not mean that school staffs were being *trained in how* to run the program.

Treviño came up next to present, and as he did so, he handed out two scientific articles to the board members. The studies had been published in the American Diabetes Association scientific journals, *Diabetes Care* and *Diabetes*. The first study showed that Mexican-American children as young as eight years of age were developing type 2 diabetes, and the second study showed that for three consecutive years the Bienestar program had decreased blood sugars in children with abnormal levels. The board members sifted through the articles and looked at Treviño as he spoke.

"We have a serious problem, and we have a potential solution," Treviño said. "The potential solution is the Bienestar health program."

Treviño next handed out copies of the colorful Bienestar health textbooks.

"But what we don't understand is why the Texas Education Agency has tried to keep our program away from children at risk for diabetes.

What we suspect is that the health of our children is not in the best interest of Mr. David D. Anderson and Tommy Fleming." [This comment was referring to Anderson the educator, and not the legal counsel.]

In a split second, the room went from calm silence to an eruption of noise, and the audience members started twisting in their chairs to talk with their nearest neighbor and also get a glimpse of the two men who had been cited.

At the time, Anderson was sitting in a table in the inner circle near the board members; Fleming was sitting outside the circle with the audience.

Treviño didn't have to explain his words, because Bernal chose to target Anderson next. In fact, Treviño got out of the way and sat down in the audience behind Fleming as Bernal started his justifiable attack.

"About a month ago, you [Anderson] visited San Antonio and saw the Bienestar program operate in two schools. You saw the studies documenting the decrease of blood sugars in children. In response to our observations, both you and Tommy Fleming said that you would send out letters to the school districts stating that the TEA does not prefer any one program. And yet, you and Fleming did completely the opposite," Bernal clearly enunciated. "In fact, the TEA staff almost immediately sent out a letter telling school districts to enroll in the Texas CATCH program right away."

As more mumbling and whispering erupted from the audience, Chairwoman Geraldine Miller jumped into the fracas.

"I have a big problem with the state mandating what health programs the school districts should and should not implement in the schools. What I hear from Dr. Treviño and Dr. Bernal is not leaving too much room for local control."

Anderson responded with a positive nod of his head, showing that he was in agreement with what Bernal and Miller had said.

While Anderson was getting this heat in front, Fleming turned around and stared at Treviño, an incensed look on his face. Treviño smiled coolly back.

MIND GAMES

After Bernal's scolding, the board members called a two-hour break, and discussions moved from the conference room to the hallways. Roger Rodriguez was scheduled to speak after the break.

About twenty minutes into the break, Treviño saw Rodriguez walking toward him with his head down. When he reached Treviño, he was pale with beads of sweat on his forehead.

Forgotten Children: A True Story of How Politicians Endanger Children

"What happened, Roger?" a concerned Treviño asked immediately. "You look sick," he observed.

Rodriguez looked Treviño in the eyes, and said, "Robert, I won't be able to present."

"What?" Treviño said in surprise. Had Rodriguez gotten ill, or was he too nervous to speak in public? "You can't let me down, Roger. The board needs to listen to the experience teachers and students have with operating the Bienestar program in the schools. And with twenty-six years experience as a school staff member and administrator, you know all about that."

Rodriguez gave no answer; he kept rubbing his forehead.

"Do you feel okay, Roger?" Treviño asked, changing his focus from the board presentation to Rodriguez's well-being.

"I feel okay," Rodriguez uttered slowly.

"You look pale," Treviño observed.

"David and Tommy just threatened me," Rodriguez said suddenly in a low tone, shaking his head.

"*Hijos de la chingada*," ("Son of a bitches,") Treviño whispered. "What did they tell you?"

"They told me that if I testified, the TEA would find a cause to investigate the San Antonio Independent School District. And if they start an investigation because of me, the superintendent will not be very happy."

"Roger, they are playing mind games with you. They are trying to scare you. Plus, they have nothing to investigate." Determined to get Roger to the podium despite these unfair tactics, he continued. "Remember Roger, we are not here for ourselves, we are here for the kids. We can't let them down."

Rodriguez was a good, upstanding man. He looked up at Treviño and said, "Let me see how I feel when the session starts again. The last thing I want is to go up there as a ball of nerves and make it worse for you."

Treviño stood silently for a moment as Rodriguez walked away. He could not believe what had just happened to Rodriguez. Obviously it was time for their side to play the same mind games, and so when Treviño saw Barnett standing by the elevators, he hurried to talk to him before the elevator arrived.

"Dr. Barnett, I can't believe you testified on behalf of the Texas CATCH program. As a pediatrician, you know better than anyone in that room that providing medical treatment to a patient with diabetes without performing blood tests to measure their response to that treatment is just as good as no treatment at all. You know that the Texas CATCH program has never measured a blood sugar, let alone lowered one. Therefore, how can you stand there and say that it is a diabetes education program?"

At his attack, Barnett got red in the face and started breathing fast. Was he weighing the difference between striking Treviño in the face or abiding by societal expectations and behaving in a civil fashion?

Barnett decided to behave civilly.

"You're a troublemaker, Treviño," he said shortly. "We're trying to help children, and you keep stopping us from doing our work."

With that, Barnett turned around and walked into the elevator.

Treviño shook off these words, and went looking for Fleming.

When Treviño walked into conference room where people were reconvening, he saw Fleming was surrounded by a group of people and standing close to the conference tables where the SBOE members sat.

This made an immediate impression on Treviño, for he knew that the closer people got to the conference tables, the more important they appeared to members of the audience. Treviño made sure to go up to stand right by Fleming, standing very close to let the group know he needed to converse with Fleming.

When his opportunity arose, Treviño bluffed, "A group of parents are getting together to set up a meeting with the commissioner. They are very upset at you and the TEA for giving special preference to a program that is not bilingual. A large percentage of children with type 2 diabetes are Spanish-speaking, and the parents are not happy their children are not getting treatment that is appropriate for them."

Fleming ignored those words, and focused on something entirely. "I can't believe you went up and embarrassed a fine man like David Anderson. To have him chastised by the board in public was disrespectful of you."

"You're worried about David!" Treviño retorted angrily. "What about the children? Have you forgotten about them?"

Fleming did not respond, but his face got red with anger.

As Treviño wasn't getting anywhere with Fleming, he walked over to Rodriguez.

"Hey, Roger, I spoke with Tommy and scared the shit out of him," Treviño bluffed again, hoping his words would boost Rodriguez's morale. "I threatened him with the fact that the parents would ask for a meeting with the commissioner if they started a sham investigation on SAISD."

Rodriguez put on a smile and said, "You know, Robert, I have enough years in the school district to retire. So I don't care about what can happen to me. I will go up and make the presentation as planned."

Rodriguez then went on to deliver his testimonial in favor of the TEA being open to the Bienestar and other school health programs. As it turned out, he was able to present very well, in a calm and unhurried fashion.

By the meeting's end, the SBOE directed Anderson and Fleming to find ways to include other school health programs, so that they too could participate in SB 19. Anderson also agreed to formulate a selection process so that other programs could ask for, and perhaps obtain, the approval of the TEA.

PUTTING ON THE MUZZLE

As Treviño had noticed during the meeting that certain high-ranking TEA staff members who would have the authority to muzzle Anderson and Fleming were not present, he decided to write Arturo Almendarez, the TEA Deputy Commissioner for Program and Instruction on February 11, 2002. He wrote him the following letter:

> We [the SHRC] have five years operating the Bienestar school-based diabetes prevention program in San Antonio elementary schools. Bienestar students, when compared with non-participating students, have significantly decreased their fat intake, have increased their fruit and vegetable intake, and have increased their physical fitness levels. Type 2 diabetes is affecting South Texas children, and the Bienestar is the only program shown to normalize high blood sugars in these children. Because of its success, the Bienestar received $2 million from the National Institutes of Health. Despite Bienestar's positive results and Institutes having personally met with David [D] Anderson and Thomas Fleming, they continue to give exclusive support to one program that is medically and culturally irrelevant to South Texas children.
>
> Senator Jane Nelson, author of Senate Bill 19, wrote (see attached letter) that no preferential treatment should be given to any one health program and that all qualified programs should be considered for implementation. David Anderson and Thomas Fleming ignored that directive. Senator Frank Madla who is on the committee

for health services, and Senator Leticia Van de Putte's aide met (12/13/2001) with David Anderson and Thomas Fleming. At that meeting, they were directed to stop giving preferential treatment to any one program and to allow other qualified programs to compete. David Anderson and Thomas Fleming, however, continued to ignore that directive. State Board of Education members were made aware (1/10/2002) of David Anderson's and Thomas Fleming's misguided efforts to push one program into schools with diverse social and health needs. At that meeting, David Anderson and Thomas Fleming were made aware that in behavior modifications programs, one size does not fit all. They were directed to stop being exclusive to any one program, and to send a letter to all school districts informing them of their freedom of choice. David Anderson and Thomas Fleming again ignored that directive.

Despite the very clear intention of SB 19 and its author, Senator Nelson, David Anderson and Thomas Fleming continue to give exclusive support to one program. Just recently (2/6/2002), Thomas Fleming told the Texas Diabetes Council board members that the TEA endorses only one program.

I have concerns because of the friendship David Anderson and Thomas Fleming have with Peter Cribb (CATCH program sponsor). The CATCH program has no proven results in preventing diabetes, and it is diabetes that is so overwhelmingly affecting South Texas children. Since there is no reasonable explanation for why exclusivity is given to one program, it leaves open the suspicion of self-interest. In the interest of children, we request the following two actions:

(1) Could the TEA send a letter to all school districts clarifying that TEA gives no preferential treatment to any one program so long as the health program fulfills Senate Bill 19 requirements?
(2) Could the TEA make site visits to school districts where supposedly the CATCH is being implemented? (We have evidence of school districts getting CATCH money without curriculums being implemented).

Your quick response to this matter will be appreciated.

Treviño sent copies of his letter to the SBOE's board members, and Senators Jane Nelson, Frank Madla, and Leticia Van de Putte.

A week after the letter to Almendarez, Fleming sent the following e-mail to Tinker Murray, the program coordinator for the TAKE 10 health program:

> I received your letter regarding TAKE 10 and SB 19. You mentioned in the first paragraph that you were 'puzzled' about this issue. Tinker, there are probably a lot of people puzzled about this particular section. Let me see if I can answer your questions...
>
> SB 19 instructs each school district to 'participate in appropriate training for the implementation of the program approved by the agency.' So, whatever program schools use to comply with SB 19 must be approved by this agency. Interestingly, that does not leave much room for locals to determine the program (it doesn't leave any room). The agency is required by legislative language to 'approve the program.' After the passage of SB 19 in May 2001, it was determined that the CATCH program was the only program approved by the agency. Technically, it was the state board that approved CATCH, not the agency. So, my office was simply following the direction of the agency to proceed with adopting a schedule at ESC [Education Service Centers] to train schools in CATCH. The point of this paragraph is that the language in that section of SB 19 very much limited TEA to develop training around the 'program approved by the agency.' That program was determined by the agency to be the CATCH program. If, for instance, the legislation said, "develop training around any program that a local school district wants"...then we wouldn't be having this conversation.
>
> Because there have been suggestions from people like yourself that the agency should consider other coordinated school health programs, I have recommended a new strategy to the Commissioner for selecting qualified, coordinated health programs that will be "approved by the agency." I have recommended that the agency establish a process for reviewing and approving

programs. The process would include establishing criteria that programs must meet, conducting a review of proposed programs, and approving programs. That internal memo went forward today.

I have asked the agency to move as quickly as possible on this new strategy because the school districts and education service centers need to fully understand this section of SB 19. As I said, the memo to the Commissioner went forward today.

I don't know if the agency will want to develop a list of criteria against which the agency would evaluate potential coordinated health programs. But, I think they will consider my recommendation. I do not know how extensive the criteria list will be. However, based upon the legislative intent of the authors of this section of the bill, I do know that the intent was obviously for the state to provide training in a program that had been shown through research evaluation to be effective in changing children's dietary and physical activity patterns. (That legislative intent is known from letters to the agency from SB 19 authors). I do know this much…if the agency is charged with approving programs for this section, and the approval process includes development of a list of criteria, I'm positive at this point that the most basic criteria will be something like this:

At a minimum, the program must provide for coordinating the elements identified in SB 19, Section 38.103 and include:

(1) Health education
(2) Physical education and physical activity
(3) Child nutrition services; and
(4) Parental involvement

That's all I know, Tinker. CATCH was a logical choice since the SBOE had previously approved it as a permissive, diabetes prevention program. TEA legal felt it was a logical extension for the agency to approve it as a required, coordinated program. That is, it made sense to them to approve the same program but for different purposes. And, the language in SB 19 indicated that it was 'one program'…and not more.

My new recommendation will allow other programs

to be considered...if the agency adopts the criteria strategy. Feel free to e-mail whenever you want.

TOO GOOD TO BE TRUE?

Based on this latest e-mail, it seemed Fleming was actually proposing a process of fair competition for program approval by the TEA. Inspired by the news, Treviño called Murray to discuss Fleming's e-mail.

"Hey, Tinker, thanks for sending me a copy of that e-mail. It's ironic how some Republicans talk 'local control' [referring to Nelson], but when it's to their convenience, they shift to 'state control'. They played with the words in that bill to accommodate the Texas CATCH program. It is amazing how they find political loopholes to keep medical interventions away from children at-risk for type 2 diabetes."

"Yeah," Murray said in agreement. " When I told Fleminig to present TAKE 10 to the State Board of Education board members, he sent me to Peter [Cribb]."

"Well, regardless of all that political crap we've both gone through, it sounds like now they will set a list of criteria by which to let other programs come in," Treviño said, in relief. "And I'm okay with that."

Murray was not as optimistic, however. "I don't trust those good old boys. I think this is a smoke screen they've created while they go to work at formalizing our exclusion."

"Well, I'm not sure about that," was Treviño's reaction. By this point, he had had enough pummeling from politicians and bureaucrats, and deep in his soul he needed and craved some good news. "I sent a letter to Dr. Arturo Almendarez. He's the TEA's Deputy Commissioner for Program and Instruction. I just got a call from his secretary saying that Dr. Almendarez would consider letting other programs participate as long as they fulfilled SB 19 requirements."

"I think Dr. Almendarez is a good guy," Murray remarked, "but Tommy and his handlers are not. I think Tommy has a direct link to the Governor, and they're gonna get their way."

Treviño was disappointed to hear these words. He wanted to believe in the encouraging information, but he also trusted Murray's judgment. So he said, "Okay, Tinker, I'll continue to keep my guard up."

Treviño received the following encouraging letter from Almendarez on March 22, 2002, in response to the letter Treviño sent him on February 11:

In May 2001, the 77th Texas Legislature passed

• DR. ROBERTO P. TREVIÑO •

Senate Bill 19 (SB 19). SB 19 addresses children's health through daily physical activity in public schools, and a coordinated school health approach aimed at reducing the risk of obesity, cardiovascular disease, and Type II diabetes in elementary school students.

SB 19 requires the Texas Education Agency (TEA) to make available to school districts a coordinated health program and to notify each district of the availability of the program. Each school district is required to implement a program approved by the agency in each elementary school in the district no later than September 1, 2007. Any organization/program that chooses to be considered for selection by the agency will be invited to send a complete description of their program to TEA. The following coordinated elements are required by SB 19 and have been established at the Agency as a program selection criterion:

> Does the program coordinate the four elements of health education, physical education and physical activity, nutrition services and parental involvement in elementary grades?

Any program that meets this criterion will be identified to school districts for their consideration. If you would like to submit your program for consideration, please send a complete set of materials that best describes the Bienestar Program to the following address:

Dr. Tommy Fleming
Health and Physical Education
Division of Curriculum and Professional Development
Texas Education Agency
1701 N. Congress Avenue
Austin, Texas 78701

In addition to the materials that best describe your program, please send information related to the following program issues:
- The cost of the program to each elementary school;
- A district and/or school contact in the district that have adopted the program;
- A description of the district and/or school training that is currently used to train school personnel in the

program;
- A description of the trainer certification process for the program.

The information that you submit will be evaluated against a checklist of program indicators. A comparison of qualifying programs will be sent to each district so they may evaluate a program more effectively. Districts can then choose the program that best fits the schools' needs and coordinate training through the regional service centers or by contacting a program provider directly.

Excited by this news, Treviño immediately called Murray.

"Tinker, I am going to fax you a letter from Dr. Almendarez. You can submit TAKE 10 and, if it fulfills SB 19 criteria, it will be approved by TEA."

"We can submit the programs, but it might not help," Murray said.

These words completely deflated Treviño's hope.

"Why do you say that?" Treviño asked quietly, his excitement abating.

"I have a friend who works in the Department of State Health Services," Murray confided. "She is privy to information about what's going on the inside of the state agencies."

"What's her name?" Treviño queried, wondering if what this person said could be trusted.

"I promised I would keep her name anonymous," Murray responded.

So Treviño simply asked about the information. "What did she say?"

"There's going to be a major shakeup at the TEA. The powers above don't like it that the doors might be opened to other programs. I think they're going to squelch our opportunity."

• DR. ROBERTO P. TREVIÑO •

Chapter 10

NOT MAKING THE GRADE. HOW THE TEA 'FLUNKED' THE BIENESTAR PROGRAM

Despite the fact that Murray had suspicions about the TEA's upcoming review process, Treviño submitted his curriculums with all the requirements to Fleming. What Murray predicted, however, began to unfold.

First came the shakeups. Commissioner of Education Jim Nelson resigned, and Almendarez, under increasing pressure, took a new position with Corpus Christi ISD.

Governor Perry, who had used a Mexican-American Commissioner of Health at the TDH to secretly push the Texas CATCH program through, must have hoped to do the same at the TEA, for he appointed Dr. Felipe Alanis, another Mexican-American, as the TEA's new Commissioner of Education.

However, Perry's plan would backfire. Alanis, a professor of education at the University of Texas at Austin, was too ethical and nice of a person to block an effective diabetes program from reaching high-risk children.

THE SHAKEUP STARTS SHAKING

Once all agencies, with coordinated school health programs, had submitted their materials for review, and the material was sitting on Fleming's desk, he decided to change the rules in the middle of the game. Fleming sent the following e-mail on June 25, 2002, to the participating candidates:

> I want to provide you with an update regarding the review process for materials you recently submitted

to TEA. Based upon letters we sent to districts in March 2002, the 'agency' was responsible for evaluating submitted materials. However, after the new Commissioner of Education, Dr. Felipe Alanis, was appointed on March 25, 2002, the process for reviewing and approving health programs submitted to TEA was reviewed by the commissioner. That is, after Dr. Alanis became commissioner, he reviewed the coordinated health program selection process that had been established prior to his appointment as commissioner. Based on his review, he is considering changing the current program selection process (outlined in letters to each of you and to districts on March 22, 2002) to include the establishment of an independent review committee.

He has asked various health-related organizations to select representatives that have expertise in coordinated school health, medicine, physical education, health education, and nutrition services. The committee would be charged with developing selection criteria and approving coordinated health programs as representatives of TEA. The organizations asked to appoint representatives are: Texas PTA, American Heart Association, Texas Medical Association, Texas Diabetes Council at TDH, American Cancer Society, Texas Association for Health, Physical Education, Recreation, and Dance, Texas School Health Association and the TEA Child Nutrition Program.

The major difference in the selection process is that the establishment of criteria and program approval would be handled by an outside group approved by the commissioner...rather than having TEA staff evaluate programs. Other elements of the process remain as explained in previous correspondence. That is, once the committee approves a program or programs, a list of qualified programs will be sent to districts. Districts will then coordinate training through their respective regional service center or by contacting the program provider directly.

Due to management reorganization at the TEA in the last two weeks, I have been unable to schedule a meeting to discuss the issue. Until a meeting is scheduled to finalize this issue, I am unable to tell you more than I have in this e-mail. I am hopeful that a meeting will be scheduled within the next two weeks. I will then write each of you and outline in detail whatever the agency decides regarding the program selection process.

Treviño sent Murray a copy of this e-mail and called him to get his insight.

Murray believed it did not look good, commenting morosely, "Just look at the organizations that will comprise that review committee. It's the TEA, the TDH, and the TMA and they'll usurp the review process! I think we've been set up, Dr. T."

"You shouldn't say that, Tinker," Treviño said, somewhat aggrieved by Murray's pessimistic view. "We still need to see the names of the individuals who are going to be evaluating the programs. These are big organizations with large staff members, and not all of the people on staff are corrupt."

Treviño adamantly refused to believe that the people who would be responsible for the selection would be that wicked.

Fleming was very friendly and encouraged Treviño, by e-mail, to submit as many updates as he wished. He also informed Treviño that the first committee meeting to develop the criteria for the selection process would be in August. So the SHRC staff provided Fleming with updates of the program's published results and dissemination in July and August 2002.

But it was this unexpected display of friendliness from Fleming that was the very thing that started making Treviño suspicious.

Treviño started to wonder about the wisdom of allowing the committee to form criteria when the group already had the Bienestar program materials and specifications in front of them. If the committee was stacked with people who were hell-bent on excluding the Bienestar program, couldn't they use that very information to deliberately form criteria based on what the Bienestar program did not have!

DOING IT BACKWARDS!

On October 10, 2002 Fleming sent Treviño the following e-mail:

I wanted to update you on the health program evaluation process. The review team has now established criteria, scoring standards, and a rating scale against which submitted programs will be evaluated. On October 22, your Bienestar program, and the three other health programs that have been received at the agency, will be evaluated. I will write you with the results.

The Commissioner also wants me to post a notice in the *Texas Register* [the journal of state agency rulemaking] by November 1, 2002. The Register notice will contain everything an individual/organization will need to know about the review process and will invite interested parties to also submit programs. The deadline for submission through the *Texas Register* notice will be December 13, 2002. After any new programs are evaluated, a list of TEA approved programs will be sent to districts. I anticipate that the letter to districts will be mailed around the first of the year.

I am also writing to ask if you have updated program material that you would like the team to review. Or do you wish for us to review the materials you sent us previously?

The very process of what the TEA was doing was strange and unfamiliar to Treviño. In the grant or program review process, this is what should happen: The criteria are set; the criteria are posted; and then applications are submitted, *in that order*. The TEA was doing it backwards! They asked applicants to submit their program materials; they reviewed what components the applicant's program had; they formed the criteria based on what components the applicant's program did or did not have; they selected a program; and only then did they post the announcement and the criteria.

Something smelled fishy, and Treviño decided to call Fleming to put him on the spot. He place the call at three-thirty in the afternoon, on the same day he received the e-mail from Fleming.

"Tommy, who are the reviewers in the committee?" Treviño jumped right to the point when Fleming answered.

"Robert, we sent you the list of organizations that comprise the committee," Fleming answered, sounding somewhat disturbed by the question.

"No, I need the names of the individuals involved."

"Why?"

"Because it's your obligation to be up front about it. This is government business, and you should keep all information transparent. And if you don't provide the list, I'll slap you with an Open Records Act."

"I will try to send you the list later this week."

"No, I need it now," Treviño demanded, running his hand through his hair agitatedly. He provided Fleming with a fax number so that he could forward the information to him.

Within an hour, Fleming sent Treviño a fax with the committee members. The committee members were Stephen Barnett, Diana Everett, Jan Ozias, Sara Williams, Chuck Mains, Linda Seewald, Ellen Kelsey, David Wiley, Sara Williams, Mike Hill, Teresita Ramirez, and Laura Garcia.

Treviño panicked when he saw the lists, and called Fleming immediately.

"Tommy, this committee is stacked on the Texas CATCH side!" Treviño noted angrily. "Stephen Barnett was paid to travel to make Texas CATCH presentations, and he testified on behalf of the Texas CATCH program at the January 10th SBOE meeting. Diana Everett is the director of TAPHERD. TAPHERD interpreted SB 19 to mean Texas CATCH only, and sends out newsletters supporting the Texas CATCH program. Jan Ozias is the director of the Texas Diabetes Council. They have the Texas CATCH all over their website and brochures—"

"I know, I know," Fleming tried to interrupt, but Treviño would not be stopped.

"Chuck Mains is Manny Najera's chief of staff. Manny was at the LULAC Health Initiative pushing the Texas CATCH, and he is the legislator that inserted 'an approved TEA program' in SB 19 to make it the Texas CATCH. Linda Seewald is the director of health curriculums at Northside ISD. She has tried to implement the Texas CATCH program in her school district, although the teachers have not chosen to adopt it. Ellen Kelsey is vice president for prevention for the American Heart Association. They gave $500,000 to the Texas CATCH program. David Wiley is a professor at Texas State University, and he invited you and Peter [Cribb] to present the Texas CATCH to his students. Sara Williams is with the TEA. And Mike Hill, he's with the American Cancer Society. According to Roger [Rodriguez], Mike is at every state-sponsored meeting pushing the Texas CATCH program."

"Robert, Robert—"Fleming tried again to interrupt but Treviño continued.

"Tommy, this means **eight of the twelve committee members have ties to the Texas CATCH program.** What is going on?" Treviño demanded.

"Robert, you need to trust me."

"I can't! Come on, Tommy, at other times, you have said one thing and done another. So how can I trust you? You need to tell me if these people signed a conflict of interest form!"

"They did not," Fleming answered slowly.

"Tommy, that is unethical!" Treviño exploded.

"You need to trust me. Everything will be okay." Fleming kept repeating.

But Treviño knew that Fleming's words were hollow, and had no meaning. There was no doubt about it now: Treviño and Murray were being set up, but it was too late for him to attempt to dismantle the committee. He had to wait for the committee's decision, and then act based on the outcome.

THE SOLE VENDOR

On October 23, 2002, the TEA sent out an e-mail to the school districts informing them that only the Texas CATCH program had been approved by the committee. When Treviño found out—from a Julia Garcia at Edgewood ISD—Treviño called Fleming.

Treviño deliberately acted naïve during the call.

"Tommy, I know the committee met yesterday," he started the conversation, "and I'm calling to see if the Bienestar got approved."

"Robert," Tommy said, then paused. "The committee was very impressed with your program—"

"Tommy, was the Bienestar approved?" Treviño interrupted, although he already knew the outcome.

"It was not," Fleming answered dryly.

"Why not?"

"It was not comprehensive enough," Fleming offered as an explanation.

"What do you mean, 'not comprehensive enough?'" Treviño asked in a stern voice. The SHRC program was one that measured blood sugars, and tested the results of the children's training in scientific procedures; therefore, how could it be, 'not comprehensive enough?'

"The committee was looking for multiple grade levels, and the Bienestar targets only one grade level."

"Let me see if I get this right. The Texas CATCH has three grade levels, and has never lowered a blood sugar; and the Bienestar has one grade level [fourth-grade], and it has lowered blood sugars?"

"That's correct," Fleming said, thinking he had satisfied Treviño's query.

"Why would the committee put more value on a *process* than on an *outcome that saves lives*?"

"I can't speak for the committee, Robert. That was the criteria they chose, and that is what they used to select programs."

"Can you please send me the rejection in writing? I need this letter so I can take it to the next level," Treviño promised before he hung up the phone.

PRESSURE ON THE COMMISSIONER

Around the time when the TEA and the 'independent review committee' were rejecting the Bienestar program for the Texas school system, the SHRC received recognitions from: the American College of Nutrition; the World Health Organization; and the American Diabetes Association.

So within a week of discovering that the Bienestar program had not been approved by the TEA, Treviño sent Alanis, the TEA's new Commissioner of Education, a copy of these recognitions, and a request that he review the flaws in the TEA's selection process. Treviño copied Mary Berlanga, Geraldine Miller, Joe Bernal, Senator Frank Madla, Senator Leticia Van de Putte, Senator Judith Zaffirini, Senator Jane Nelson, Margaret Moran, and Vincent Ramos on the letter. (Moran and Ramos were with the Texas LULAC chapter.)

After receiving calls from Ramos and Bernal, who suggested a meeting with Treviño to discuss the matter, Alanis set up a meeting between Treviño and Dr. Paul Cruz, the TEA's Deputy Commissioner for Instruction. The meeting was set for December 2002.

Murray and Rodriguez accompanied Treviño to the meeting; Joey Lozano, an executive assistant with the TEA who was very familiar with the TEA's policy and regulations, accompanied Cruz.

Treviño started the conversation with the following courtesies.

"Dr. Cruz and Mr. Lozano, I want to thank you for meeting with us and listening to our concerns. We at the Social and Health Research Center have seven years of experience in operating the Bienestar Health Program in the poorest neighborhoods of San Antonio, and over that time period we have seen children as young as eight years of age develop type 2 diabetes. But more importantly, we have seen these students decrease their blood sugars to normal by their participation in our program! With the review committee's decision, the TEA is keeping an effective, scientifically-proven program away from the children who desperately need it! Why is, the TEA tying our hands like this?"

"The Bienestar has operated in the San Antonio Independent School District since 1999," Rodriguez added, "and the students like it, the food service staff likes it, the teachers like it, and the parents like it. What the

TEA is trying to do is take away local choice from the schools, and place it all on the state. That is not good for our children."

"We are not here simply to represent the Bienestar or TAKE 10," Murray made sure to note. "We're here to represent these, as well as ten other good programs that may have been developed, or are going to be developed. You see, I'm a professor of health and kinesiology at Texas State University, and I would like to encourage my students to design their own program. Maybe someday, one of them will develop a better program than all the existing diabetes education programs out there. But what incentive is there for them if the state says, 'No, the schools can only use the Texas CATCH program'? That cuts off all creative input that could be directed towards program development! And in the end, it is the children who will be affected negatively, for they will be receiving mediocre school health programs that do not benefit their bodies."

Cruz and Lozano were very attentive as they listened to each of the guests voice their concerns. Treviño then pulled out the list of reviewers Fleming had faxed over to him. He went through each individual, noting how each was connected to the Texas CATCH program. Cruz and Lozano shook their heads in disbelief when they heard of these connections, and both agreed to meet with Alanis and Fleming to discuss opening up the process to other programs.

Later, the same week, Lozano called Treviño.

"Dr. Treviño, we talked to Tommy Fleming, and he stated that his rational for not selecting the Bienestar was because it was too costly. Could you please send me a summary on your program so I can try to help you?"

In response to Fleming's newly-raised objection, Treviño sent Lozano the following letter:

> I will provide evidence showing that CATCH did not meet the objectives its investigators expected. The CATCH decreased dietary fat intake, but it took three years to decrease it by two units; from 32% in third-grade to 30% in fifth-grade (*Preventive Medicine* 1996;25:465). The Bienestar, in turn, decreased dietary fat intake by three units over one year alone; from 34% to 31% during the fourth-grade (*Diabetes* 1999;48:305). What the CATCH did in three years, Bienestar did in one. This is why CATCH needs a multi-grade curriculum, and the reason why the selection committee set the arbitrary criteria of multi-grade levels. With respect to fiber intake

(fruit and vegetables), Bienestar showed a significant increase in fiber intake and CATCH did not (*Diabetes* 1999;48:305, *J. Nutr. Educ.* 1998;30:354).

Another finding of CATCH is that it increased self-reported physical activity but not physical fitness (*Preventive Medicine* 1996;25:423). The Bienestar, in turn, showed significant increases in physical fitness (*Diabetes* 2000;49:17). There is a big difference between self-reported physical activity and physical fitness. In physical activity, the measure includes a survey, and data collection staff ask children to self-report how often they walk or exercise a week. Children either do not remember or they answer what is socially acceptable ('Yes, I did!'). In physical fitness, the measure includes getting heart rates before and after an exercise test. After the exercise, the lower the heart rate, the more physically fit is the child. The scientific literature confirms that it is physical fitness, and not self-reported physical activity that is more related to health outcomes.

The bottom line in health promotion/disease prevention programs is to change the child's biology that was indicative of disease. The CATCH never decreased blood cholesterol, body mass index (a measure of overweight), body fat, or blood glucose levels (*Preventive Medicine* 1996;25:378). On the contrary, African-American children that participated in the CATCH had gained more weight (overweight) and had increased their blood pressure (hypertension) than African-Americans in the control (*Preventive Medicine* 1996;25:432). In the Bienestar, all children decreased their abnormal glucose to normal levels without medications (*Diabetes* 2002;51:430).

The last factor is cost. During their experimental phase, CATCH cost $3,725 per student ($19 million for 5,100 students) and the Bienestar cost $357 per student ($500 thousand for 1,400 students). When cost and effects are considered, Bienestar appears to be a more a cost-effective program than CATCH. Despite science and economics supporting the Bienestar, we do not understand the rationale behind the TEA giving preferential treatment to the CATCH. Our suggestion is that it should not be just the CATCH or just the Bienestar, but instead it should be both as well as say ten more programs. This would promote competition, which is the engine for self-improvement and would promote variety, which gives the schools choices so they can select the best fits for their children populations.

At this point in time, Treviño surmised that Alanis, Cruz, and Lozano had their hearts in the right place. They wanted to help—but the CTN would prove to be too powerful. Not only did the CTN have bureaucrats 'pulling down' the SHRC, they also had the powerful association that represents Texas physicians—the Texas Medical Association (TMA)—as well as politicians pressing down on the SHRC's throat.

THE MEDICAL INDUSTRY HAD MUCH TO LOSE
The TEA's selection committee had four of their meetings at the TMA offices. What business did the education agency have setting their meetings at the medical association office? Who knows? The dates of the meetings were, August 23, September 10, October 1, and October 22, 2002. It was within the confines of the TMA that the biased selection process was contrived. Because type 2 diabetes is a $174 billion dollar industry in the U.S, and the children being affected were not those of the corporate directors, Treviño figured that it would be counterproductive for them to stop the disease.

The TMA started supporting only the Texas CATCH as early as 2001, and they were using Dr. Stephen Barnett, a retired pediatrician, to get the message out. Barnett had become involved with the TMA in several capacities. For example, in the TMA's January 2001 *Texas Medicine* issue, there was a paragraph that read as follows:

> Dr. Barnett points out that children, parents, and schools will see immediate results from the CATCH. Parents will see increased physical activity levels, better eating habits, healthier weights among children, and a reduced likelihood to use tobacco, alcohol, and other drugs. This will have a definite influence on family health as well. "Schools will see less absenteeism, more positive attitudes toward class work, and less failure and lower dropout rates. There are a number of indicators that aren't direct results of this curriculum but have indirect outcomes," Dr. Barnett said.

Forgotten Children: A True Story of How Politicians Endanger Children

Barnett sounded like a traveling medicine man selling drug compounds from the back of his wagon which he claimed were cure-alls for everything.

Barnett was also paid to travel around the state pushing the Texas CATCH program to schools. He spoke about the Texas CATCH program at the January 10, 2001 SBOE meeting, and at the Texas Health Institute conference, that same year.

Treviño had wanted the TMA's support for the Bienestar program, so he sent them the Bienestar books and studies for their review and approval back in September 2001. It was in December of 2001 that Treviño received the following response from the TMA. It was signed by Stephen Barnett:

> Karen Batory forwarded me your letter of September 10th, 2001, requesting TMA's review and recommendations of the Bienestar school-based health promotion program. I apologize for the delay in not responding sooner. However, we shared your correspondence and data on the program with several pediatricians I handpicked to review and advise. I also understand that Dianna Burns, MD, TMA Chair of the Committee on Child and Adolescent Health, met with you to discuss Bienestar.
>
> In general, we were pleased with the preliminary findings of the Bienestar program. We strongly encourage you to continue this program and to set up trials in other parts of the state. I believe you may be doing this in Laredo.
>
> The pediatric comment was very supportive of the Bienestar program goals to reduce type 2 diabetes in children and improve the health of Texas' children. However, the ad hoc reviewers agreed that more data is needed, and we look forward to findings from future trials.
>
> Please let me know when this data is available, and we would be happy to review it further.

There was nothing wrong with Barnett reviewing this material if he had no conflict of interest. But he did. He was paid to travel the state to present the Texas CATCH, and then sat on this committee that rejected the Bienestar.

Treviño decided it was time to use some of his connections to combat this conflict of interest. Not only had he, along with Dr. Roberto Ross, founded a medical group with sixteen physicians, but he was past president of the Mexican American Physicians Association. Through this association, he could get in touch with, and influence, the 400 physicians who were responsible for coughing up $300,000 in annual membership dues to the TMA. He was going to use that, plus the science behind the Bienestar program, to loosen up the TMA's support for 'one program'.

On November 1, 2002, he wrote a letter to Lou Goodman, Executive Director of the TMA. The letter started with the Bienestar's program description, the scientific merit, and the following paragraph:

> ...Although the Bienestar is recognized by the World Health Organization, the American College of Nutrition, the American Diabetes Association, and funded by the National Institute of Health (see attachments), the TMA (Dr. Stephen Barnett) has favored a school program that is culturally insensitive to minority children. The program favored by Stephen Barnett has no bilingual material designed for South Texas Children, and African-American children that participated in that program were more likely to drop out, were more likely to increase their body mass index, were more likely to increase their skin-fold thickness and were more likely to increase their blood pressure than African-American children in the control arm. Diabetes in children is an alarming medical problem that needs intense and culturally-appropriate medical intervention. Only Bienestar provides that comprehensive service to Texas most at-risk children. We kindly request that TMA reconsider its position regarding the Bienestar children's diabetes program.

Copies were sent to Frederick Merian, M.D. (President, TMA), Kay Peck (Executive Director, Bexar County Medical Society), Marc Taylor, M.D. (President, Bexar County Medical Society), Barbie Hernandez (Executive Director, Mexican American Physician Association), Eddie Flores, M.D. (President, Mexican American Physician Association), and Jesse Moss, M.D. (President, C.A. Whittier Medical Society [African-American Medical Association])

Sixty-nine Mexican-American physicians then either called or wrote to TMA in support of the Bienestar. After this, the TMA seemed to have second thoughts about endorsing program adoption in Texas schools.

In April 2003, Dr. Andrew Eisenberg (TMA Chair for Council on Public Health) sent Treviño the following letter:

> Thank you for your letter regarding the Bienestar Program. The Council on Public Health has previously invited you to the Council on Public Health and we have asked for your participation again at our next meeting in September. The Council has been encouraged by the early positive results in identifying fourth graders at risk for diabetes and the implementation of nutrition and exercise activities in the target schools.
>
> It is not the role of TMA to endorse school health curricula, but rather the role of the Texas Education Agency. Our policy is clear on that point and reads as follows:
>
>> **55.0022—Comprehensive School Health Education in All School Districts:** The Texas Medical Association believes the Texas Education Agency should have statutory authority to require comprehensive school health education in all school districts of the state, and that the process should begin with implementation of the TEA-developed modules on physical education, nutrition, substance use, and sexuality (Council on Public Health, pp 104-107, I90; amended CM-CAH Rep. 2—A01).
>
> The Council encourages you to adapt your program to meet criteria set forth by TEA that incorporates the elements listed in SB 19 applicable to all elementary grades and coordinates health education, physical education and activity, nutrition services, and parental involvement. A significant component of the TEA criteria is that approved curricula must address grades K-6. Council members have spoken with you about the fact that Bienestar focuses exclusively on the fourth grade.
>
> Thank you again for your interest and support of public health programs to address the obesity epidemic

• DR. ROBERTO P. TREVIÑO •

and to reduce the number of Texas children being diagnosed with Type 2 diabetes. Childhood obesity is one of our top public health priorities. As we develop the Council meeting agenda for September, our staff members will contact you regarding your availability and any handouts that you would like the Council to receive.

Interestingly, the month before this letter, TMA gave the Bexar County Medical Society Alliance $10,000 to try to extract the Bienestar program from local schools. The Bexar County Medical Society Alliance is the association for doctor's wives discussed on page 86.

Then, in the same month that Eisenberg's letter went out, claiming that the TMA did not want to endorse school health curricula, the TMA published in their journal, *Texas Medicine*, a report titled, "**TMA Foundation promotes CATCH to local Schools.**" The report stated that the TMA and TMA Foundation provided some schools with $45,000 to implement the Texas CATCH program. In this same issue, Cribb was quoted saying, "the law [SB 19] essentially was written to support the Coordinated Approach to Child Health (CATCH) in public schools."

In the very same month—the TMA said one thing and did another.

OCCASIONALLY, SUGAR IS SWEET

The other group CTN sent out to suffocate the SHRC was politicians. Senator Eliot Shapleigh, D-El Paso, is a tall, gregarious Texan. At about six feet two inches, he makes an impression in the Texas Capitol, especially when he sports a cowboy hat and boots, an outfit he wore frequently.

Shapleigh is a good man who supports noble issues, but he made some unfortunate choices. He got together with Ann Pauli and the CTN people to bring in their program to children along the Texas-Mexico border, a place which has the highest rates of hospitalization for diabetes in the country. Hospital costs are the most expensive component of all medical care and by providing children with a placebo program, they would be using the children to supply that industry.

The Texas legislature meets for six months every two years. In 2001, Nelson introduced SB 19 during this time period; in 2003, Shapleigh would introduce SB 343. [Note: A sister bill was also introduced in the House by Representative Arlene Wohlgemuth, R-Burleson. It was called HB 764). Shapleigh and Pauli announced SB 343 in the *El Paso Times*. It stripped power away from the people and the local school districts, and gave it to the government. Components of SB 343 read as follows:

> ...Section 38.013 (a) The agency [TEA], with the assistance of the Obesity Prevention Coordinating Council, shall make available to each school district a coordinated health program designed to prevent obesity, cardiovascular disease, and type II diabetes in elementary school students."
> Section 112.001. DEFINITION. In this chapter, "council" means the Obesity Prevention Coordinating Council.
> Section 112.002. COUNCIL. The department [TDH] and the Texas Education Agency shall jointly establish and support the council.
> Section 112.003. COMPOSITION; TERMS. (a) The council is composed of six members who serve staggered two-year terms. (b) The department and the Texas Education Agency shall each appoint three members to the council.
> Section 112.007 PERSONNEL AND FACILITIES. The department and the Texas Education Agency are jointly responsible for the administration of the council.
> Section 112.051. COORDINATION WITH STEERING COMMITTEE; STRATETIC PLAN. The council shall coordinate its activities with the Statewide Obesity Task Force Steering Committee established by the department. To the extent possible, the council shall ensure that its activities are consistent with the Strategic Plan for the Prevention of Obesity in Texas issued by the task force steering committee.
> Section 112.052. COORDINATED HEALTH PROGRAM FOR ELEMENTARY SCHOOL STUDENTS. (a) The council shall assist the Texas Education Agency in developing and facilitating the implementation of the coordinated health program for elementary school students...

Note the wording of the bill, which refers to a singular program (i.e., the Texas CATCH), and the people who would be at the controls: Fleming was at the TEA; Sanchez was at the TDH; and the Statewide

• DR. ROBERTO P. TREVIÑO •

Obesity Task Force, as already shown (Chapter 5) was full of people whose intent was to support and fund the Texas CATCH program.

Treviño called Andrea Varnell, Shapleigh's legislative aide, to inquire more about their bill.

"Andrea, this is Dr. Treviño with the Social and Health Research Center."

"Hi, Dr. Treviño, I've heard of the good work you do," Varnell responded warmly.

"Andrea, I'm calling to ask if we could meet with you or Senator Shapleigh to discuss Senate Bill 343?"

"Sure, let me look at our schedule."

After putting Treviño on hold momentarily, she suggested, "Dr. Treviño, we're putting a committee together to discuss this bill."

"When?"

"It will be next Thursday at one p.m., at the Texas Capitol Extension. Conference room E1.024."

"Who will be attending?"

"The beverage industry lobbyists are not happy with our bill, and they want to discuss removing some sections," Varnell informed Treviño as she also explained the details of bill. "Senator Shapleigh is putting together a panel of health experts to help us repel these lobbyists. Would you care to join us?"

"I will be there," Treviño promised before he walked over to Oralia Garcia's office to discuss the upcoming Shapleigh meeting.

"Oralia, I just got off the phone with Andrea Varnell from Senator Shapleigh's office. We were discussing a meeting about SB 343."

"How did it go?"

"Well, apparently a section in the bill says to remove beverages with added sugar completely out from school campuses. And that has gotten the beverage lobbyists all stirred up."

Upon hearing this news, Garcia smiled and said, "A-ha! Let's let them cannibalize Shapleigh's bill."

"Yes, exactly!" Treviño agreed. "We stood behind state comptroller Susan Combs when she took on the beverage industry. She passed and enforced policies to remove beverages with added sugar from the school cafeterias. But we're not going to stand behind Shapleigh. If we do, his bill, when it comes into effect, will cannibalize the Bienestar program."

The strategy worked. Sure enough, the beverage industry dogs chewed Shapleigh's bill to pieces.

ATTEMPTING TO RIGHT A WRONG

Forgotten Children: A True Story of How Politicians Endanger Children

During the same legislative session, Treviño begged Nelson's staff to undo the damage they had done during the 2001 session with SB 19. At the beginning of the 2003 session, Treviño sent Amy Lindley, Nelson's aide, an e-mail asking Nelson to write Smisko (TEA Associate Commissioner of Curriculum, Assessment and Technology) a letter suggesting that the TEA be open to other coordinated school health programs. Treviño was even willing to draft the letter for her, but Nelson did not respond. In April 2003 (three weeks later), Treviño followed up with an e-mail to Lindley:

> Just to make you aware of two publications that came out regarding the selection process at TEA. The first is by *Texas Medicine* (TMA Journal), quoting Peter Cribb from CATCH, saying that SB 19 'essentially was written to support the use of CATCH' (see fax). It surprises me that a bill would be written just to favor one vendor, and I know that that was not the intention of Sen. Nelson (her letter to us and the attorney general's ruling says otherwise). The second was published in the *S.A. Express-News* (this Sunday) by Cindy Tumiel. In her article, two things stand out. One is how Bienestar is backed by <u>science</u> and TEA backs their decision by <u>politics</u>. Second is that Cindy did her own investigation and, indeed, finds that Texas CATCH proponents are sitting in state agency review panels and supporting their own program. I am receiving many calls, and people are getting fed up with cronyism. Please, we need Sen. Nelson to intervene and put a stop to all this conflict of interest.

After receiving frequent calls and e-mails from Treviño, Lindley finally called Treviño to set up a meeting. Treviño and Garcia drove in to the Capitol for the meeting.

The room where Lindley met with Treviño and Garcia was small and crowded. They greeted Lindley, a tall, large-boned woman with wavy brunette hair. She listened carefully to Treviño, and when she spoke, she revealed she was exceedingly knowledgeable about state politics.

"We really want to thank you for making time to hear our concern about how SB 19 has been manipulated by the staff of the TEA," Treviño started politely. He selected his words carefully to show his respect for the aide of such a powerful woman in state politics. "We know it was not the intention of Senator Nelson that SB 19 be exclusive to any one program."

"We have seven years operating the Bienestar coordinated school health program in the poorest neighborhoods," Oralia offered smoothly. "Over those years, we have found five to seven percent of the children have high blood sugars, and year after year our program has been able to normalize the blood sugars on these children."

"The Bienestar might not be perfect, but then there is no perfect program out there," Treviño admitted. "School health interventions are still in their infancy, so it seems unusual for the TEA to start pruning the programs by supporting one to the exclusion of others."

"Why do you say that, Dr. Treviño?" Lindley asked carefully.

"In May 2002, members of the TEA staff asked all agencies with coordinated school health programs to submit their programs. But it wasn't until September 2002 that the TEA formed a panel of reviewers to evaluate these programs, and when they did, the majority of the panel members already had prior affiliations with the Texas CATCH program. In October 2002, they ended up approving one and only one program, the Texas CATCH program. And it was not until November 2002 that they posted the criteria for selection in the *Texas Register*. They did the selection process all backwards."

Lindley shook her head, her facial expression showing her disbelief.

"Are you telling me that they reviewed the programs without criteria, and they only posted the criteria in the *Texas Register* after the selection?"

"Yes," answered Garcia firmly, and without hesitation.

"I see," said Lindley, as she shook her head again. "I will discuss this with the senator and get back to y'all."

At the end of April, Lindley faxed Treviño a draft of SB 1357, which was meant to rectify SB 19. In the cover letter she stated, "I think you [Treviño and the SHRC] will be pleased with the added language of this new bill."

The bill was remarkable in the way it would make improvements in children's health. In a time of diminishing physical activity in schools, SB 1357 mandated at least 30 minutes per school day, or 135 minutes per school week of physical activity. It changed from singular to plural the following statement that the "agency shall make available to each school district one or more coordinated health programs." But while it also rectified the timing for forming criteria and selecting programs, it still placed the control in Fleming's lap. The revision that concerned Treviño read as follow:

> The [TEA] commissioner by rule shall adopt criteria for evaluating a coordinated health program before making the program available under Subsection (a). Before adopting the criteria, the commissioner shall request reviews and comments concerning the criteria from the Texas Department of Health's School Health Advisory Committee. The commissioner may make available under Subsection (a) only those programs that meet criteria adopted under this subsection.

Quickly Treviño wrote Amy the following e-mail:

> Recent findings emerged that made us concerned about SB 1357's last paragraph. On May 1st, I spoke with Dr. Paul Cruz (TEA, Dep Comm) and he acknowledged that it was Dr. Tommy Fleming that wrote the CATCH & GBS [Great Body Shop curriculum] ONLY letter and it is he who sent it to all the school districts. This gave us the impression that when SB 1357 gives the authority to the commissioner, it is really Dr. Fleming that is in the driver's seat in this area. Second, SB 1357 gives authority to TDH's School Health Advisory Council. Yesterday, it clicked in our mind to search to see who sits on that committee and sure enough it is Dr. Fleming (see fax). So the last paragraph of SB 1357 goes back and puts all the power again on Dr. Fleming. Please distribute the power. Please give me a call.

As it turned out, the wording in this bill's draft paragraph would not be changed. But since mandating daily physical activity in the elementary schools would allow for an enormous advancement in the field of children's health, Treviño testified in favor of the bill at a SBOE meeting.

SB 1357 became part of Texas law in September of 2003. As wonderful as this occurrence was, the fact that changes had not been made to the language which designated the Commissioner of the TEA as the person in charge would become a burr under the saddle of the SHRC.

Chapter 11

UNDER INVESTIGATION

Fortunately, the fact that something did not smell exactly right in the state of Texas was coming to the attention of honest, ethical politicians. It would be State Representative Mike Villarreal (page 110) who introduced the Bienestar program and the Texas CATCH case to State Representative Pete Gallego (D-Alpine) and Garnet Coleman (D-Houston) in October of 2002.

Gallego was a tall man with pearl-colored skin. He was preppy-looking with his conservative, shorter haircut and rimmed eyeglasses.

Villarreal had been visiting with Gallego for months asking him to review the Texas CATCH case. Villarreal's concern was that the CTN was setting themselves up to be the sole vendor of health textbooks in the state of Texas. Gallego would be the right person to approach about the problem, as he was Chair of the House Committee on General Investigation. And Coleman got involved because he and Houston's UTSPH were usually at odds on different issues, and he did not trust them.

A HARPOON STRIKE

It was a cold afternoon in December 2002 when Treviño picked up the phone.

"Dr. Treviño, this is Jacquelyn Plyler with Representative Gallego, and here with me is Monica Faulkner with Representative Coleman's office. We heard about your case, and both representatives are very interested in hearing about it. Can the two of us meet with you to hear more about what kind of treatment your program has received by the state agencies? We would like for you to bring any documents you may have that shows that your program has been treated unfairly."

Treviño was thrilled at this unexpected offer of help, even though in his mind, the voices at the other end of the phone sounded too young to belong to those of seasoned people working at the state capitol. The meeting was set for the following day.

Treviño and Oralia Garcia went to Gallego's office. After they introduced themselves to the front office secretary, Plyler and Faulkner came out to greet them. Both were attractive young ladies who looked like they might have been college freshman.

When the women walked away to locate an available conference room, Treviño turned to Garcia, and said with a grin, "These girls sounded like college students in the phone, but now that I see them, they look more like high school students."

"I think we took a long drive for nothing," Garcia joked. "I don't think these young girls will be able to take the CTN people off our backs."

"Actually, I can't believe the representatives put these girls to the task," a worried Treviño admitted. "Starting an investigation into the CTN dealings is a daunting task. I'm concern they will be like little fish in a shark's tank."

Despite their trepidation, Treviño and Garcia presented to the women the components of the Bienestar program, as well as the studies and the results. They also showed the letters and e-mails that went back and forth between SHRC and TEA. And as it would turn out, these teenage-looking professionals would strike the CTN as acutely as a harpoon.

First, the women set a follow-up meeting the following week in the State Capitol with Gallego, Coleman, and Villarreal. Garcia drove up to Austin with Treviño.

"What can we do for you," Gallego asked, getting right to the point once everyone was seated in the room.

"I will cut to the chase," Treviño said. "You don't need to be a scientist to know about the problem we have in Texas with too many kids being overweight and developing type 2 diabetes. You see that in the news almost every week."

Treviño paused to pull out some of the SHRC's publications and put them on the conference table.

"This paper showed that students in the Bienestar program decreased their dietary fat intake and increased their dietary fiber intake. This paper showed that students in the Bienestar program increased physical fitness levels, and students not in the Bienestar program decreased their physical fitness levels. This last paper showed that students in the Bienestar program had high blood sugar levels at the beginning of the school year, and normal blood sugar levels at the end of the school year.

What is noteworthy is that the Bienestar program is the only program in Texas showing evidence of reversing high blood sugars."

The state representatives' eyes shifted back and forth between Treviño and the studies.

"But something that is so very simple has been complicated by the interference of the government and politics," Treviño continued.

"What do you mean?" Coleman asked, an anxious tone in his voice.

"We have an available and effective program that obviously has the potential to prevent occurrence of type 2 diabetes in Texas children, but the TEA is limiting the reach of our program so that we cannot improve the health of our children. It seems like the TEA would rather see our children go blind and lose limbs from the diabetes complications than let our program operate in the schools in our state."

"That's horrible." Coleman snarled. "Why on earth would they do that?"

"Could it be that diabetes is big money for the medical industry, and that the people who fill the hospital beds are black and Latinos, while the people who make the money from treating their medical conditions are white?" Treviño suggested.

Treviño had no firm evidence to back up his statement, but hoped the race card might stir the black knight to enter the battle.

Coleman, an outspoken black politician and son of a Houston physician, understood the problems minorities had receiving medical care. He became incensed upon hearing Treviño's hypothesis. He spoke the words that followed in a clipped tone of voice: "Who the hell is behind all this?"

"It's a group out of Houston," Treviño explained. "Houston's UT School of Public Health. The School of Public Health literally sits in the middle of the largest medical conglomerate of hospitals and health institutions in the world. The medical industry profits from illness. There is nothing wrong with that, but it is wrong when they hold back treatment so that they can make profits."

"Peter Cribb and some other men were in my office early this morning, and I told them to get the hell out," Coleman interjected bluntly.

Treviño was not that surprised to hear this. It had seemed to him for a long time that the CTN had a way of knowing beforehand who was meeting with whom at the State Capitol.

"Those guys from Houston's UT School of Public Health are usually up to no good," Coleman continued.

Treviño did not know why Coleman made that comment, and he did not ask. He simply knew Coleman was fired up and ready to attack, and that's all that mattered.

"Well, what has the TEA done to hold back your program from our schoolchildren?" Gallego quizzed.

Treviño explained the distressing experiences the SHRC already had in dealing with the TDH and the TEA.

Coleman turned and looked at Gallego afterwards. "This sounds like sole vendor stuff," he summarized.

Gallego returned the look, and said quietly but decisively, "I'll get the Attorney General to rule on it."

Gallego turned to Treviño and asked, "Could you please make the formal request in a letter?"

THE FORMAL INVESTIGATION

On January 10, 2003, Treviño wrote Gallego a letter requesting a formal investigation of the matter. The first paragraph of the letter was the following:

> I have a concern with Mr. Tommy Fleming (TEA Director of Health Curriculum) giving preferential treatment to one school-based health program (the Texas CATCH). There is strong lobbying by the Texas CATCH proponents to convince state agencies to only approve and adopt their program and to exclude all others. The potential benefits for having exclusivity are several. The $200 million grant the CDC will provide to state educational agencies for school health funding would only go to the Texas CATCH, all funding by state agencies for school health would only go to the Texas CATCH, and all educational material bought by school districts for school health would only be purchased from the Texas CATCH people. This appears to have a self-interest motive, and we would ask for a formal investigation into this matter.

Copies were sent to Senators Frank Madla, Leticia Van de Putte, Judith Zaffirini, Jane Nelson and Representatives Mike Villarreal and Garnet Coleman.

Senator Madla's office asked Steve Kelder, a professor of Houston's UTSPH and the Texas CATCH program coordinator, to respond to

Treviño's request for an investigation. He sent this letter to Gallego dated February 24, 2003 to Gallego:

> Pursuant to an invitation from Senator Madla's office to respond to the letter you received from Dr. Roberto Treviño, I would like to provide an explanation of CATCH's participation in the process of implementing Senate Bill 19. Additionally, some background information relative to the research and dissemination of CATCH will address the continued misrepresentation of the program by Dr. Trevino. The following information and documentation will also confirm the validity of CATCH as an educational program that reduces risk behaviors in children that lead to obesity, cardiovascular, diseases, type II diabetes, and other chronic disease. And finally, this correspondence will confirm that the CATCH program and personnel have followed exemplary professional and ethical practices in our quest to serve the State of Texas, as well as the school children in this state.
>
> As you know, Section 38.014 of SB 19 requires each school district to 'participate in appropriate training for the implementation of the program approved by the agency'. After the passage of SB 19 in May, 2001, Texas Education Agency (TEA) leadership determined that the CATCH Program was the only program 'approved by the agency' and began the process of implementing SB 19. TEA support in this early phase of SB 19 implementation included explaining CATCH program implementation plans to regional education service centers (ESC's) at a meeting of ESC curriculum specialists referred to as the "Core Group" in October, 2001. The TEA endorsement of the CATCH Program as the only program approved by TEA was challenged by Dr. Trevino in a letter to Commissioner Nelson in December 2001. As a result of the controversy, beginning to increase around the 'intent' of SB 19, TEA developed a new plan for implementing coordinated health program in school districts.
>
> The new plan was outlined to districts in a March 22, 2002 letter from Deputy Commissioner for Programs and Instruction of TEA, Dr. Arturo Almendarez. The

following part of that letter highlights the change in TEA policy regarding the SB 19 directive to TEA to approve coordinated health programs: 'Beginning this spring, any organization/program that chooses to be considered for selection by the agency will be invited to send a complete program description of their program to TEA. TEA will then develop a list of qualified programs that will be distributed to school districts.' This plan opened the SB 19 process to any program that coordinates the four components of health education, physical education/physical activity, nutrition/cafeteria service, and parental involvement. At this point, TEA no longer endorsed one program, but rather, any program that met the requirements set forth in the legislation.

After the new Commissioner of Education, Dr. Felipe Alanis, was appointed by the Governor in March 2002, a third mechanism for SB 19 evaluation, review, and approval of submitted programs was established at TEA. Dr. Alanis decided to establish an independent group of experts to evaluate health programs submitted to TEA. As of this letter, the review committee has approved two health programs, the CATCH Program and The Great Body Shop.

Aside from the issue of implementation of Senate Bill 19, on a separate sheet I have listed the main points of rebuttal to Dr. Treviño's current letter. I might add, that I wrote the bulk of this fact sheet in October, 2000, in answer to his October 3, 2000 letter of complaint to then Commissioner of Health, Dr. Ryen Archer. Since that time, the following events have taken place that have bearing on this issue:

(1) On January 18-19, 2001, CATCH was reviewed by an appointed panel of cultural and minority experts to determine if CATCH was culturally relevant to Texas children of all ethnic and racial backgrounds. This panel met in person for two days and concluded CATCH would be acceptable for all children.

(2) In 2001, the US Department of Defence (DOD) adopted CATCH PE for worldwide implementation across all DOD elementary schools.

(3) In 2001, the Texas Medical Association vigorously

supports the CATCH program.

(4) In 2002, the Centers for Disease Control and US Department of Health and Human Services formally announce CATCH as an exemplary program for improving child health.

(5) In 2002, CATCH was nominated for the William T. Grant Foundation Youth Development Prize by the Texas Governor's Advisory Council on Physical Fitness.

(6) CATCH currently is part of the statewide plans of the Texas Council of Cardiovascular Disease and Stroke, the Texas Obesity Task Force, and the Texas Department of Health Diabetes Council.

(7) HHS Secretary Tommy G. Thompson was briefed on CATCH during a Town Hall meeting on January 23, 2003 in Austin.

(8) I would also like to note that in 1997 CATCH was cited as an example of 'Best Practices' by the Canadian Health Behavior Research Group in the International Scan for Best Practices in Heart Health demonstrating not only national, but international recognition for the quality of the work.

My point is, Representative Gallego, if CATCH is as ineffective as Dr. Treviño suggests, how could we possibly gain endorsement from so many medical, community and state agencies, as well as receive international recognition?

This is especially true when you consider, to date, we have received only $1,200 in royalties derived from the sales of CATCH. This money and any additional royalties that might ensue are relegated to a University of Texas state program income account at the center for Health Promotion and Prevention Research: these monies can only be used for further research, development and support of CATCH materials and activities. In fact, there is virtually no profit evident in our location within a state university system, our research with CATCH, and the many other youth-oriented research and service projects conducted at the Center for Health Promotion and Prevention Research. In contrast, Dr. Trevino's research is conducted at an independent foundation, which is not subject to the same controls and public access as a state entity. The state of Texas has no public access to the accounting system and finances of Dr. Trevino's foundation, so there is no way to determine if, for example, a conflict of interest exists between his NIH funded study and referrals of Bienestar students to his diabetes clinic.

We welcome innovative research and the development of new projects that have a positive impact on children's health. However, as scientists, we rely on stringent evaluation and peer review to maintain high standards and to distinguish effective programs from those that do not work, or which work in a limited setting. Bienestar is currently in its main trial, which is in contrast to the CATCH main trial conducted in 1991-1994. Until Dr. Trevino's study has passed the same rigorous standards for quality and evaluation that CATCH has, it is premature to disseminate it widely. In contrast, there are over 80 peer reviewed CATCH publications. The CATCH study investigators did not try to widely disseminate CATCH until we were certain of the program effects.

Thank you for the opportunity to respond to Dr. Trevino's repeated, unfounded accusations. I personally believe Dr. Trevino, with his persistent calls for investigations of CATCH, has delayed full implementation of SB 19 by nearly two years, time with which we could have been saving children of Texas. For his detrimental efforts in blocking wide implementation of the CATCH program (or any other approved and deserving program), he should be held responsible, in part, for the rising level of childhood obesity.

You can see I am passionate about this topic. My interest is to serve the children of Texas and to avoid any further delays in meeting the mandates of Senate Bill 19. I believe in the process that has been followed and am quite proud of the work my team has accomplished with the CATCH program. We stand by our record. I welcome your questions and am ready to provide any information you require.

Forgotten Children: A True Story of How Politicians Endanger Children

Copies of this letter were sent to Frank Madla, Jane Nelson, Leticia Van de Putte, Judith Zaffirini, Eddie Lucio, Gonzalo Barrientos, Eliot Shapleigh, Mike Villarreal, Garnet Coleman, Jamie Capelo, Jim Dunnam, Eduardo Sanchez, Susan Combs (Commissioner of Agriculture), Felipe Alanis, Ann Smisko, Paul Cruz, Janet Russell (TEA), Philip Haung, Jan Ozias, Karen Batory (TMA), Paul Carrozza (Governor's Advisory Council on Physical Fitness), Ellen Kelsy (American Heart Association), Mike Hill (American Cancer Society), Diana Everett (TAPHERD), George Carmel (Flaghouse, Inc. owner), Ann Pauli, Joan Miller (Bexar County Community Health Collaborative), Rene Nuñez (SBOE), Mary Helen Berlanga (SBOE), Joe J. Bernal (SBOE), Alma Allen (SBOE), Dan Montgomery (SBOE), Terri Leo (SBOE), David Bradley (SBOE), Linda Bauer (SBOE), Don McLeroy (SBOE), Cynthia Thornton (SBOE), Patricia Hardy (SBOE), Geraldine Miller (SBOE), Mavis Knight (SBOE), Gail Lowe (SBOE), and Bob Craig (SBOE).

Treviño was not going to sit back and have Kelder have the last say. Treviño responded to Kelder's letter by sending Gallego the following letter on March 10, 2003:

> The letter we mailed January 10th, presented concerns about the conduct at TEA and not the conduct at the University of Texas' Center for Health Promotion and Prevention Research. The concern about the TEA was due to their exclusive support for a sole vendor. The CATCH educational program has many accomplishments. At the school-level, the CATCH has improved menus in school cafeterias and it has increased moderate to vigorous physical activity time in school health class. At the student level, the CATCH has increased perception of how often students do physical activity, it has improved students' health beliefs, and it has decreased students' self-reported percent intake of total fat. Although the CATCH educational program has modified positively students' self-reported health knowledge, beliefs and behaviors, it has not modified unhealthy biological markers. It is high cholesterol, high blood pressure, and high blood glucose that will kill children, and it is lowering high cholesterol, high blood pressure and high blood glucose that will save children.
>
> The Bienestar is a school-based medical program aimed at treating and preventing diabetes in at-risk,

low-income children. It is high blood glucose that will cause their blindness, amputations, and dialysis, and it is lowering blood glucose that will prevent their blindness, amputations, and dialysis. The Bienestar, in its NIH-funded randomized control trial, has prevented high blood glucose levels and has treated abnormal blood glucose levels without medications. The aim of the CATCH educational program is to reduce risk behaviors associated with chronic illness, and the aim of the Bienestar medical program is to modify biological markers associated with illness. An educational intervention and a medical intervention are not exclusive—they are inclusive—they complement each other.

Again the question is why the TEA shifted the decision for selection away from the local school districts (which SB 19 endorses) and placed it on the state? Why produce artificial protection of one program instead of letting it compete with others? Shouldn't it be local school districts deciding which program best fits their students' needs and which programs produces best outcomes? Interrupting competition and best fits will only produce poor quality programs and ultimately affect the health of Texas children. Who then will be made responsible?

Treviño sent copies of the letter to the same individuals whom Kelder copied.

This contest put the Republican Party at odds, because the Governor and the Attorney General were both Republicans, but the Governor wanted government control so he could impose his will, while the Attorney General needed to rule for local control to protect the Republican ideals.

Attorney General Greg Abbott's ruling [Opinion GA-0038] came back addressed to Representative Kevin Bailey on March 13, 2003 . The first paragraph read:

Your predecessor in office [Gallego] asked whether Education Code section 38.013, which requires the Texas Education Agency ("TEA" or "agency") to make "a coordinated health program" for elementary school students available to each school district in Texas",

> authorizes TEA to choose only one single coordinated school health program for all the school districts in Texas...

In the middle of five pages of legalese, the following statement opened up the process to other school health programs:

> ...The statue does not state that TEA must make available to each school district identical teacher's guides, student workbooks, videos, posters, and other educational materials, nor does it state that only one provider may supply educational materials that implement the coordinated health program...

The TEA must have known this was coming because Kelder, in his February 24th letter, mentions for the first time that the Great Body Shop school health curriculum was also approved by TEA. The Great Body Shop, from Connecticut, was a program submitted to the TEA after the announced deadline—and as the SHRC staff would soon discover, it was not even a program that met the requirements of SB 19.

On March 6, 2003, Roger Rodriguez e-mailed Roxanne Burns, who was with the Great Body Shop, to ask if their program included PE, parent and food service components. Burns sent Rodriguez the following e-mail in response:

> The TEA said that they approved us even though those other activities [PE, parent and food service] hadn't been added yet—so the copies that you have are the ones they reviewed and approved. But if you want, I can send you the other PE activities when they are completed and submitted by our PE specialist. Let me know, Rox.

Shaking his head, once again, in disbelief at this news of the Great Body Shop program being approved after the deadline, Treviño called Ozias. Ozias was a member of the October 2002 Coordinated School Health Program selection committee (see page 163). He wanted to drill down on the reasons as to why the selection committee would choose a program that clearly did not meet the requirements of SB 19.

"Hi, Jan. Do you have a minute?"

"Hi, Dr. Treviño," Ozias responded pleasantly. "It is nice to hear from you."

"Jan, I just heard your committee approved the Great Body Shop. When did y'all meet, and why would the TEA approve it even though it was missing the PE, parent, and food service components?"

For a moment, there was silence on the end of the phone line. Then Ozias responded in a voice that trembled, "Dr. Treviño, the committee has *not* met."

"Well, were you aware that the selection committee has approved the Great Body Shop?"

"No, I wasn't," Ozias answered, sounding perplexed.

"Okay, thank you Jan."

Treviño hung up and walked over to Oralia Garcia's office and told her of his findings.

"We need to call the other members of that committee, to find if they met and were they informed of the selection," Garcia said thoughtfully.

"Can you call Laura Garcia and Carey Dabney?" Treviño asked. "Both were members of the 2002 Coordinated School Health Program selection committee and neither has ties to the Texas CATCH. If these guys did something improper they would've left them out."

Garcia got on the phone immediately, and was able to contact both committee members. Laura Garcia and Dabney both indicated that they were unaware of any meeting or of any approval being given to the Great Body Shop.

"*Estos desgraciados nos fregaron otra vez*, Oralia," ("These scoundrels have screwed us again, Oralia,") Treviño said afterwards. He was so disappointed in what was happening in the state in which he lived. "Here's the Bienestar program showing positive results in the poorest Texas neighborhoods, and yet the TEA goes all the way to Connecticut to pull in another program without the SB 19 requirements or any evidence of decreasing blood sugars. How can this be happening?"

At that moment, Garcia and Treviño decided to apply more pressure on the TEA.

Chapter 12

THE BUILDUP TO ATTACK THE TEA

After four long months since the TEA review committee had announced that the Texas CATCH was the only program approved by the state (Chapter 10, back on page 164), Ann Smisko, the TEA Associate Commissioner of Curriculum, Assessment, and Technology, finally had the courtesy of sending Treviño a rejection letter about the Bienestar program submission. The letter was dated February 20, 2003 and it read:

> The Senate Bill 19 state review committee met in Austin, Texas, on October 22, 2002, to evaluate several health programs, including *Bienestar*. The purpose of this letter is to inform you that the *Bienestar* program is not approved.
>
> To ensure that programs continue to be submitted for review by the agency, a *Texas Register* notice will be published periodically. You are encouraged to review the evaluation process when published and resubmit your program.
>
> Should you have questions about this issue, please contact Dr. Tommy Fleming, Director of Health and Physical Education.

A fervent believer in both science and free enterprise, Treviño fired back a letter at Smisko that started off detailing the scientific merits of the Bienestar program. The letter, sent on February 24, 2003, concluded with the following:

> ...Because we are confused, we need your clarification. SB 19 clearly wrote the law and set the

criteria by which a program can participate. SB 19 states "...may require a student enrolled in k-6 to participate in daily activity," which is being done in all Bienestar schools. SB 19 states the implementation of "a coordinated health education program designed to prevent obesity, cardiovascular disease, and type 2 diabetes through the coordination of: A) health education, B) physical education, C) nutritional services, D) parental involvement, and E) instruction to prevent the use of tobacco," which the Bienestar does. SB 19 states, "A school district must consider the recommendations of the local school health education advisory council before changing the district's health education curriculum or instruction," which Bienestar has the approval by.

The question is, why is TEA writing criteria when **SB 19 already wrote the criteria? Shouldn't TEA be enforcing those criteria?** Why would TEA shift power away from local school districts and place it on the state? Isn't free enterprise and individualism the foundation of this country? Why produce artificial protection of a single program instead of letting it compete with others? Shouldn't it be local school districts deciding which health program best fits their students? Interrupting competition and best fits will only produce poor quality programs and, ultimately, this will affect Texas children. Who then should be responsible for this?

Treviño sent copies to Felipe Alanis, Rene Nuñez, Mary Berlanga, Joe Bernal, Alma Allen, Dan Montgomery, Chase Untermeyer, David Bradley, Grace Shore, Don McLeroy, Cynthia A. Thornton, Richard Watson, Judy Strickland, Sen. Jane Nelson, Sen. Frank Madla, Sen. Leticia Van de Putte, Rep. Garnet Coleman, Rep. Pete Gallego, Rep. Mike Villarreal, and Marty De Leon.

In response, Bernal asked that Alanis set up a meeting at which Smisko and Fleming should be present to answer questions directed at them. Smisko and Fleming were reluctant to attend such a forum, but what brought them to the table was a phone call they received from Dr. Ruben Olivarez, superintendent of SAISD.

At the time, Rodriguez and Treviño were in Olivarez's office to report an improper act previously conducted by the CTN people. When Rodriguez reported to Olivarez that the CTN people had offered him

Forgotten Children: A True Story of How Politicians Endanger Children

money if he pulled the Bienestar out of the schools in his district, and brought in the Texas CATCH program, Olivarez got very upset and immediately called Smisko.

Olivarez and Smisko had worked together at the TEA before he took the position of superintendent at SAISD. He bluntly told her that if she and Fleming did not meet with Treviño and Rodriguez, he would take news of the bribe Rodriguez had been offered to the authorities.

It turned out that Smisko and Fleming called Joe Bernal to set up an appointment for the following day.

MANIPULATIONS BEHIND THE SCENES

Treviño and Bernal invited Oralia Garcia, Roger Rodriguez, Linda Urrutia from National Council of La Raza, Nina Perales from the Mexican-American Legal Defense and Educational Fund (MALDEF), and Vincent Ramos from LULAC to attend the meeting on March 6, 2003. It would be held at four in the afternoon at the TEA.

On the day of the meeting, all of the invitees were present, except for a representative who came in place of Vincent Ramos.

After asking everyone to identify themselves and say who they represented, Bernal started by saying, "Dr. Smisko and Dr. Fleming, I want to thank you for taking time from your busy schedules to hear our concerns."

He then looked at Treviño, and signaled him to take over.

Treviño looked right at Fleming and asked, "Why did you present the Texas CATCH program to the State Board of Education as a diabetes education program, when it didn't even have a diabetes lesson plan?"

"At that time, that was the only program I was aware of," Fleming answered.

"But Dr. Murray from Texas State University asked you to present the TAKE 10! program to the board, and you refused. I also had asked you in two prior letters to come and visit San Antonio to observe the Bienestar program, and you refused."

"Dr. Treviño, I'm the only person in the department," Fleming sighed, "and I can't be everywhere doing everything for everyone."

"I must admit, it's hard for me to hear such excuses when we have type 2 diabetes affecting children as young as eight years of age," Treviño said with a glare in his eyes. "This is a medical illness that needs medical treatment, and the staff members of the TEA are not medical experts. The TEA has taken it upon itself to assume a responsibility its staff are not trained for, or prepared to handle."

"We agree with you," Smisko said, nodding her head and looking at Fleming.

"Well, then why were you sending school districts e-mails telling us that we had to implement the Texas CATCH program because the legislature mandated it?" Rodriguez queried as he looked at Fleming. "SB 19 doesn't even have the words "Texas CATCH" in it."

"I misread the bill," Fleming said as his defense.

"How could you have misread the bill?" Bernal questioned in disbelief. "A high school student could've read that bill correctly," he chided.

"I didn't appreciate it when you [Fleming] and David Anderson threatened me at the January State Board of Education meeting," Rodriguez said boldly. "You told me that if I testified against the Texas CATCH program, the TEA would find a reason to investigate SAISD and change the selection criteria to exclude the Bienestar. Now it is obvious that you guys did indeed change the rules to exclude the Bienestar."

The reaction to his words first came in facial expressions of disbelief and shock in the room. Fleming's face got red, and Smisko turned to look at Fleming to re-direct the blame away from her.

"We had nothing to do with the selection criteria," Fleming shot back. "The criteria were set by an outside panel."

"Wait just a minute!" Treviño spoke up. "That review committee was stacked on the Texas CATCH side, with eight of its twelve members having affiliations to the Texas CATCH. And you know it, because I called you about it, and you responded with, 'Don't worry, everything will be okay.' Well, now I understand! You meant, okay for the Texas CATCH."

Fleming's face got red again when he heard the charge, but he sat quietly and offered no verbal rebuttal.

"Dr. Almendarez, TEA's former Deputy Commissioner for Program and Instruction, had sent Dr. Treviño a letter informing him that if the Bienestar met the entire SB 19 requirement it would be approved," Garcia noted to Fleming. "Then we got an e-mail (page 159) from you informing Dr. Treviño that the rules were changed. Why were they changed?"

"Well, back in April, Representative Manny Najera asked Dr. Alanis to get an outside panel of reviewers to select the programs," Fleming responded.

"That's not what I heard," Treviño interjected. "When I met with Dr. Cruz, he told me you and Manny Najera walked into Dr. Alanis's office and suggested both the change of rules and the formation of that sham review committee," Treviño added.

Forgotten Children: A True Story of How Politicians Endanger Children

Fleming made no comment after these words.

"No wonder," Garcia almost yelled as she supported Treviño's version of events. "Manny Najera was at the September 2002 LULAC Health Initiative meeting trying to get LULAC members to endorse the Texas CATCH program. But when its members endorsed the Bienestar program, he walked out upset while saying, 'It doesn't matter; the TEA will take care of it anyway.' They sure did!"

"And who became the facilitator for the review panel that TEA put together?" Bernal asked, already knowing the answer.

"Tommy," Smisko answered, again shifting all the blame away from her and wiping her hands of the matter.

"Tommy!" Treviño said in a loud voice, acting as if he were surprised at the news. "He has five years' experience facilitating the Texas CATCH program, and he becomes the *facilitator*!"

"I'm just an employee here, and I do as I am told," Fleming muttered in defense.

"Where were the meetings of the review panel held?" Bernal asked, being careful not to point out what was up his sleeve.

"We had four meetings, and they were held at the Texas Medical Association office," Fleming answered.

"What were the dates?" Bernal asked again.

"August 23, September 10, October 1, and October 22, 2002," Fleming responded after looking at some notes.

"So your last meeting was on October 22nd?" Treviño asked.

"Yes," Fleming answered.

"Well, then, how is it that the Great Body Shop was selected in February 2003, or four months later, if the review panel's last meeting was in October 2002?" Treviño questioned.

"Oh. We did it by conference call," Fleming said, a false smile on his face.

"Interesting. You see, Oralia and I called Jan Ozias, Laura Garcia, and Carey Dabney, who are members of the review panel, and they all denied having met about the approval, or about even being aware of the Great Body Shop being selected by the committee," Treviño said (page 189). "I find this very strange."

"I can't remember all the details, and who was on the call. It could have been a sub-committee," Fleming answered. As he said these words, his face became flushed, and his hands started to shake ever so slightly.

By the time the meeting ended at six p.m., Smisko and Fleming would admit to those present that major mistakes had been made in the TEA's review process. They would also agree to take the matter up with

Drs. Felipe Alanis and Paul Cruz. Bernal and Treviño also asked them to be sure to open up the selection process to other programs, and for the future workings of the TEA to be as transparent as possible.

MORE THREATS

But the future did not look all that promising for the following week, which became apparent to Treviño when he received a call from Rodriguez.

"Hey, Robert, Tommy called me," Rodriguez said in a sad and low tone of voice.

"What did he want?" Treviño queried.

"He said he was going to sue me."

"What!" Treviño exclaimed loudly. "For what?"

"For libel. He said, I said things about him at the meeting that was not true."

"Well, then, he can sue me too," Treviño said in solidarity, "because I am going to stand in the middle of the street, and scream out loud about all the improprieties he's done to our children."

"I don't know what to do, Robert. Should I get an attorney?" a worried Rodriguez asked.

"No, no," Treviño assured him. "I'll talk to Nina Perales, from MALDEF, for you. The Mexican-American Legal Defense and Educational Fund attorneys will defend you."

At the time, Treviño didn't even know if MALDEF did that kind of law. He just wanted to comfort Roger.

And, as it turned out, nothing came out of it at all. It had only been another threat from Fleming.

THE MEETING GOES INTO DEAF EARS

A month after the meeting with Smisko and Fleming, the TEA sent the school districts a letter—signed by Ann Smisko—to inform them about the two programs which had been approved by TEA as coordinated school health programs. While the Texas CATCH and The Great Body Shop programs were mentioned in the cover letter (dated April 9, 2003), only the Texas CATCH program was promoted in the attached three pages that followed the cover letter. One of these pages—a letter of support for the Texas CATCH program—was attached and signed by Steve Kelder (Houston's UTSPH), Peter Cribb (CATCH program project director), Karen Lyon (President, American Heart Association), and Jennifer Smith (Director, Cardiovascular Health and Wellness Program, TDH).

Treviño called Dr. Paul Cruz, the TEA's Deputy Commissioner, to inquire about the letters. He faxed over the letters beforehand so that Cruz could be prepared to answer his questions.

"Dr. Cruz, did you get the letters I faxed over to your secretary?" Treviño inquired first.

"Yes, I did."

"The cover letter signed by Ann Smisko mentions both the Texas CATCH and Great Body Shop programs, but then the following three pages are all about the Texas CATCH," Treviño said angrily. "On the third page, there is even a quote saying, 'By joining the CATCH Network before June 30, 2003, schools can receive the CATCH curriculum at a highly reduced cost.' My question is, why would the TEA get into the business of selling books for a special interest group? It makes the agency sound like a used car salesman trying to make a quick deal."

"Yeah, I'm reading that," Cruz replied, in a low tone of voice. "That's not something the TEA should be doing," he agreed.

"It seems like a special interest group—Texas CATCH—is using public agencies and state stationery for their own financial interests. Why would Dr. Alanis, our Commissioner of Education, allow that?" Treviño asked impatiently.

Cruz hedged a bit when he replied, "I know for sure that it was Tommy [Fleming] who wrote this letter, and Smisko who signed it."

"Well, did Dr. Alanis ever approve these letters?" Treviño wondered in response.

"He couldn't have," Cruz said in a disbelieving tone of voice.

"It's like Tommy is running the Texas CATCH program out of the TEA," Treviño noted furiously. "The only two people who can grant that much authority are the governor and the commissioner, and you just told me it wasn't Alanis."

In response to this observation, Cruz was mute.

After the phone conversation, Treviño sat down to study the signatures of the staff from the other agencies which appeared on the letter which gave support to the Texas CATCH. He noticed that they appeared similar in penmanship style, and he became suspicious. Knowing now that members of the TEA staff might have sent the letter without the approval of Alanis, he wondered if they also could have sent it out without the approval of the other persons whose signature were on the letter?

Treviño decided to try and contact Jennifer Smith at the TDH to ask her if she had signed that letter of support.

• DR. ROBERTO P. TREVIÑO •

"Hello, may I speak to Jennifer Smith?" Treviño asked the TDH staff member who answered the phone.

"Yes, may I ask who is calling?" the TDH staff member asked.

"Dr. Roberto Treviño with the Bienestar health program."

After this response, the staff member put Treviño on hold.

Minutes later, a male voice picked up the line. "Hello, Dr. Treviño, what can we do for you?"

"Who is this?" Treviño wondered. Hadn't he asked for Jennifer Smith?

"This is Phil Huang."

"Oh," Treviño said in surprise. "Dr. Huang, how're you doing?"

"Fine. I'm sorry Jennifer can't come to the phone, but what is it that you need?"

"I read the letter the TEA sent out to school districts—"

"What letter?" Huang asked before Treviño could finish.

"The letter to inform the school district of the school health programs they needed to choose to comply with SB 19."

"Oh yes, what about it?"

"If the TDH does not support any one program, why would a TDH representative sign a letter of support for the CATCH program?" Treviño probed Huang. "Why didn't they write one for The Great Body Shop? It is an approved program too."

"Dr. Treviño," Huang said, losing patience with him. "You need to go to the TEA to get your program approved! The TDH only supports programs that are TEA-approved," he emphasized.

Treviño continued with his questioning undeterred. "Dr. Huang, did Jennifer sign that letter?"

Huang had a surprising response to this question. "They forged that signature, and we already talked to them about it," he said crisply.

"Thank you," Treviño said upon hearing this news, and hung up.

Treviño then saw Karen Lyon's signature had the same penmanship as that of Jennifer Smith's. He called Lyon, and she also disclosed that it was not her signature.

From that moment on, the American Heart Association disengaged itself from all CTN activities.

In September 2003, Midge Epstein, president of the Texas Chapter of the American Heart Association, came to visit the SHRC facilities. The meeting was kept positive and she left impressed with the SHRC operations. Then, in May 2005, Dr. Fernando Lopez, President of the San Antonio Division of the American Heart Association, would send out a letter to Governor Perry in support of the Bienestar program.

ALANIS TAKES A STANCE

After six years of pelting from politicians, bureaucrats and special interest groups, Treviño felt tired. It was exhausting to try and tackle three fronts—that of the TMA, the TDH, and the TEA. So the staff of the SHRC decided to focus their limited energies on one specific goal: to remove Fleming, who had behaved dishonorably and unethically, from his position at the TEA. After all, it was quite possible that it was only Fleming who stood between the Bienestar program and the TEA's approval of it.

In April 2003, the *San Antonio Express-News* wrote an article about the controversy surrounding the TEA's approval of school health programs. When Smisko was interviewed for this article, she acknowledged there was confusion on how the process for program selection unfolded. Smisko claimed, however, there was no cronyism in the selection of the review panel. Cindy Tumiel from the newspaper did her own research, and she found some of the individuals in the review panel were already advocates and supporters of the Texas CATCH program (page 163). A week later, the *San Antonio Express-News* wrote the following lead editorial:

> Obesity, cardiovascular disease, and type 2 diabetes have become so prevalent in schoolchildren that the 2001 Texas Legislature mandated measures to attack the problem. Unfortunately, rules developed by the Texas Education Agency exclude one of the most promising local programs aimed directly at Hispanic children, where the risk is high.
>
> The Bienestar program has successfully reduced blood sugar levels in fourth-graders in the San Antonio and Edgewood school districts and motivated the students and their families to adopt healthier lifestyles.
>
> The program, whose name means well-being in Spanish, is funded with a $2 million grant from the National Institutes of Health and is in use in 63 schools.
>
> Unfortunately, because the program is in its infancy and does not yet have the historical data necessary to chronicle long-term successes, TEA has rejected it as a qualified program under the state's new mandate for diabetes prevention and physical education in elementary

schools.

Preliminary findings show that after one year, Bienestar has reduced blood sugar levels and improved nutrition and fitness in program participants.

Three more years of study for the program, started by local physician Dr. Roberto P. Treviño, are planned.

TEA administrators cannot be faulted for wanting what is best for the schoolchildren of Texas, but the rules should be flexible enough to allow innovative programs, such as this one, an opportunity to work.

Treviño developed Bienestar seven years ago after working in the barrio, where diabetes was widespread. His program is motivating youngsters and their parents to develop healthier, more active lifestyles to fight the onset of diabetes.

Treviño, a doctor familiar with the Hispanic culture, knows how to get the message to a segment of the community where language sometimes can be a barrier.

The TEA should keep in mind that one size does not always fit all.

This was just the stick Treviño needed to bang on the TEA's door—and be heard. Treviño called the TEA's Commissioner of Education, Dr. Felipe Alanis, in May 2003.

"Dr. Alanis, I'm glad you could come to the phone and talk to me briefly," Treviño began. "Did you get the editorial the *San Antonio Express-News* staff wrote?"

"Yes," Alanis responded, sounding a bit rushed.

"Did you get the letters the children from Edgewood ISD wrote you?"

Copies of the letters the Edgewood ISD children had sent to the Governor (see page 117) had also been sent to Alanis.

"Yes. It is amazing the stories they told, and how happy they are with the program."

"Dr. Alanis, the *Express-News* did its own investigation and found some of the members in the review panel were tied to the Texas CATCH program," Treviño observed.

"I spoke with Paul [Cruz] and Joey [Lozano; TEA executive assistant] and they agree," Alanis said. "The review panel was stacked on the Texas CATCH side."

"What are you going to do about it?" Treviño questioned, glad to hear these other parties agreed with him, but feeling desperate in terms of there ever being a fair solution.

"We're going to dismantle that committee and form a new one," Alanis responded.

"Since the Texas CATCH program came in unfairly, will they need to re-apply too?" Treviño asked.

"I...uh...I...," Alanis stuttered, surprised by this suggestion, "I am under a lot of pressure to leave them alone."

Treviño did not pressure Alanis further about kicking out the Texas CATCH, but he did put the pressure on about Fleming.

"Fleming has taken it upon himself to make decisions based on personal preferences instead of best practices," Treviño said. "Children as young as eight years of age are being diagnosed with an adult disease, and he is no physician and no health expert in type 2 diabetes. He has performed many activities to keep the Bienestar program away from high-risk children, and blames it to misreading a law and misunderstanding legal counsel. That needs to stop!"

Alanis got quiet for a short while. "I spoke with both Smisko and Fleming, and they've agree many mistakes were made," he finally said. "Let me see what I can do."

But when Treviño did not hear from Alanis, Treviño organized a group of individuals to send Alanis a barrage of requests. Treviño wrote him a letter in the middle of May questioning the conflict of interest between the review panel members and the Texas CATCH program. He also told him to get the Bienestar program approved by the TEA so it could operate in schools located in socially deprived neighborhoods, where the risk of type 2 diabetes is higher.

Treviño sent copies of the letter to the members of the SBOE board and Bexar County's (Republican and Democrat) senators and representatives. He found it galling when no one responded.

At Treviño's request, on May 16, 2003, Margaret Moran, the LULAC state director, sent Alanis a letter urging him to consider including other coordinated school health programs.

On June 5, 2003 Nina Perales from MALDEF sent Alanis, and the TEA an Open Records Act requesting all documents related to the review process of coordinated school health programs.

On June 9, 2003, Treviño sent Alanis the following letter:

> Bienestar just had six abstracts published and these will be presented at the American Diabetes Association meeting in New Orleans (see attachments). In summary,

these results show that the Bienestar participants are at-risk for diabetes and vulnerable; Latino children have higher mean fasting glucose than non-Hispanic White and African-American children; Bienestar normalized high blood glucose for three consecutive years; and it has decreased the chances of getting high blood glucose by half. All children, regardless of their racial/ethnic background, have benefited from the Bienestar program. It is beyond our understanding why anyone would withhold medical treatment and prevention education from youth with type 2 diabetes.

Again Treviño copied the members of the SBOE board and Bexar County's (Republican and Democrat) state senators and representatives.

On June 21, 2003, the *San Antonio Express-News* wrote an article with the heading, "**State's education chief suddenly quits. Alanis gave no explanation for his decision.**"

Treviño's opinion of Alanis was (and remains today), that Alanis was truly an honest person, one who had enough dignity to move out of the way and not follow the commands of his superiors to suppress a program with the potential of preventing diabetes in children of color and those living in poverty. Unfortunately that was not the case with his counterpart at the TDH—Eduardo Sanchez.

TELLING IT LIKE IT WAS

On July 8, 2003, Treviño called Fleming intending to leave a message but a female voice answered the line.

"Hello, is Tommy Fleming in?" Treviño asked after her gretting.

"Let me see. I just saw him across the hallway," the female voice responded.

Minutes later she returned to the phone. This time her words were, "He's not in. Do you want to leave him a message?"

If it had been another individual he had been calling, Treviño would not have left this particular message. But since it was Fleming, a person whose ethics were in question, he did not care if the whole world knew what was going to happen.

"Please let him know that Dr. Treviño called, and that I will be testifying at this Thursday's State Board of Education meeting. I will bring up some allegations that involve him, and he will need to be there if he wants to defend himself," Treviño said crisply.

He then thanked the woman for taking down the message before he hung up.

On July 10, 2003, the SBOE's board members met in the morning; the public hearings began at one o'clock. Mia Morris, the SHRC coordinator for the NEEMA program, and Bianca Treviño, Treviño's daughter and a volunteer at the center, drove up to Austin with him. When he entered the room, Treviño spied Fleming in the audience, but Fleming avoided making eye contact with Treviño.

When it was Treviño's turn to approach the podium, he began, "Good afternoon, Chairwoman and board members. The reason I'm here is to present allegations about the improper acts of a staff member at the TEA."

Although lots of people had been talking amongst themselves quietly when Treviño took the stand, the phrase, "improper acts of a staff member at the TEA" stopped everyone in their tracks, and the voices quieted immediately.

"Since 1999, Dr. Tommy Fleming and the TEA have used political means to keep the Bienestar health program away from high-risk children. I will not bore you with the high rates of type 2 diabetes among low-income children, and the success the Bienestar program has had in decreasing their blood sugars. I have presented these findings in previous State Board of Education meetings. Instead, I will present specific allegations of Dr. Fleming's improprieties.

"In 1999, he misled the board by asking you to approve a 'school diabetes education program,'" Treviño said, lifted two fingers from each hand to make the quotation marks, "even though that program had no lesson plans in diabetes and never lowered a blood sugar. When Dr. Tinker Murray from the Texas State University asked Dr. Fleming to present another curriculum to you, Dr. Fleming refused and sent him to the legislators for an approval. He showed a personal preference for one program instead of looking out for the best interest of our children.

"In early 2002, Dr. Almendarez, the Deputy Commissioner for Programs and Instructions, had sent out letters to agencies operating coordinated school health programs inviting them to participate in the schools if they met all the SB 19 requirements. Later that year, Dr. Fleming and state representative Manny Najera walked into Dr. Alanis's office and coerced him into changing the rules. They convinced him to form a review panel to select the coordinated school health programs, but Fleming and Najera made sure to stack this panel first with Texas CATCH program advocates and supporters. And Dr. Fleming, who had a conflict of interest because of his loyalty to the Texas CATCH program, became the facilitator of this review panel. These two individuals took advantage of the fact that Dr. Alanis had been new in his position.

"After forming the panel, the panel asked all the agencies to submit their programs. Only once all the programs were in front of them did they form the criteria—a backward way of doing things. They then made sure to form criteria that would exclude all the submitted programs—with the exception of the Texas CATCH program, which was then approved. These men had tried to form a monopoly by protecting a sole vendor for coordinated school health programs, from competition. They took away choice from the schools, and gave it all to the state.

"This case was referred to the Texas Attorney General, and weeks before he made his ruling on the matter public, asking that SB 19 require multiple programs rather than just one, Fleming and the Texas CATCH people brought in the Great Body Shop program, which the 'panel' suddenly approved even though it did not have all the components required for SB 19 and even though it had been submitted after the deadline."

Treviño distributed the e-mail from the Great Body Shop staff, which indicated their surprise over the approval (see page 189). He also distributed to the board members an e-mail Fleming had sent to the school districts on January 2001.

"Dr. Fleming sent out this e-mail to school districts telling them to implement the CATCH program because legislation mandated it," Treviño said. "But when we met with him this past March, he told us that he sent out this letter because he had misread SB 19. The bill stated that any program that had parent, food service, physical education, and health educations components, which the Bienestar program had, could participate. Fleming, instead, interpreted this bill as saying that 'only the Texas CATCH' could participate. This is a man with a Ph.D. degree working for the highest house of education, and he misread a legislative bill?" Treviño evaluated bluntly as he turned around to point at Fleming in the audience. "Maybe Dr. Fleming can comment on these allegations."

Smisko, who was sitting in the front with the TEA rank and file, shook her head to signal to Fleming not to answer. Fleming caught on, and did not rise from his seat. He too shook his head to indicate he had no comment.

Treviño turned back to the board members and concluded with, "I believe I have made my allegations very clear, and I beg you to please investigate this matter, and take appropriate action. Thank you."

At the meeting, Treviño had taken notice of the acting Commissioner Education recently appointed by Perry: Robert Scott a young-looking attorney who dressed in expensive suits. Scott had no experience in the classroom, but as a former aide to Perry, he had strong political ties. He would be an important person for Treviño to get to know.

Bernal was able to set up an appointment for Treviño to meet him. The meeting was set for July 30, 2003. When Bernal and Treviño arrived at the TEA, a TEA staff member guided them to a conference room. When all the members arrived, Bernal and Treviño sat in the middle, Scott to the left, and Smisko and Cruz, who were also attending, were on the right side.

"Good morning, Mr. Scott," Treviño said, deliberately not offering greetings to either Smisko and Cruz. At this point Treviño was chosing not to deal with Smisko and Cruz at all because of his previous meetings with them had been futile, in terms of any progress. "You were at the last State Board of Education meeting, where you heard about Fleming's improper activities. We have children as young as eight years of age with type 2 diabetes, and we have a program that can reverse high blood sugars. But certain staff members from the TEA have put roadblocks between the Bienestar program and those children."

"Robert," Bernal noted to the new acting Commissioner, "we met with Fleming and Smisko, and we questioned those activities."

At this point, Bernal turned to look at Smisko, but she turned her face away.

"At our meeting, they admitted mistakes had been done and they promised to get them fixed. Well, it has been four months, and they have done nothing to clean up their mess. Enough is enough," Bernal said with intense indignation.

Treviño deliberately took on the polite, 'good cop' role because Bernal was being the forceful one.

"Mr. Scott, since 1999 the TEA has told us many times how good the Bienestar program is, but then the TEA's staff simply do an about-face, and they engage in conduct where they make sure to reject our program. They tell us one thing, but then they go on to do another," Treviño summarized.

At this point, Treviño's face got red and his forehead wrinkled. It was difficult for him to hide his anger at the unfairness of it all.

"I know about the mistakes, but I don't think Fleming acted alone," Smisko suddenly interjected.

This comment caught Bernal and Treviño by surprise. But Smisko refrained from commenting further on the matter, or even indicating the parties to whom she was referring.

"I'll assure you I will investigate this matter, and get to the bottom of it," were Scott's first words. "I'm a father, and I wouldn't want my children to be excluded from a good program like the Bienestar."

"You can investigate what has happened as much as you want, but what we really need is for you to find a mechanism to get the Bienestar program approved so it can operate in the schools without restrictions," Bernal told him.

"Let me check with our legal counsel to see what mechanisms exist to get the Bienestar approved," Scott offered.

When Treviño and Bernal walked out, they were optimistic that Scott saw the dishonesty of Fleming's acts, and that he would find a way to propitiate those acts. They were uncomfortable, however, with the fact that he had mentioned he was going to ask David A. Anderson, the TEA's legal counsel, to find a way to make a judgment on a medical treatment. As always, Treviño believed a medical expert should be making the decisions on a health treatment or adoption.

The other concern the two men had was the comment that Smisko had made about other parties being involved.

"I wonder what Smisko meant when she said Fleming did not act alone," Treviño whispered to Bernal in the hallway.

"Maybe she meant David D. Anderson, the director of Curriculum and Professional Development," Bernal answered.

"Everyone knew that David, Fleming, and Smisko were acting together," Treviño evaluated, "I think she is trying to smear the blame on someone else."

They kept walking along when all of a sudden Treviño stopped and grabbed Bernal back by the arm.

"Oh, shit!" Treviño nearly yelled.

"What?" Bernal inquired, startled.

"I bet they're going to put the blame on Alanis! He's out of the organization now, and not around to defend himself. They're going to use him as the scapegoat, and this will allow them to protect and keep their foot soldiers in place. I'll have to write Scott tomorrow, to make him aware that we won't go for that."

Treviño wrote Scott the following letter on July 16, 2003:

> First I want to thank you for hearing our case, and I have no doubt that Bienestar will soon be approved by the agency. Under Section 504 of the Rehabilitation Act of 1973, the Individual with Disabilities Education Act

1991 and the American with Diabetes Act, it reminds us that diabetes is a disability, and that it is illegal for schools and/or daycares to discriminate against children with disabilities, and mandates that appropriate diabetes care be made available in these facilities. Attached is a National Institutes of Health response to Bienestar results, and a list of experts in the field of health education, pediatric endocrinology, nutrition, and fitness. I hope you get their professional opinion too.

The concern I do have is that no disciplinary action will be taken against the TEA individual who may have tried to exclude Bienestar unfairly. As the documents show, Dr. Tommy Fleming presented to the State Board of Education a diabetes education program that had no lesson plans on diabetes, had never measured a diabetes marker, and had never lowered abnormal blood glucose. This appears misleading. Second is his e-mail stating that SB 19 mandated the CATCH program. As you read in Sen. Jane Nelson's letter, it was never her intention to write a bill that would support a sole vendor. This appears deceitful. Last is how Fleming got involved with a selection committee that was formed by an improper process. Knowing he had a personal preference for another program, why would he become the facilitator? This appears unethical. Furthermore, once the attorney general ruled that SB 19 meant multiple programs Fleming was involved in bringing in a program that disregarded SB 19 criteria. This appears unlawful.

An intriguing comment at our meeting was made by Dr. Ann Smisko saying Dr. Fleming did not work alone. This gave the impression of another member of the TEA being involved. I suspect that they may try to use Dr. Alanis as a scapegoat. If you look at the documents I have provided, these alleged improprieties go back to 1999 and 2001. [Alanis had only been commissioner from March 2002 to June 2003.] Hope to hear from you soon.

Treviño copied Smisko, Cruz and Bernal—the meeting's attendees—on this letter.

On July 30, 2003, Scott responded with the following letter:

• DR. ROBERTO P. TREVIÑO •

I enjoyed the opportunity to discuss your health program, *Bienestar*, and how it may serve the students in local school districts in Texas.

As you know, Senate Bill 1357 requires the commissioner of education, under the rulemaking authority granted in Texas Education Code (TEC), Section 38.013, to make available to each school district one or more coordinated health programs designed to prevent obesity, cardiovascular disease, and Type 2 diabetes in elementary schools. The Agency will move forward with the development of commissioner's rule to fulfill the requirements of Senate Bill 1357. According to the requirements of Senate Bill 1357, before adopting criteria, the commissioner must request review and comment concerning the criteria from the Texas Department of Health's School Health Advisory Committee. Once the review and comments are complete, and the criteria established in rule, we will review new programs that are offered for consideration. We will notify school districts of the programs that meet the criteria.

During our meeting, I raised the possibility that districts may be able to request a waiver to use the Bienestar program. Following review by the agency's general counsel, such a waiver is not possible as Section 7.056 of the Texas Education Code does not allow waivers of health and safety issues under Chapter 38 of the education code. We are currently exploring alternatives and will keep in touch.

Thank you for the suggestions you made regarding the advisory committee in your letter of July 16. I will consider them carefully.

I appreciate your interest in helping the children of Texas. If you have other questions or concerns, feel free to call Ann Smisko.

Scott also copied Smisko, Cruz and Bernal.
After this receipt of this letter, Treviño called Bernal so they could both analyze the contents of the letter.
"Dr. Bernal, did you get the letter Scott sent us? It was dated July 30th."

"Yeah," he answered dryly. "He took us through a legal psychobabble path."

"I'd say more like a psycho-path!" Treviño agreed. "They all say they like the Bienestar health program, but then they give us these legal loopholes to keep it away from children. The TEA points to the Texas Department of Health for selection comments, and then the Texas Department of Health points to the TEA for approval comments, and in the middle is the Bienestar program, stuck in this mud."

"I'm sure Scott took it to David A. Anderson [the TEA's legal counsel], and Anderson opened a law book to find the right clause to keep the Bienestar program out," Bernal said.

But, on a positive note, two days following the receipt of Scott's letter, the TAPHERD newsletter broke the news about Tommy Fleming's resignation.

The staff of the SHRC celebrated that Friday August 1st, like it was New Year's Eve.

Fleming's resignation would be effective August 31, 2003.

Chapter 13

THEY HAVE POLITICS, SHRC HAS SCIENCE

A HELPFUL HAND

The time the SHRC staff had to spend removing political fetters, was time taken away from developing new and better products. The content of their program's educational material was getting outdated, and the books needed new designs. It was stressful times for the SHRC staff; the work was plentiful, and the time available was short.

Irene Hernandez was working in the Program Building when a professionally dressed woman with short dark hair, entered the building.

Hernandez saw her, and went up to greet her.

"Hi I'm Liz Flores," the woman greeted Hernandez, and handed her a business card.

Hernandez looked at the card, and her eyebrows raised at the pleasant surprise.

"You work for McGraw-Hill," she said with a big smile.

"Yes," Flores said. "Macmillan/McGraw-Hill is interested in publishing your books."

Hernandez almost hit the floor at the news. Macmillan/McGraw-Hill (MMH) was a well-respected publisher, and they could publish and help distribute the Bienestar program books throughout Texas and even the nation.

"You need to meet Dr. Treviño," Hernandez said with excitement. She quickly walked Ms. Flores across the parking area to the Evaluation Building.

"Dr. Treviño, this is Liz Flores, the local sales representative for MacMillan/McGraw-Hill." Hernandez explained, the big smile still on her face. "They're interested in partnering with us to publish and distribute our books."

Treviño was happy to have such a welcome, although unexpected guest.

"Please sit down." Treviño invited both Flores and Hernandez.

The two women settled comfortably around his turn-of-the-century mahogany and leather Duncan-Fief table.

"How did you hear about us?" he asked carefully.

"I've read about your program in the local newspaper, and our corporate staff has read your studies," Flores replied. "We are very impressed with the program results. Our regional manager asked me to visit with you, and find out if your research center is interested in exploring a partnership with McGraw-Hill."

"Of course," Treviño answered without hesitation. "Who is your regional manager?"

"His name is Wayne Rider," Flores answered. "He saw you present at the July 10, 2003 State Board of Education board meeting. He was very impressed with your presentation."

Treviño felt a little embarrassed because at that meeting he seemed more like a Central American fighter rather than a mainstream businessman.

In thinking back, Treviño began to recall an image of a particular man at the meeting. He had noticed a nicely dressed middle-aged man with short blond hair who was standing by the door when he exited the conference room. The man was staring at Treviño with a big smile, but Treviño did not return the smile because many in the audience were still observing him, and he wanted to maintain a serious demeanor. At the time he had wondered who that man might have been.

Treviño looked over at Flores and queried, "Is he a middle aged man with short, blond hair?"

"Yes," Flores said as she further described the man Treviño had seen at the TEA conference room exit door.

"I think I saw him at the board meeting as I was walking out. I don't know why he was impressed with my presentation. I was there fighting with people."

"That's why he was impressed with you. You stood up to unfairness." Flores declared simply.

Before Flores left the SHRC office, she made plans for a follow-up conference call between Treviño, Hernandez, and the McGraw-Hill editorial staff located in New York.

After the encouraging meeting with Flores, Treviño called Roger Rodriguez to give him the good news. Rodriguez was very familiar with health textbook publishers, due to his twenty-five years experience as an educator.

"Hey Roger, you'll never guess who gave us a visit," Treviño said excitedly into the phone.

"Who?"

"Macmillan/McGraw-Hill."

"Nooo!" Rodriquez responded, surprised to receive this information.

"They're interested in publishing our Bienestar books."

"That's great!" Rodriguez said supportively.

"Do you know Liz Flores?" Treviño inquired.

"Yeah, she's our sales representative for McGraw-Hill. In fact, I've been telling her about the Bienestar program for years."

"Do you know Wayne Rider?"

This was a name Ms. Flores had mentioned at the SHRC meeting.

"Yeah, he's Liz's boss. He works out of the Dallas area. He's like their government representative. He's always going to at the State Board of Education meetings," Rodriguez informed Treviño.

"Ahh! No wonder he was there," Treviño replied to this unexpected tidbit of news.

"No wonder, what?" Rodriguez quizzed.

"When I testified against Fleming at the State Board of Education meeting, there was a man standing at the door who looked like he wanted to talk to me."

"He probably wanted to give you a hug," Rodriguez remarked with a smile in his voice.

"Why?" Treviño asked, puzzled. "I was trying to take out Fleming, and it certainly wasn't pretty!"

"Well, you didn't know this, but your fighting was helping a big New York publisher!" Rodriquez said with a laugh. "You did their dirty work, and blew away their biggest enemy.

"What do you mean, Roger?" Treviño wondered. This was news to him.

Rodriguez started to explain. "The TEA is going through their health textbook adoption process. The process started a year ago, and the TEA will approve the textbooks by the end of next year [2004]. Right now, there's fierce competition going on among a number of large health textbook publishers.

"The largest textbook publishers in the country are Harcourt & Brace and Macmillan/McGraw-Hill. Harcourt & Brace has a contract with Tommy Fleming; he is a contributing author to their health textbook, and is also responsible for promoting it. Can you imagine the purchasing power Harcourt & Brace would have had by having the TEA director of Health and Physical Education in their marketing wagon? They had the market cornered, until you came along and knocked him out of his position!

"Now, all of a sudden, McGraw-Hill's regional market has gone from nothing to the possibility of $370 million. That is how much the state is expected to appropriate for school textbooks."

"Wow, Roger! So while Tommy and I were slugging it out in the streets, these guys were in nice corporate offices waiting for the winner. Well, now that the dirty work is done, maybe the kids and I can benefit from this possible partnership," Treviño commented.

"You make sure you ask them for the moon and the stars," Rodriguez suggested. "They owe you."

"I've already checked them out on the web. McGraw-Hill owns the largest textbook publishing company in the world! They also own Standard & Poor and *BusinessWeek*. So they'd be a pretty formidable partner. We've always had to use a toothpick to defend ourselves here. Now we might have a sword!" Treviño hypothesized.

The editorial conversation with MMH went well, especially as MMH foresaw another advantage in partnering with the SHRC. The Latino market in Texas was growing exponentially, so having a bilingual health textbook in the MMH sales package would be a big plus. There would be a lot of pickup.

Treviño ended up signing not only a contractual agreement which allowed MMH to publish the Bienestar health textbooks in Texas and nationwide, but a contributor agreement with MMH to write the introduction to their health textbook. The agreement also called for Treviño to promote their health textbook as well.

The Bienestar books had moved from the neighborhood Kinko's to the printing facilities of a New York publisher. The books that came off the printing press were colorful, bilingual, high standard, and of high quality. In addition, MMH provided 150,000 copies of the Bienestar program's four intervention components to the SHRC at no cost.

The SHRC had become much better armed—not only because of the beautifully produced books, but because MMH was a formidable partner with strong lobbying resources.

It would only help the SHRC that Joe Bernal, the SBOE board member, and Roger Rice, a Boston bilingual education lawyer, would continue putting pressure on the TEA.

THE NEW SELECTION PROCESS

Treviño got on the phone with Bernal to tell him about the new partnerhship with MMH and about the call Roger Rice had made to David A. Anderson, the TEA legal counsel.

"Dr. Bernal, Roger Rice called David A. Anderson to ask him if the TEA was complying with the federal law to provide bilingual curriculums to Spanish-speaking children. Pancho [Velaszquez] had called Roger to ask if he could put some pressure with that law."

"What was Anderson's response?" wondered Bernal.

"That he was not sure; that he was going to check into it; and that he thought the Texas CATCH was bilingual. And guess what!" Treviño added. "When Rice told Anderson that he was calling on behalf of the Bienestar program, Anderson's first comment was that 'the Bienestar was too political'." Shaking his head in frustration, Treviño continued, "These guys have used the political system to protect the Texas CATCH program from competition, and they call us 'political'! What do you think we should do next, Dr. Bernal?"

"We need to do is what Rice did, keep pressuring," Bernal responded. "We cannot let our kids down."

Undoubtedly this situation reminded Bernal, who had been an outspoken civil rights leader in the early sixties, of old times, and the importance of not shying away from the right fight. Bernal had never been one to turn away from injustices.

"I will get the State Board of Education to pressure Scott into forming another review panel to select more coordinated school health programs. We're not done with these bureaucrats," Bernal promised.

"I will continue operating the Bienestar program in the school districts," Treviño said indignantly. "And if they want us out, they'll need to call in the Texas Rangers. We're not going to leave those children without appropriate medical care."

At the time, SHRC investigators were detecting five to eight percent of the children with positive screens for type 2 diabetes, and were referring them to Dr. Daniel Hale, a pediatric endocrinologist, for medical treatment. (Dr. Hale's offices were located at the University Health System on the west side of San Antonio.) These children needed awareness education and treatment—treatment that was monitored by experts. And if they do not get it, many of them would be losing their health and lives to a preventable disease.

Treviño sent Acting Commissioner Scott the following letter on October 21, 2003:

> Attached is a newspaper article announcing the expansion of Bienestar. Over one year, the program has

> expanded from one school district with sixty elementary schools to four school districts with ninety elementary schools. Positive results and easy adaptability are the reasons for its growth. The messages are simple—decrease saturated fat, increase fiber, and increase physical activity. It is beyond understanding why the TEA would set up barriers to prevent these three simple messages from reaching vulnerable populations of children. I am a father too, and I cannot see any law in the book that will stop me from teaching my children those messages. The article does mention TEA politics obstructing science. Hopefully under your guidance we can all see beyond self-interest and focus on children's health. Could you please provide me an update on the new selection process?

Treviño sent copies of this request to, once again, Bernal, Smisko, and Cruz.

Although the Bienestar was not a TEA-approved curriculum, the San Antonio ISD, Edgewood ISD, South San Antonio ISD, and the Archdiocese Catholic School system continued to implement the Bienestar health program. Because of two large NIH grants to the University of Texas Health Science Center at San Antonio and the SHRC, the children in these school districts were being examined, referred for treatment, and provided with school health curriculums. This was a comprehensive medical service the children needed, and received, at no cost. The school districts were not going to let the state remove those services from their needy children.

Meanwhile, Bernal continued calling and e-mailing Scott and Geraldine Miller, chairwoman of the SBOE asking for the TEA to start another process to review and approve more coordinated school health programs. Miller supported Bernal in this request.

On November 11, 2003, Scott sent Treviño the following letter to give him an update on the new selection process:

> Thank you for your letter and newspaper article announcing the expansion of Bienestar. You are to be commended for your efforts to teach students the benefits of exercise and a healthy diet.
>
> With regard to the new selection process for school health programs: During the summer of 2003, I appointed

> an advisory committee to review the criteria used in the last selection. Senate Bill 1357, enacted by the 78th Legislature, requires that the commissioner of education adopt, by rule, the evaluation criteria used in approving programs. The committee met on August 20, 2003 to review the criteria and determine whether modifications to the criteria were required.
>
> On September 26, 2003, the first draft of commissioner's rules was sent to the committee for review. On October 16, 2003, a second draft was sent to the committee for review. The rules are now being prepared for submission to our Rules Division. The Rules Division will finalize the rule text for submission to the commissioner prior to publication in the *Texas Register*.
>
> Following publication in the *Texas Register*, a 30-day public comment period begins. Agency staff will prepare responses to all public comments submitted. Following review of comments and staff responses, the commissioner authorizes final publication of the rule in the *Texas Register*. After the rules are published in final form, school districts and potential vendors will be invited to submit products for review. We intend to have new programs approved and announced prior to the end of the 2003-2004 school year.
>
> If you have additional questions related to the rules or selection process, you may contact Dr. Robert Leos.

When Treviño read about the appointed advisory committee, his heart began to race. They had screwed the SHRC too many times via advisory committee members with conflicts of interest, so Treviño immediately requested the list of committee members for the selection process from Scott.

Jack Williams, from the TEA, faxed Treviño the minutes from the August 20, 2003 advisory committee meeting. And indeed, when Treviño saw the list of invitees, guests, and committee members, his heart rate shot up even further.

It was loaded with the names of TDH staff members, such as Michelle McComb, Jennifer Smith, and Martha McGlothlin. Peter Cribb, who was with the Texas CATCH, and Ellen Kelsey and David Wiley, who were on the 2002 review panel, were there as *guests*.

Fleming, whose last day was August 31, 2003, was being invited to come back to explain the rules.

Veronica Ford, a Perry appointee and wife of Tom Ford, a high profile Republican lobbyist, was also part of the committee, but was later removed. The press uncovered that Perry had given her a high-paying position in health although she had no credentials in that field.

And making matters worse, Houston's UTSPH Steve Kelder, a member of the committee, seemed to be calling the shots! For an e-mail Robert Leos sent out on September 9, 2003, about the August 20, 2003 minutes, read as follows:

> ...Please take time to review the minutes and let me know if there are any glaring omissions or required corrections. In addition, please review and comment on Dr. Kelder's work: do you agree with his rewirte of existing criteria? Do you agree with the addition of the new criteria, #9?...

On September 10, 2003, the staff of the TEA sent Treviño another e-mail that read as followed:

> **Suggested Rewrite of Criteria 5, 7, and 8 by Dr. Stephen Kelder**
> To participants in the August, 20, 2003, meeting: Please offer your comments on the following. Comments may be sent to rleos@tea.state.tx.us
> #5. The program is supported by peer review empirical evidence of effectiveness.
> #7. The program is based on health education theory and national standards for instructional best practices in the four components.
> #8. The program allows for tailoring to schools' individual needs and can be adapted to a variety of specific situations: ethnic diversity, children with disabilities, school schedules, socioeconomic status, and gender differences.
>
> Dr. Kelder also offered a suggestion for #9 (new criterion).
> "I also have a suggestion for a new criterion which is intended to address the implementation issue. If schools make use of the SHI [CDC School Health Index], they

will understand what the best practice guidelines are and have a method for systematic improvement."

Proposed criteria 9: The program trains schools in the annual use of the elementary school version of the [CDC's] School Health Index, a free self-assessment and planning tool of school programs and policies. http://www.cdc.gov/nccdphp/dash/SHI/index.htm.

Not only was Kelder raising the bar, he was bringing in the CDC to build a wall.

For the 2004 review process, the list included thirty-eight criteria under nine different categories. The Bienestar and other new school health programs now had to meet over seven printed pages of specific criteria.

Because in the 2002 review process, the Texas CATCH program had gained approval for Texas schools without meeting *any* criteria, Treviño drafted and sent the following letter to Perry and Nelson on November 24, 2003:

> An increasing number of low-income Black and Latino children are being diagnosed with type 2 diabetes. If glucose-lowering programs are not implemented now, these children will be blind, lose limbs, or be on dialysis before they reach adolescence. Attached is a newspaper article and letters of recognition for the Bienestar program from the International Diabetes Federation, the National Institutes of Health, the American College of Nutrition, and the American Diabetes Association. They demonstrate that the Bienestar school-based diabetes control program is growing because of its local acceptance and solid scientific basis. Despite positive outcomes, lobbyists for the Texas CATCH program and Dr. Thomas Fleming (former TEA director of health curriculums), have used Senate Bills 19 and 1357 to exclude all other programs from participation. In October 2002, a selection committee with ties to the CATCH self-selected themselves to be the only TEA-approved school health program. Program selection was made in October 2002, and selection criteria was made public only in November 2002. Later, under pressure from an attorney general ruling, selection committee

• DR. ROBERTO P. TREVIÑO •

members approved another program not complaint with SB 19. [Great Body Shop lacked P.E., parent, and school cafeteria components.] The Bienestar, on the other hand, with eight years' experience producing positive results in the poorest neighborhoods, was bypassed. Because of its biased position, the committee has since been disbanded.

Now with SB 1357, we were hoping for a fair process, but that is not the case. Dr. Steve Kelder, coordinator for the CATCH program, sits on this new selection committee, and he has increased the number and standards of the new criteria (see attachment). Our problem is not the higher standards that Bienestar needs to pass; our problem is the double standards by which programs are being judged. We ask that either Dr. Steve Kelder be removed from this selection committee or have the Texas CATCH program be reviewed using these higher standards.

The letter was copied to state senators and representatives (David Dewhurst, Frank Madla, Jeff Wentworth, Judith Zaffirini, Rodney G. Ellis, Royce West, Eddie Lucio, Jr., Gonzalo Barrientos, Mike Villarreal, Garnet Coleman, Joaquin Castro, Frank Corte, Pete Gallego, Elizabeth Ames Jones, Trey Martinez Fischer, Ruth Jones McClendon, Jose Menendez, Ken Mercer, Robert Puente, and Carlos Uresti); TEA staff and SBOE members (Robert Scott, Robert Leos, Geraldine Miller, Rene Nuñez, Mary Helen Berlanga, Joe J. Bernal, Alma A Allen, Dan Montgomery, Terri Leo, David Bradley, Linda Bauer, Don McLeroy, Cynthia A. Thornton, Patricia Hardy, Mavis B. Knight, Gail Lowe, and Bob Craig); and *S.A. Express-News* editor (W. Lawrence Walker).

Nelson and Perry never responded to Treviño's letter.

A fierce battle between <u>science</u> and <u>politics</u> was building up. Who would win? Treviño had <u>science</u> and *they* had <u>politics</u>. The showdown was set for October 18th and 19th of 2004. These were the dates set for the review committee members to meet and select new coordinated school health programs.

Treviño continued targeting the staff of the TEA in his attempt to get the Bienestar program where it needed to be—in the schools. Since Robert Leos, TEA Senior Director of Textbook Administration, was put in charge of the 2004 coordinated school health program selection process, Treviño sent him the following e-mail on July 26, 2004:

> All we ask is for fairness and in the recent review panel Steve Kelder was part of that committee. He is the person behind the Texas CATCH program and it would be an enormous conflict of interest for this individual to sit and review other programs that may compete with his. Thanks.

Leos, who was not in the CTN loop, thanked Treviño for the information.

Bernal did not relent either. He wrote Scott the following e-mail on August 3, 2004:

> The time has come for the TEA to select health programs which would meet criteria defined by SB 19 and 1357. Over the years I have personally observed one specific program, the Bienestar, which has not only met all the requirements under state law, but has gone a very important step beyond, that it is the only program that on a solid scientific basis has reduced life threatening risk factors for type 2 diabetes among children.
>
> The problem however is that TEA has not ever conceded that point. Now it seems that the committee which will be writing new criteria and selecting programs acceptable to the state has a very key individual, Dr. Steve Kelder, who is also the coordinator for the CATCH program, the only health program so far acceptable to the state. Will Dr. Kelder's involvement mean that he will be able to write standards which would narrow the state program to the point that only CATCH will be acceptable?
>
> So far I know, CATCH has never printed any results from its program stating unequivocally that it also can reduce type 2 diabetes among children. My concern is that type 2 diabetes is increasing among children and it seems to affect African-American and Hispanic children to a greater degree than the overall population.
>
> Before commissioner Neeley came on board, I brought this problem to your attention and I recall you stated you would take care of it. At that time, the TEA had put together a committee to set standards and after the

question of whether the law called for only one program, the TEA proceeded to agree to accept another program (an out-of-state program—The Great Body Shop) which didn't even meet the basic standard of providing PE programs.

We now have time to correct the sloppy standards of the past, and I know that with your sense of fairness, the situation can be corrected.

Thank you for your consideration on this very important matter.

In the SBOE's Operating Rules, under Section 5.4 Rulemaking Authority Delegated to the Commissioner of Education, Scott had the authority to approve a health care program if he assessed that the children's public health or safety were in peril.

This was something he chose not to do.

ON TO PRIORITY # 2

The SHRC and Treviño had a number of priorities. The need to remove those individuals on the selection committee who had conflicts of interest had to be first. Determining if the Bienestar program met the criteria was second.

To tackle priority #2, Treviño arranged a sit-down with the SHRC's Associate Director, Irene Hernandez, to review the lengthy list of criteria and determine if Bienestar program components fulfilled all of the items. While he had met with Hernandez because her primary role at SHRC was program implementation, he was also taking into account that it was Hernandez's nature to find solutions to problems. And that was a big plus.

And so, Treviño had to grin when he heard Hernandez's response to the following question, "Irene, does the Bienestar program meet the new TEA evaluation criteria?"

"Dr. T., we're blessed that God has put the CTN people in our way. Every hurdle they've put in front is a challenge for us to improve our program. Thanks to them, we have developed a better and stronger program that can compete with any in the country."

"I don't know if I'm ready to give them a hug yet, Irene," Treviño said dryly, "but I do appreciate you're taking the silver lining into account here, and you're right: All those years of rejection has made us take the Bienestar and NEEMA to a higher level. We had to—to survive!"

"The program staff and I wrote down all the components of the Bienestar program before we reviewed the list of criteria," Hernandez said, with a big smile. "We've discovered that we just need to update our training manual, and that is it. We should be able to jump over this hurdle easily."

"Thank God, Irene," Treviño burst out, letting out a loud sigh and leaning back in his chair. "We always argue for keeping the bar high, so the last thing I would want to do is ask them to lower it."

The two Bienestar advocates smiled in harmony before they adjourned their meeting. Hernandez left immediately to brief key staff members about updating the training manual.

The exercise of reviewing the criteria had actually helped the staff of the SHRC to update and improve the components of the Bienestar program. At the end, children would benefit from this exercise.

CLEAR SKIES AHEAD

Although a dark cloud had loomed over the SHRC in 2003, in 2004 the sky had began to clear up.

Dr. Shirley Neeley was appointed Commissioner of Education in January 2004. She was the first female to ever head the TEA.

Neeley had been the superintendent of Galena Park ISD. As superintendent, she had done an outstanding job in improving the academic test scores of underperforming students. A bubbly, carrot-haired lady, she used a cheerleading-type enthusiasm to get everyone behind her projects.

Neeley was an individual who possessed a high regard and respect for matters of health. At the TEA, she was responsible for developing the new Department of Health and Safety, and she named Jeff Kloster associate commissioner of this department. Kloster had been a corporate attorney working with a large law firm before he took this position. An avid runner, he had a type A personality that gave him the agility to finish what he started. That is why he was chosen for this position. Neeley and Kloster understood that to improve student's performance in school, academics and health had to go hand in hand.

With Neeley at the helm of the TEA, the CTN's influence on the TEA would become severely restricted. On August 13, 2004 Leos sent the following e-mail:

> Thank you for submitting your coordinated school health program for review and approval by the Texas Education Agency. Our plan was to evaluate the programs

during the week of August 16, 2004, using members of the committee that was convened to review and revise the evaluation criteria.

Due to scheduling conflicts, we have postponed the evaluation until a more suitable time. I will keep you informed of our plans as we progress.

When Treviño spoke with Joan Reeves and Wayne Rider, MMH's regional directors, to find out what was really going on, they had their sources check with TEA insiders. Their sources informed them that the advisory committee formed by Scott was being dismantled, and that another group would be formed to review the programs. The new committee would be chosen from the education and academic field, and would be experts in children's health. Clearly, more than a conflict of scheduling was going on; no doubt Neeley had taken note of the conflict of interest issue, and was moving to do something about it.

To further clear the sky, Leos sent out an e-mail to the new panel of reviewers on September 22, 2004. The last paragraph read as followed:

...<u>Disclosure</u>. In addition to specifying your preferred dates, we ask that you inform us if you have received compensation in the past five years from any of the four companies submitting new programs for consideration or from the companies/organizations publishing The Great Body Shop or CATCH, approved in 2002. We will ask that members who have or have had a professional association with any of these companies not participate in the upcoming evaluation. This includes reimbursement of expenses....

The new review period was set for late October 2004. This couldn't have come at a more opportune time, for in September 2004 the SHRC paper, "Impact of the Bienestar School-Based Diabetes Mellitus Prevention Program on Fasting Capillary Glucose Levels. A Randomized Controlled Trial," was published in the *Archives of Pediatrics and Adolescent Medicine*. This paper showed that children who participated in the Bienestar program increased their fitness levels, increased their dietary fiber intake, and decreased their blood glucose levels. Those children who did not participate in the Bienestar program had the opposite effects: their fitness levels and dietary fiber intake decreased, and their blood glucose levels increased.

Although Neeley was the new Commissioner and seemed fair, Treviño was still doing everything he could to keep Scott honest and fair. Scott had been moved from acting commissioner to associate commissioner. Treviño sent Scott the following e-mail on the first of October:

> Attached you will find our new Bienestar study published in the *Archives of Pediatrics and Adolescent Medicine*. In this randomized controlled trial, the nearly 700 students that participated in Bienestar decreased their blood sugars and, increased their fitness levels and dietary fiber intake. The nearly 700 control students had the opposite effect: increased blood sugars and decreased fitness levels and dietary fiber intake. We have a serious problem of obesity and diabetes in Texas youth, and the Bienestar is the only program impacting favorably unhealthy biological markers of children. It is beyond understanding why the TEA, since 1998, has made every effort to exclude this valid program from participating in schools with high-risk children. Why would anyone want to withdraw an effective treatment away from high-risk children? We support our program with science and the TEA blocks it with politics. I hope this cloud of unfairness is removed from this new process. Could you please provide me the list of reviewers and their affiliations?

The new study must have struck the CTN people like a bomb, for they used Lucina Suarez, from the TDH, to try and find errors or weaknesses in the SHRC paper. When they found nothing that impacted the results, they had to move out of the way of the review process.

The actual review of the programs was set for October 18 and 19, 2004. A week prior, the SHRC received an e-mail from Leos inviting all agencies that had submitted programs to attend the review process.

This shocked everyone at the SHRC; in the past, an open review process had been unheard of at the TEA.

Hernandez and Treviño drove in to Austin on the 18th to sit in on the meeting. They were allowed in the room as the panel of experts reviewed the programs.

The review started at nine o'clock in the morning, and ended at four. The reviewers could and did ask Hernandez and Treviño questions about the study results, and for help in locating components needed for the evaluation criteria. The training manuals were reviewed and no questions were asked. No one indicated any serious questions or concerns about the Bienestar program and its suitability for school district adoption. Hernandez and Treviño left with a good feeling about reviewers, and the new review process initiated by Neeley, the TEA's new head.

THANKSGIVING IS HERE
On November 22, 2004 the SHRC received the following letter from Neeley:

> Thank you for submitting the *Bienestar Health Program* for approval as a coordinated school health program. The program was reviewed for alignment with criteria included in 19 TAC Chapter 102, Subchapter CC, Commissioner's Rules Concerning Coordinated School Health Programs.
>
> We are very pleased to inform you that the *Bienestar Health Program* has been approved and may be used by school districts to comply with the coordinated school health requirements in Senate Bill 19 (SB 19). SB 19 requires that school districts participate in appropriate training for the implementation of approved coordinated school health programs by September 1, 2007. See the Texas Education Code, Sections 38.013 and 38.014 for additional information.
>
> Congratulations and best wishes for success with the *Bienestar Health Program*. Please contact Dr. Robert Leos, Director of Textbooks.

The happiest day of Treviño's professional life had always been the day he received his medical diploma. The next happiest day now qualified as the day he received this letter.
And for the rest of the staff at SHRC?
It was their Thanksgiving.

Forgotten Children: A True Story of How Politicians Endanger Children

Chapter 14

AMBUSH

As Treviño already knew, Governor Perry was no advocate for early-age health interventions, particularly if they benefited children of color and the poor. Fortunately, this was something the media would notice.

On April 22, 2005, the *San Antonio Express-News* wrote an article titled, **Perry isn't joining fellow govs on Pre-K funding bandwagon**. A two-year study by the National Governors Association advised states to create stronger early childhood education paths, particularly for children of color and the poor. Based on that study, nineteen Southern state governors led a national charge to spend more to educate pre-kindergarten children, specifically those who qualified for free or reduced lunch, who were homeless, and who spoke limited English. Perry refused to join that movement.

Kathy Walt, a Perry spokeswoman, said about his reluctance, "… it would be a great pool of added kids whose educational services would have to be paid for." She then added, "Perry does consider early childhood development important, having launched the Early Start Initiative in 2003."

Well, "initiatives" are generally one- or two-day meetings where experts gather, talk big, and exchange business cards. Many times, nothing is accomplished.

Given Perry's position, it was not all that surprising that when the Bienestar health program finally received the TEA's approval, the governor and legislators suddenly shut the purse that funds health textbooks. Perry vetoed the Education Article, which funded school health textbooks and the Republican-led legislature refused to re-work the state budget to fund the books.

It seemed that if the Texas CATCH program could not get all the coordinated school health textbook funds, no one else could.

• DR. ROBERTO P. TREVIÑO •

NOT TAKING IT SITTING DOWN

Fortunately, MacMillan/McGraw-Hill (MMH) had a big stake in the holdup. They had warehouses full of up-to-date health textbooks, and were simply waiting payment for them from the state.

In April 2005, a woman named Nancy Siefken called Treviño to ask him a favor. Siefken worked for McDonalds' public relation firm, which had been retained by MMH to conduct their lobbying.

"Dr. Treviño, the legislators dodged the issue of funding health textbooks," Siefken said, focusing on the poor children. "I am worried that these children will not get the most up-to-date knowledge about nutrition and health. Many of their health textbooks date back to the 1990s."

"I've been worried about that for five years," Treviño said in agreement, "and no one has ever paid attention."

"But now I think we've reached epidemic proportions of childhood obesity," Siefken countered. "I think now the public is more aware."

"I don't know what a little center like ours can do; wouldn't a big corporation like the one you represent be more effective if it comes to having to flex some muscle?" Treviño questioned.

"Dr. Treviño, the legislators are holding back $378 million to fund the textbooks," she specified. "I think McGraw-Hill and the Social and Health Research Center can become formidable partners to compete for those dollars. But we need the legislature to release the funds."

"Well, we need McGraw-Hill to get our good health information across," Treviño responded. "Our little center has been bullied by giants for a long time, and it's difficult for us to take them on alone. What is it that you think I can do?"

"Dr. Treviño, you are an accomplished physician and investigator in children's health. An opinion editorial from you would carry a lot of weight. Can you write an opinion editorial for the *San Antonio Express-News*?" Siefken finally asked. "I can draft a letter and send it to you today."

"You could," Treviño smiled, "but I already have some ideas of what to write."

What Siefken was suggesting was easy enough for him to do, and Treviño wrote the following opinion editorial, which the *San Antonio Express-News* published on July 7, 2005:

> The Texas Legislature left Austin in May without paying for public school children's textbooks that were

scheduled to be used in classrooms this fall. Now that legislators are back in Austin for a special session on education, they have the chance to fix that.

These instructional materials were requested by the State Board of Education in 2002, approved by the board last fall, selected by educators this winter, and approved by school districts this spring.

Some of these textbooks are on the very important subject of health education for elementary school children.

I have been working on childhood obesity in Texas during my entire career, specifically as it relates to the alarmingly high rates of diabetes in schoolchildren.

Childhood obesity rates in inner-city schools in San Antonio are among the highest in the nation.

The amount of obesity and adult disease in Texas schoolchildren is an enormous health concern, and there is increasing evidence that school-based interventions can improve students' eating habits, attitudes toward exercise, and even their glucose levels.

In a recent study we conducted and published in the September 2004 issue of the *Archives of Pediatrics and Adolescent Medicine*, we showed that children participating in the Bienestar school health program significantly decreased their blood sugars and increased their fitness levels and dietary fiber intake.

Control students, on the other hand, experienced the opposite effects: increased blood sugars, decreased fitness levels and decreased dietary fiber intake.

Our state's largest expenditure is health, and diabetes is the illness with the most rapid growth rate.

Between 2001 and 2004, diabetes rates grew by 55 percent. In 2004, we estimated 1.6 million people living in Texas had diagnosed and undiagnosed diabetes.

Once the undiagnosed enter the health care system, the cost for all diabetes health care in our state will add up to $21.3 billion a year.

At this rate, there will not be enough money in our state agencies to pay for these health costs, and we will all need to pitch in more.

What do we do? Prevention.

A large national study, the Diabetes Prevention Program, reported that high-risk individuals who practiced health lifestyles were able to reduce diabetes risk by fifty-eight percent.

Early intervention works, and we need to give educators the tools to help.

We haven't had new health books in Texas for twelve years, and the material in the current health education textbook adoption are designed, and have been scientifically proven, to improve the health of children.

I am very disappointed in the Legislature's shortsighted actions this spring, and I hope our governor and legislators make the right decision this summer.

The decision is simple: Either pay $378 million now for the health and other textbooks, or pay $21 billion later to care for the illnesses we could have prevented by early-age interventions.

The letter had the desired effect. After pressure from many, the legislators approved—and the governor signed—the bill to fund the health textbooks in August 2005.

BACK AT THE TEA

After that experience with the Governor, Treviño got concerned that Perry would mandate the TEA to change its policies of openness and inclusiveness. As the state's Chief Executive Officer, he had the power to influence bureaucracy.

Treviño and SHRC staff decided not let their finger off the TEA pulse, even though with Neeley at the helm, TEA was another organization. For example, in September 2005, the TEA sent letters to school districts informing them about the Bienestar program being an approved coordinated school health program. The TEA included information about the Bienestar program on their web site, and the TEA kept the staff of the SHRC updated on any activity related to coordinated school health programs.

This proved helpful, because back on April 8, 2005, SB 42 had started moving in the Texas Legislature. SB 42 was similar to SB 19 but it required school districts to implement a TEA-approved middle school coordinated school health program. So the SHRC was working on a middle school initiative.

Dr. Tammy Wyatt, professor of Health and Kinesiology at the

University of Texas at San Antonio, put together the 6th, 7th, and 8th grade drafts, while Treviño and the staff at the SHRC did the editing and revising. The SHRC's books geared for middle school children were submitted to the TEA in January 2007, and set for review in April 2007.

Treviño wanted to keep his guard up, so he called Marissa Rathbone, the TEA's Director of the School Health Division, to set up a meeting with her and Kloster, associate commissioner of the TEA's Department of Health and Safety. Treviño wanted to meet Kloster personally and make him aware of the science behind the Bienestar program.

Kloster, Rathbone, Saldaña, and Treviño met in February 2007.

"Good afternoon, Dr. Treviño," Kloster said in a loud and friendly manner. "I've heard a lot of good things about your program. I've also heard you're one of the top NIH investigators in the state. I congratulate you for all your work."

"Thank you," Treviño said simply.

"I'm new at this position, and I'm interested in learning more about diabetes in children and what we need to do to prevent it," Kloster said, settling back to listen. "I'd like to tap into your brains," he joked.

Treviño presented briefly the rates of type 2 diabetes among children, then dwelled extensively on the studies showing the Bienestar program's results. He put several of the Bienestar program studies in front of Kloster.

"We have a big problem with obesity and diabetes among our youth," Kloster agreed. "As you're a physician with extensive research in diabetes and children's health, how do you think the state should approach this problem?"

"Let me start first by telling you how *not* to approach this problem," Treviño started. "The state should not get involved in protecting one program. It should get involved in evaluating multiple programs. The children would be better served if the state lets multiple programs compete, with the state playing the role of evaluator.

"The state should develop the criteria by which school health programs are evaluated. Examples would be fitness test; food frequency questionnaires; and measures of adiposity such as body mass index or percent body fat. The state then should collect these results, and set minimum standards, adjusted for age. Schools whose students pass those standards, should be commended, and schools whose students do not, should be provided assistance and be monitored.

"Local school staff then can use these data to help them select coordinated school health programs that are more appropriate and produces better results for their student population. It might be that for some schools one program is best, but for other schools other programs are best. If the state keeps this competitive edge, it will put all the school health programs on a self-improvement course."

"That makes sense," Kloster nodded.

"We would be glad to share our evaluation training manuals," David Saldaña offered. "Those are the manuals we use to train staff in data collection methods."

During the meeting, Treviño and Saldaña did not ask for information on how the middle-school review process was doing. Their intention at the time was just to personalize a relationship with Kloster and Rathbone.

Throughout the meeting, Kloster and Rathbone were friendly and courteous, and Treviño and Saldaña walked out with the impression that they were dealing with fair and honest persons.

THE SCHOOL PLAYGROUND IS OPENNED

In April 2007, Rathbone called Treviño.

"Hi, Dr. Treviño, how're you doing?" Rathbone started in a happy and friendly tone of voice.

"Doing great," Treviño responded anxiously. Would he be hearing from Rathbone the results from the TEA's middle school program review?

"Jeff would like to set a meeting with you, Steve Kelder, and Sylvia Winker. He has some good news for all of you."

Treviño knew of Winker; she was with the Healthy & Wise program, the third coordinated middle-school curriculum that had been submitted for the review. The Healthy & Wise was a health curriculum written and distributed like a newspaper. It had no evidence of effectiveness but it was an example of a school program that, if allowed to participate, could eventually demonstrate good results after a trial-and-error process. And if it did, the Bienestar and Texas CATCH programs would need to be improved to stay competitive.

When Treviño heard there was going to be good news, his whole body relaxed.

"Oh sure," he eagerly agreed. "Does he have a date in mind?"

"We were looking at Thursday, April 19th at nine a.m.. Will that work for you?"

"It's perfect," Treviño replied. There was no way he would not be there!

Since Rathbone would also call and invite Rodriguez to the meeting,

Forgotten Children: A True Story of How Politicians Endanger Children

the two men would drive together to Austin for the meeting.

Rodriguez and Treviño were the first to arrive. Treviño noted they were put in the same conference room where he had testified against Fleming (see page 202). Minutes later Kelder and Cribb from the CTN, and Winkler from Healthy and Wise, walked into the conference room.

Since there were two rows of tables facing each other, Rodriguez, Treviño, and Winkler had sat on one side. Now, on the other side of the other table, were Kelder and Cribb, facing them.

This was the first time Treviño had encountered Kelder in person. Back in 2002, Joan Miller with the Bexar County Hospital Collaborative had tried to get Kelder and Treviño to meet, but Kelder never gave Miller a date. The next year, in 2003, Tom Baranowski from Baylor University also had scheduled a meeting between Kelder and Treviño, but Kelder ended up cancelling the appointment.

Kelder was an elegantly dressed man who had neatly-groomed, shoulder-length, snow-white hair. He kept a smile on his face during the meeting, but he would not give Treviño any eye contact.

The meeting started with Rathbone and Kloster going to stand in the front of the room. They stood like schoolteachers about to lecture their students.

A lean and fit man, Kloster was the first to speak. His voice was harsh; his words and message, blunt.

"I will tell you why you are here, but first I will tell you who I am," Kloster said in a loud voice as he paced back and forth in between the two columns of tables. "I was a high-paid attorney working with one of the most prominent law firms in the state of Texas. I had it all. But I couldn't keep up with life in the fast lane, and before I knew it, I had developed some bad habits that were difficult to shake. I had become a drug and food addict. In fact, I was weighing over 250 pounds."

The room remained very quiet as Kloster shared his incredible life experiences.

"My life was out of control, and I had to get it back on track. I went through rehabilitation, and that helped me with the drug addiction. I got into cycling and jogging, and that helped me lose almost 100 pounds.

"That whole experience has taught me a valuable lesson. If I could rehabilitate myself out of that deep mess, anyone can be rehabilitated. That means we can rehabilitate any student in the state of Texas. But we at the TEA cannot do it alone. And that's why you're here.

"I know there's been a lot history between two programs in this room. That shit needs to stop," he said forcibly, shaking his head to provide emphasis for his words. "I don't give a shit about who was at fault, and who did what to whom. There's a lot of talent in this room, and some of you have tremendous credentials in the field of children's health. I want you to look forward from here on out, and think about how we can work together to improve the health of Texas children."

As he was talking, the new Commissioner of Education walked in and sat down on top of one of the tables. When Kloster finished talking, she took over.

"I want to thank you for joining us in this meeting," Neeley said with a big smile as she swung her legs back and forth from the table's edge. "I have doctor friends who tell me they see children nine and twelve years of age who weigh more than an adult. They tell me these kids are being diagnosed with high blood pressure and diabetes. It's a shame to see children this young having to be treated with adult medicines. Mr. Kloster, Ms. Rathbone, and I have a commitment to these children. With your help, we want to bring the best health programs to these children's schools. Does anyone have any questions or comments?"

"Dr. Neeley, I'm a physician, and our center published one of the first studies to show that children as young as nine years of age were developing type 2 diabetes," Treviño said. "But the solution is not in my clinic or in the hospitals. It is in this room. A teacher is more important than any doctor or physician specialist to stop the increasing rates of diabetes and all its complications. I commend you, Jeff, and Marissa for moving health education up to the level of academics. We at the Social and Health Research Center will work together with you, and the staff of the TEA, to teach children in Texas about healthier lifestyles."

Kelder and Cribb sat quietly and had no comments at this point.

Neeley thanked everyone again, and gestured to Kloster to take over the meeting.

"Well, gentlemen and ladies," Kloster said, "the review panel has approved the three curriculums, pending some minor revisions. Marissa Rathbone will meet with you individually to inform you of the revisions your program needs. If you resubmit your programs with the suggested changes, your program will be approved."

There was a five-minute break before Rathbone would meet with each of the groups. At this point, Treviño walked over to Kelder and Cribb.

Kelder remained there, but Cribb turned and walked away at Treviño's approach.

"Steve, I'm so happy Kloster brought us together," Treviño offered. "We *do* need to work together. The day we learn to work together is the day we will make a significant change in the children."

Kelder gave Treviño an angry stare before he said shortly, "It needs to stop!"

Treviño's startled eyes opened wide in response before Kelder then turned around and simply walked away.

Kelder's words had unsettled Treviño. He had been hoping for some conciliatory comments from Kelder after his pleasant greeting, but all he had received was an angry, vague remark. Kelder had sounded threatened, and if that was the case—why?

As he was walking back to his table, Rathbone called over to Treviño, and asked to meet with him first. As always, she was nice and friendly.

"Dr. Treviño, your program received the highest score from our review panel," she noted. "The only comment was that it needed some clarifications in lesson plans six and eighteen in your P.E. pad. If you can make those corrections and send it back to us within two weeks, your program will be approved."

That was all Treviño needed to hear. He returned to the SHRC headquarters, where the revisions were made and sent back to TEA within a week.

On May 16, 2007, the SHRC received its formal letter from the TEA stating that the Bienestar middle school curriculum had been approved as a coordinated school health program. The other two curriculums were also approved.

When the news was announced through the intercom at the SHRC buildings, joy and laughter was heard throughout all the buildings. Members of the SHRC staffs were ecstatic to have two school health programs curriculums now approved by the TEA!

AFRICAN-AMERICAN CHILDREN NEED HELP

Even more good news lay ahead for the SHRC.

As mentioned prior, while the Bienestar program had been designed for Mexican-Americans, African-American children also had high diabetes risk factors, and were being diagnosed with type 2 diabetes. So a team of African-American researchers led Dr. Mary Shaw-Ridley, Director of Texas A&M's Center for Health Disparities, had translated the Bienestar program into instructional material more compatible to African-American family life and culture. Shaw-Ridley called the new program "NEEMA", which meant "wellbeing" in Swahili. Pilot testing of the program began in the fall of 2005.

In 2007, Shaw-Ridley and Treviño published a study about the NEEMA program in the *Journal of the National Medical Association*.

It showed that twenty percent of African-American children living in socially deprived neighborhoods had pre-diabetes, but that those children who participated in the NEEMA decreased their blood sugars by six percent—a significant finding!

Because NEEMA was directed towards children in kindergarten through eighth grade, and a mirror image of the Bienestar program, Treviño asked Kloster to consider it for TEA approval in the Spring of 2007. Kloster and Rathbone asked for all the NEEMA material, and by July 20, 2007, the SHRC received a letter from the TEA approving the NEEMA program.

This was fantastic news, and the head of the TEA seemed in large part responsible. The Bienestar k—5th grade, the Bienestar 6th—8th grade and the NEEMA k—8th grade curriculums all were approved by the TEA during Neeley's tenure. [The Bienestar curriculum had been expanded from fourth grade to k—5th grade in late 2002].

TOO GOOD TO LAST

Yet Governor Perry must have had enough of Neeley, her open-mindedness, and her work towards approving school health programs for children of color and the poor.

On June 21, 2007 the *San Antonio Express-News* wrote an article with the heading, **TEA chief leaving – at governor's request**. According to the article, when Neeley had asked Perry's staff what she had done wrong and what she could do differently to keep her job, she received no answers. The first woman to lead Texas's education system thus was gone in July 2007.

Neeley listed in the *San Antonio Express-News* establishing a new department and associate commissioner for student health and obesity prevention as one of her top accomplishments.

Perry brought Robert Scott back as interim commissioner of the TEA despite questions raised in an inspector general's report which specified that a number of no-bid contracts in the TEA had gone to Scott's friends. Specifically, the inspector general report chronicled instances during Scott's tenure as interim commissioner (the period between Alanis and Neeley) when millions of dollars in contracts that were not competitively bid upon went to Scott's friend, Austin attorney Emily Miller, or to his former executive assistant, Cory Rountree. Yet a few months later, on October 16, 2007, Perry named Scott as the Texas Commissioner of Education.

On that same day, a report from the *Dallas Morning News* stated teacher associations and some education groups were hesitant to support

Scott as full-time commissioner because of his close ties to Perry. (This report did not give any more specifics.)

Treviño also had his own share of concerns about the new Commissioner of Education. He remembered having to beg Scott back in 2004 to approve the Bienestar program for the Texas schools (page 205), and that ultimately, Scott had rejected the Bienestar program based on an attorney's decision, and without ever consulting with any health experts. How would Scott's perspective affect the Bienestar program's approval status by the TEA in the future?

• DR. ROBERTO P. TREVIÑO •

Forgotten Children: A True Story of How Politicians Endanger Children

Chapter 15

PROTECTING THE BORDER CHILDREN: THE HOUSE

CHILDREN OF THE POOR DO NOT CONTRIBUTE

Texas is a state where the "the less government, the better". That is why the Texas Legislature meets only for 140 days every two years. The legislative sessions begin in January every odd-numbered year.

During the 2007 legislative session, 6,374 legislative bills were introduced, and of these, 1,495 (23%) were passed. There are fourteen basic steps by which a bill must go through before it can become a law. At every step, legislators have the opportunity to weed it out.

Following are the fourteen steps, and each represents a decision node where bills can be turned off or on (the order may vary):

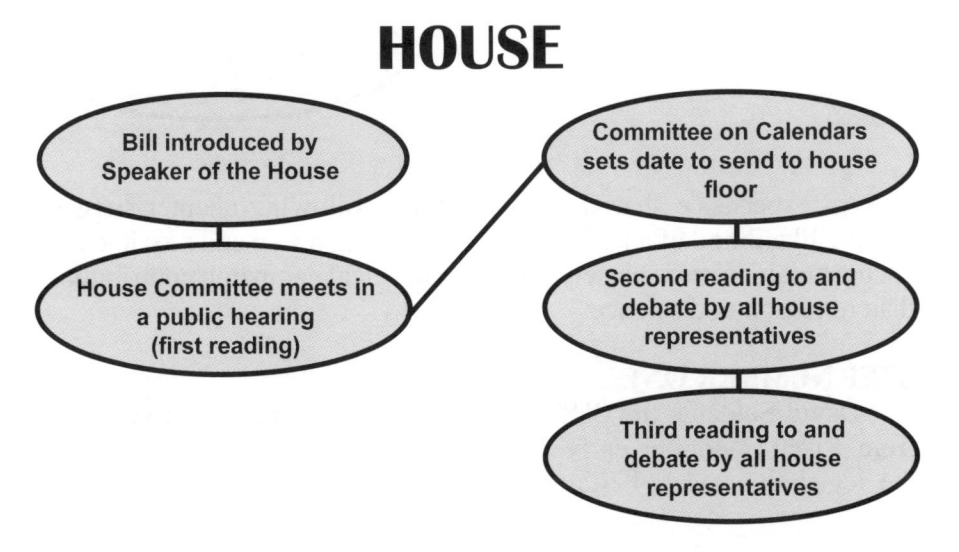

HOUSE

- Bill introduced by Speaker of the House
- House Committee meets in a public hearing (first reading)
- Committee on Calendars sets date to send to house floor
- Second reading to and debate by all house representatives
- Third reading to and debate by all house representatives

• DR. ROBERTO P. TREVIÑO •

SENATE

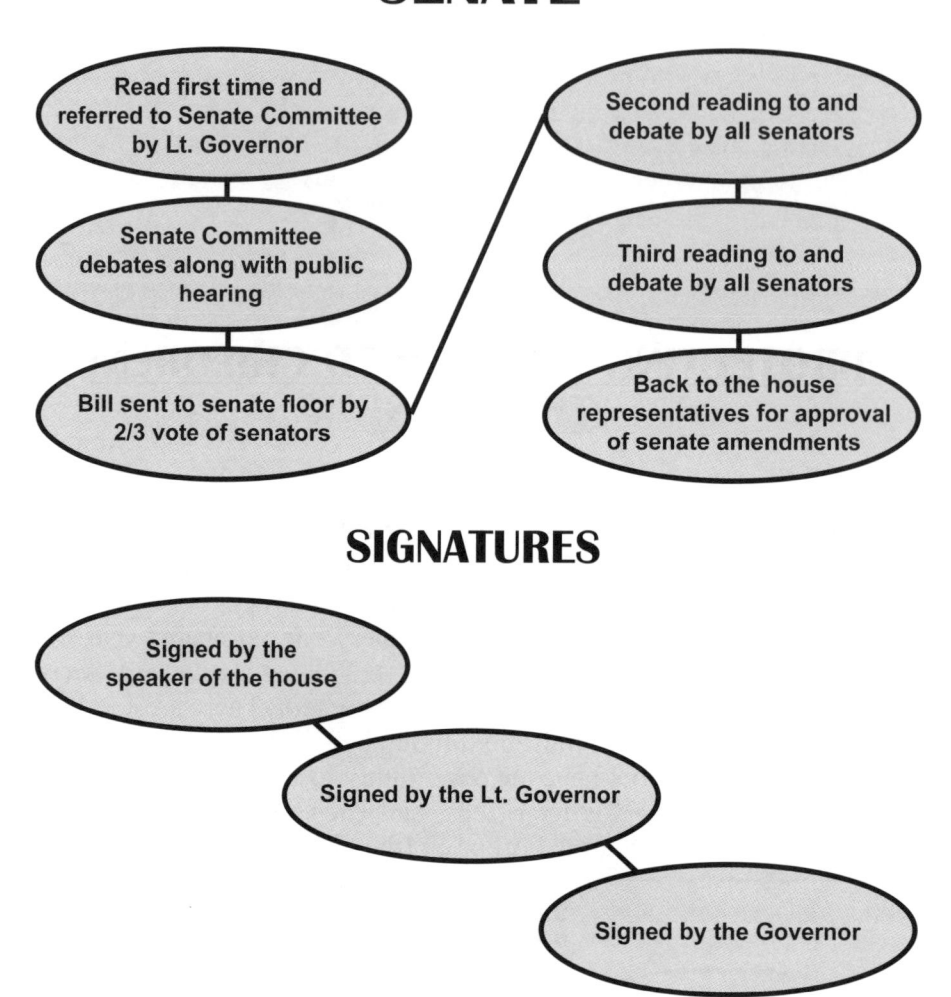

- Read first time and referred to Senate Committee by Lt. Governor
- Senate Committee debates along with public hearing
- Bill sent to senate floor by 2/3 vote of senators
- Second reading to and debate by all senators
- Third reading to and debate by all senators
- Back to the house representatives for approval of senate amendments

SIGNATURES

- Signed by the speaker of the house
- Signed by the Lt. Governor
- Signed by the Governor

An experience shared in this and the following chapter suggests that the likelihood of a legislative bill surviving a step and moving up to the next may be more closely related to political campaign contributions than to reason and science.

STEP NUMBER ONE

David Saldaña, the SHRC's marketing consultant, received a call from Lizette Montiel early January 2007. Montiel was serving as the legislative aide of State Representative Richard Raymond, who represented the city of Laredo, the prinicipal port of entry into Mexico.

Montiel was calling to set a conference call meeting to discuss a legislative bill that Raymond wanted to introduce. He was hoping to carry a bill that would fund and evaluate a pilot program to prevent type 2 diabetes in youth along the Texas-Mexico Border. The conference call was set for January 24, 2007, at 2:30 p.m. Raymond called in from his Laredo office to the SHRC, where Saldaña and Treviño were participating in the conference call.

"Good afternoon, Dr. Treviño, this is Richard Raymond from Laredo. Dr. Hector Gonzalez, the Director of the City of Laredo's Health Department, has spoken very highly about your program. He presented some results from your NIH study being conducted here in Laredo. Obviously, we are concerned about the high rate of diabetes that is present in our youth. We want to do something about it, and we turned to you because of your expertise."

"Yes sir," Treviño replied. "We found four percent of your third grade children had blood glucose levels above the normal levels. That means the possibility of eight-year-olds walking around with an adult disease!"

"We want to do something about it," Raymond strongly reiterated.

"Well, we are willing to help," Saldaña added. "You can depend on us for any support you need."

"I want our office attorney to write the first draft of the bill. But we will need your input to make sure our children get the best interventions out there to prevent diabetes," said Raymond.

The first draft of this bill, which Raymond wanted to introduce in the 2007 legislative session, included a description of the program to be implemented in the schools. Upon his review of the material, Treviño added an evaluation component, which provided for testing for program effectiveness.

House Bill 3618 (HB 3618) read as follows:

> A BILL TO BE ENTITLED
> AN ACT
> relating to a coordinated health program for school districts located in the border region.
> BE IT ENACTED BY THE LEGISLATURE OF THE STATE OF TEXAS:
> SECTION 1. Section 38.013, Education Code, is amended by adding Subsection (d) to read as follows:
> (d) The commissioner of education, in consultation

with the Department of State Health Services, shall adopt criteria to require that at least one program available under Subsection (a) be designed to prevent and detect obesity and type 2 diabetes by taking into account the needs of school districts described by Section 38.0131 that has a student population identified by the commissioner as at risk for obesity and type 2 diabetes. An evidenced-based program designated under this subsection must provide that:

(1) each school district must distribute to each school in the district:
- health curriculum teacher's guides for each grade level;
- health curriculum student workbooks for each student in each grade level;
- a physical education activity pad;
- cafeteria program teacher's guides and student workbooks; and
- a newsletter for the family of each student in the district;

(2) for each student in kindergarten through grade eight, each school in the school district must:
- measure the height and weight of the student at the beginning of the school year and at another appropriate time during the implementation of the program; and
- track the measurements of the student and the progress of the student under the program through a data entry system provided over the internet; and

(3) the coordinated health program components must consist of bilingual materials.

SECTION 2. Subchapter A, Chapter 38, Education Code, is amended by adding Section 38.0131 to read as follows:

Sec. 38.0131. REQUIRED COORDINATED HEALTH PROGRAM FOR CERTAIN SCHOOL DISTRICTS.

(A) This section applies only to a school district located in a municipality that;
- has a population greater than 11,000; and

- is located within one-half mile of an international border.

(B) A school district to which this section applies shall implement a coordinated health program that meets the criteria of Section 38.013 (d).

(C) In the first year a school district implements a program under this section, the district shall report the measurements of student height and weight and the progress of a student under the program to the entity that administers the program. The administering entity shall evaluate and analyze the measurements to determine the effectiveness of the program in the first year.

(D) The Department of State Health Services shall, from money appropriated for that purpose, distribute money to each school district required to implement a coordinated health program under this section to cover the cost associated with the program.

Saldaña and Treviño met the following day after they had received this draft to discuss the impact that the legislative bill could have on Texas-Mexico border children.

"David, if this bill is not accompanied by money and an evaluation component, it will be a waste of everyone's time," Treviño said at the time. "I don't want this to be a situation where politicians just look good for bringing the matter up, but the children's lives stay unchanged."

"I agree, Dr. Treviño," Saldaña replied. "What Raymond's staff has asked me to do is put together some cost-effectiveness numbers. I hope you can help."

"Well, how many students in kindergarten through eighth grade do you estimate are in the school districts along the Texas Mexico border?" Treviño asked.

"Denise and I researched the populations, and we estimated 214,217 students." (Denise Jones was Saldaña's associate in their marketing firm.)

"That's a lot. What cities did you include?"

"Brownsville, Del Rio, Eagle Pass, El Paso, Laredo and Hidalgo."

"What will it cost to implement the program?"

"About $3 million"

Treviño pulled out his calculator. "That works out to be about fourteen dollars a student. What services and materials did you include in the budget?"

"The schools get books for the four components, training, evaluation, and reports," Saldaña responded.

"Since in our Laredo study we found nearly four percent of the children had high blood sugars," Treviño reported, "I estimate 8,000 children along the Texas-Mexico border are walking around with undiagnosed diabetes right now."

"That's ugly, Dr. Treviño," Saldaña said, and shook his head.

"It'll get even uglier, Dave, if we have to foot the bill to cover their medical expenses."

"What do you mean?"

"An American Diabetes Association study showed that the medical cost for treating a patient with diabetes is $13,000 a year," Treviño said as he kept inputting numbers into his calculator. "If you multiply that number by 8,000, it works out to be...$103 million dollars."

Saldaña raised his eyebrows and shook his head. "Shit, that's a lot of money. Does that mean we can save the state $103 million a year?"

"No," Treviño clarified, "not every kid in the Bienestar program reverses their blood sugars to normal. Our studies show that forty-five percent do. But that would work out be a savings of $46 million annually!"

"Representative Raymond should have an easy sale," Saldaña concluded.

To make Raymond's job even easier, Treviño and Saldaña agreed to provide Raymond with data and testimonials.

TRYING TO BE OPEN

Since Jeff Kloster from the TEA had been so up front with Treviño (page 233), Treviño wanted to make sure to be the same way with Kloster. Slipping a legislative bill through for self-interest purposes would make SHRC staff no different to the CTN people. In addition, as the Bienestar middle school curriculums were in the process of being reviewed by the TEA, the TEA was the last organization SHRC staff would want to upset.

So Saldaña called Marissa Rathbone, TEA Director of Health and Physical Education, and set an appointment with her and Kloster for March 21, 2007.

It was 7:55 a.m. when Saldaña and Treviño got off the elevator on the fifth floor of the TEA building in Austin. Not many people were there that early. As the two men entered the hallway, they noticed that the office spaces looked cramped with furniture and the desks stacked high with papers.

Rathbone walked out of an office and gave Treviño and Saldaña a warm welcome. She walked them to Kloster's office, where he greeted them with a friendly handshake. He had just come in from a morning run and seemed in a happy mood.

Treviño, Saldaña and Rathbone sat down around the rectangular conference table in Kloster's office. They appreciated the view from its windows, as there was a view to the opulent state government buildings surrounding the state capital.

"Hi, Dr. Treviño," Kloster started. "I'm glad you called to make an appointment because I wanted to talk to you too."

"Good, I just want to keep you informed about a legislative bill we are supporting—"

Treviño was about to give a detailed explanation of the house bill when Kloster cut in.

"House Bill 3618," he said, nodding his head. "I'm well aware of it."

"Oh. Do you have any questions from us?"

"No."

"Well, that's our reason for the visit," Treviño said as he shrugged to gesture that was all they had on their agenda. "I will send you e-mails to keep you informed, Jeff."

As the TEA's commissioner of health, Kloster needed to stay abreast of all legislative bills related to children's health in the schools. And he was frequently called in to public hearings to provide his expert opinion. After Treviño's mention of the bill at their meeting, he did not ask the attendees any more questions about HB 3618, and shifted to the questions he had on his own agenda.

"As you might know, I just joined the TEA in January, and I'm eager to learn everything there is about childhood obesity and diabetes. I know you are an NIH investigator and a diabetes expert. Can you tell me a little bit about your work?"

"I'm a physician, and I make a living seeing patients in the office," Treviño explained. "We have opened up five offices in the poorest neighborhoods of San Antonio, and brought in sixteen wonderful primary care doctors to care for that population. But despite providing our patients with the best medical care, and introducing the newest medicines and insulins, the number of people with diabetes walking in through my front door is growing by nine percent every year.

"Furthermore, when we start patients on medicines for high cholesterol, hypertension, and diabetes their expenses add up to the point of not being able to afford the medicines. I have patients who take up to nine drugs a day. They walk in to my office and tell me 'Doctor, I don't have the money to buy the medicines, and have not taken them for two weeks'. I can predict the onset of diabetes complications when I see the results of their blood tests, and I don't sleep at night because I know what's going to happen to them. These problems won't be happening if we raise healthier children."

"What do you think the solution should be?" Kloster asked.

"Early age interventions," Treviño replied quickly. "Adult disease and obesity levels are being programmed developmentally between in utero and age nine. If we don't make the corrections at those early ages, it will be nearly impossible to correct the problem once they become adults. Unless we invest in early age interventions and quantify the results, diabetes morbidity and health care costs will continue to climb."

"How do you see the role of the TEA in guiding health programs in the schools?" Kloster inquired.

"I think the role of the TEA is to produce an environment where school health programs can compete," Treviño said, reemphasizing the same advice he had given Kloster a month ago (page 231). "If the TEA could set benchmarks or expected outcomes for the programs, it will drive all school health programs to higher standards."

Kloster sat quietly contemplating the suggestion and nodding his head. "I can tell you that with me at the helm of the TEA's Department of Health and Safety, there will be accountability," he stated.

Treviño and Saldaña left the meeting impressed with Kloster, and the openness and inclusiveness of the TEA staff.

DIFFERING RECEPTION

Since they were close to the state capital building, Treviño and Saldaña walked over to Raymond's office after their meeting with Kloster to speak with Lizette Montiel. Treviño and Saldaña felt ill-informed when it came to the legislative process, and thus had some questions about the passage of HB 3618.

Because the one-hundred and twenty year old Renaissance Revival Texas State Capitol was built for a smaller legislative body, Texas legislators were cramped in small office spaces. The offices, although small, were aggrandized by high ceilings, 15th-century Italian woodwork and turn-of-the-century American furniture. As the two men opened the door to Raymond's office, they needed to stand one behind the other to simply fit in through the narrow entrance hallway. The first person they met was Montiel. Montiel was in her mid-twenties, and she was an attractive young lady with big round eyes.

"Hi, Lizette," Saldaña said, greeting Raymond's aide. "This is Dr. Treviño, the expert in childhood diabetes who spoke with Representative Raymond about House Bill 3618 recently. Lizette, we drove here to have a meeting with Jeff Kloster at the TEA, and so we just stopped in to ask how the bill is doing. Do you know when it will go to the special house committee? Is that where they also have the public hearing?"

She stared at them for a moment, before she replied with a stolid expression on her face, "I don't know."

"Do you know to what special house committee it'll go?" Saldaña asked.

"I don't know," she repeated.

Since they were getting no useful information from Montiel, Saldaña requested, "Is it possible to speak with Representative Raymond?" Is he here?"

"No, sir, it's not possible," she replied in a dry tone of voice.

"I'm the investigator conducting the *Proyecto* Bienestar Laredo, and as of yet we've detected eighty children from Laredo and United ISDs with type 2 diabetes," Treviño said forcefully but politely, in the hope that offering this information would elicit more of a helpful response from her. "One child is too many; eighty children are unacceptable. Can you get us more information on the bill? We'd like to help in whatever way we can, to make sure it goes through."

She stared up at Treviño and in an indifferent tone of voice said, "I will look into it and give you a call."

Treviño and Saldaña walked out of her office with somber expressions on each of their faces.

"If this is the aide assigned to House Bill 3618, the children ain't got a chance," an upset Saldaña declared to Treviño.

"I think the children got themselves a bad horse," Treviño agreed, shaking his head ruefully.

To see if they could get any information at all, they walked over to Representative Ryan Guillen's (D-Laredo) office. Guillen, a rotund man with a personality and a smile to match, was a co-author of the bill. Guillen was close to Tom Craddick, the Speaker of the House.

Craddick was the complete opposite, thin, squared jaw, and a no nonsense republican. Craddick, as Speaker of the House, was responsible for controlling how the bills moved through the house. He had the power of taking a bill from the Calendars Committee and sending it to the house floor. If bills were not chosen, they died in the Calendars Committee.

When Treviño and Saldaña walked in to Guillen's office, a young lady with honey-colored skin and a big smile received them. She got out of her chair and in a friendly voice asked what she could do for them.

This reception was very different from what the two men had received from Montiel.

Saldaña introduced himself and Treviño, and asked if she could help him get information on HB 3618.

Without losing her smile, the young woman responded, "Oh, yes. Representative Guillen is very interested in this bill, and he has asked me to follow it closely."

Indeed, Laura Salcedo, Guillen's legislative aide, proved very knowledgeable about the intricate legislative process. For Saldaña and Treviño, she would be a welcome conduit in terms of receiving accurate information regarding HB 3618. They would always be welcomed in her office.

In fact, on March 30, 2007, Salcedo called Saldaña to inform him that HB 3618 had been referred to the Border and International Affairs Committee [a special house committee], and that that committee was set to meet on April 10, 2007. She asked Saldaña and Treviño if they could come to testify.

Members of that committee were state representatives Joe Pickett, Tommy Merritt, Rick Hardcastle, Joaquin Castro, Tracy King and Ana Hernandez. Stephen Frost was the chairman.

Besides Treviño and Saldaña, Hector Gonzalez and Roger Rodriguez had signed up to testify. Kloster also would be present at the meeting to provide his expert opinion to the legislators if they had questions.

ROUND ONE

The meeting started at two o'clock in the afternoon, but HB 3618 was not heard until seven o'clock. At that point, Representative Raymond went up and introduced his bill.

"Good evening, I'm here to introduce House Bill 3618," he said. "The Texas-Mexico border has the highest rates of poverty and diabetes in the state. What concerns me the most is a study from Laredo that found children as young as eight years of age with type 2 diabetes. This is an adult disease now affecting children.

"I'm a father, just like many of you in this committee. And like me, I am sure you want the best for your children. Well, we can ask no less for those children living in poverty along the Texas-Mexico border. That is why I am here: to introduce evidence-based programs to educate children about diabetes, and how to prevent it."

Raymond looked at Representative Joe Pickett with a smile and said, "Representative, you are an educator and have written children's books. I'm sure you can appreciate how important books are for children in teaching them about healthier lifestyles."

Pickett, a tall, slim and curly-haired gentleman, had some of the Bienestar studies in his hands when Raymond directed that comment at him. Pickett looked up at Raymond, grinned and nodded his head.

The chairman of the committee, Stephen Frost, asked all the people that would testify to go up to the front. Kloster, Gonzalez, Rodriguez, Treviño, and Saldaña sat together on a long table in the front, although Kloster was only there to answer questions, not to make a presentation.

The first to go was Gonzalez. He distributed to committee members an article from a medical journal. "I'm Dr. Hector Gonzalez, Director of the City of Laredo Health Department. A new study from the Centers for Disease Control showed that among states along the U.S.-Mexico border, Texas had the highest rates of hospitalizations for diabetes. Texas had 26 patients hospitalized for diabetes per every 10,000 of the population. This compares with 12 in California and 15 in Arizona. When the CDC looked at the border counties in Texas, for every 10,000 of the population, 35 patients of those hospitalized for diabetes were Hispanic and only 14 were non-Hispanic. Obviously we have a serious problem in Texas, and it's more pronounced along the Texas-Mexico border and among Mexican Americans. Children along the Texas-Mexico border cannot wait any longer. We hope you give serious consideration to House Bill 3618. Thank you."

Rodriguez spoke next about his experience implementing coordinated school health programs in the San Antonio ISD, and the favorable impact those programs had on the health of the children.

When Treviño's turn arrived, he spoke about the medical model not being able to stop the number of new cases of type 2 diabetes being diagnosed among adults and children.

Last to go was Saldaña, who presented the Bienestar health textbooks to demonstrate what a coordinated school health curriculum consisted of. The committee members looked through the books with interest.

When the vote came back, the committee was unanimous in its support of the bill (5 Yeas and 0 Nays).

'EXPERT' OPINION

Legislators depend on the expert opinion of state agency staff to guide them in their decision-making of what bills to accept or reject.

Without the support of state bureaucrats, a bill passage is almost unlikely.

It was Monday morning, April 23, 2007 when Saldaña walked into Treviño's office. Treviño immediately handed Saldaña the newsletter of the Texas Diabetes Council.

"Look at page two," Treviño asked Saldaña. "What do you see missing there?"

Saldaña read through the bills listed under the "Diabetes on the Agenda for Texas Legislature" section of the newsletter.

"I don't see HB 3618 here," Saldaña said, clearly confused. "How could the Council miss mentioning something so relevant to their mission?"

"Every legislative year, the Texas Diabetes Council people go through the entire agenda, and study in detail every bill related to diabetes surveillance, screening, and education," Treviño explained. "They know about Raymond's bill, and if they didn't mention it here, it is because they don't support it," he analyzed.

"Why not? I don't get it," Saldaña responded, totally perplexed. "House Bill 3618 addresses the high levels of type 2 diabetes of children along the Texas-Mexico border, it asks for evaluation measures, and any evidence-based program is welcome to participate. Why would they have a problem with the bill?"

"Because the Texas CATCH program has no evidence of decreasing blood sugars, and the people running the Texas Diabetes Council don't want it excluded."

"Tough shit," Saldaña declared.

Three days later, Saldaña received a call from Laura Salcedo.

"Hi Dave, I just got a visit from a Margaret Pacillas. She is from El Paso, and a member of the Texas Diabetes Council."

When Saldaña heard, "Texas Diabetes Council," he remembered his recent conversation with Treviño. He immediately asked, "What did she want?"

"She has a problem with House Bill 3618."

"What's her problem?"

"That it's too narrow in scope."

"It's too narrow in scope?" Saldaña echoed.

"I think she meant geographically," Salcedo clarified.

Saldaña shook his head. "The bill focuses on the Texas-Mexico border, which has the highest rates of diabetes in the world. To go statewide with the implementation would be cost-prohibitive and self-destructive. No legislator would go for the exorbitant budget that would be needed to cover the entire state."

"The Texas Diabetes Council endorsement of House Bill 3618 is important for other legislators to support it. She left me her cell number and e-mail. Please call her as soon as you have an opportunity."

Saldaña paid Treviño a visit to inform him about the phone conversation.

"It doesn't make sense," Treviño exclaimed. "She's from El Paso, and this bill is for El Paso. Why would she cast aside programs that could offer favorable health outcomes for the children in her territory?"

"We need to call her now, Dr. Treviño," exclaimed Saldaña in an exasperated tone of voice. "Maybe she can explain to us better what the problem is."

Treviño picked up the phone and called Pacillas's cell number. The voicemail picked up, so he left a message. Pacillas did not return the call immediately, and he waited an hour before calling Dr. Phil Huang. Huang was the Department of State Health Services' Chief of the Bureau of Chronic Disease Prevention and Control and the state agent that oversaw the TDC. His secretary answered and responded that he was in a meeting next door, and not available.

Treviño then called Dr. Victor Gonzalez, a TDC board member, at his office in McAllen; his secretary also said that he was in Austin at a meeting.

Treviño looked at Saldaña with sudden suspicion. "Dr. Huang and Dr. Gonzalez are in Austin at a meeting, and Pacillas is not answering. I can almost bet these guys are together plotting a plan to derail House Bill 3618."

Treviño picked up the phone again and called Huang's secretary and firmly told her that it was very important for Huang to call him right after he came out of his meeting.

Saldaña and Treviño were sitting in Treviño's office waiting by the phone when Dr. Hector Gonzalez, the Director of the Laredo Health Department, unexpectedly walked in around five in the afternoon.

Saldaña and Treviño were surprised and happy to see him.

"What are you doing here?" Saldaña asked Gonzalez.

"I was driving to Laredo from Austin, and just stopped by to say hello," Gonzalez answered.

"What an opportune time!" Saldaña said loudly. "You're not going to believe it."

"What is it now?" Gonzalez replied suspiciously.

"The Texas Diabetes Council people are going around the Texas

Capitol questioning legislators about their support for House Bill 3618."

"Well, why didn't they call me?" Gonzalez said, his face making a grimace. "I brought the idea to Representative Raymond, and if they had any questions they should've called me."

It was five-thirty in the afternoon when Treviño got a call on his cell phone; the caller ID read Department of State Health Services.

"This is probably Huang," Treviño said, and rapidly answered the phone.

"Dr. Treviño, this is Phil Haung, and I am here with Dr. Larry Harkless and Cassandra De Leon," Huang said through a speaker phone.

Harkless was the chairman of the TDC board, and De Leon had replaced Ozias as Director of the TDC.

"Hey Phil, I'm here with David Saldaña and Dr. Hector Gonzalez," Treviño said. "I'm going to put you on a speaker phone."

Treviño put his cellular on speaker phone and laid it on his round conference table. Saldaña and Gonzalez moved in close about the table.

"We got a call from Representative Guillen's office informing us that Margaret Pacillas was there representing the Texas Diabetes Council," Treviño said in a polite manner. "Their understanding was that the Texas Diabetes Council had a concern with House Bill 3618. That's why I called. Maybe we can answer some of your concerns or questions."

"We have two concerns with the bill," Huang responded. "One is that it's too narrow in focus and it does not address the problem statewide. And second is that there is already another program operating in the border, and this bill would exclude the other program from participating."

"This bill is to prevent diabetes, and the Texas-Mexico border has the highest rates of diabetes," (Hector) Gonzalez replied. "That's why it's being proposed. Also, to take this bill statewide would be too costly. It just wouldn't fly."

"Does the other program have any evidence of lowering blood glucose in children?" Treviño asked directly, already knowing the answer.

"I, ahh, I don't know," Huang stuttered but then asked, "Would the authors be willing to remove the words 'evidence-based' from the bill?"

Treviño looked at Gonzalez and Saldaña, while Saldaña, without saying a word, made an angry facial expression and shook his head and right index finger violently.

Treviño put his two hands on the edge of the round table and bent over to get closer to the cellular phone. "Why would the authors want to lower their standards for these children?" he answered.

"Listen, Roberto," Harkless burst out angrily, "you made a big mistake in going around us. You should've brought that bill to us first. If you would've come to us, we would've reviewed and considered it."

"Larry—" Gonzalez tried to interject, but Harkless wouldn't allow it.

"Roberto, just because you get these large NIH grants you think you can tell the state what diabetes programs to implement," Harkless blasted.

"Larry—"

Treviño tried to speak up too, but Harkless simply raised his voice and began shouting. Treviño looked at Gonzalez, shrugged, and raised his hands in disbelief.

"Roberto, you need to understand that it's the Texas Diabetes Council that decides what diabetes programs operate in Texas, and not you. You come across very strong pushing your programs forward, but without our authority you are not going to succeed," he emphasized. "The pharmaceutical companies come through us to get their drugs on the Texas Diabetes Council treatment algorithm. If you want your programs in the schools, you're gonna have to come through us."

"Larry," Treviño finally got a comment in, "it should not be who's got what power, it should be about effective performance."

This comment incited Harkless even further.

"You don't tell me what it's about! I'm the chair of the Texas Diabetes Council, and I don't need the director of a small non-profit telling me what it's about."

Harkless went on for another five minutes without letting the others talk.

"Larry, Dr. Treviño didn't originate this bill," Gonzalez finally was able to interject. "*I* did. *I* went to Representative Raymond and planted the seed. The Texas Diabetes Council has done nothing for the Texas-Mexico border. We just hear needs assessments and surveillance from the council, but no one talks about interventions. The South Texas population is fed up with assessments and surveillance. What we need is evidence-based programs, and that is why we approached Dr. Treviño. It was not the other way around."

There was silence at the other end of the line after the callers

• DR. ROBERTO P. TREVIÑO •

heard that Dr. Treviño was not the initiator of the bill, as they had envisioned.

"And about not keeping you informed," Gonzalez continued, "I spoke with Dr. David Lakey in early March. I told him about House Bill 3618, and he was supportive of it."

Lakey, as the new commissioner of health, was responsible for overseeing the TDC.

Treviño brought the conversation back to where they started. "Phil, how can we work together to take school health programs with best practices to high-risk children living along the Texas-Mexico border? We need a position from the Council on House Bill 3618. You know and we know that legislators put a lot of weight on what you guys have to say about a legislative bill," Treviño acknowledged. "I know you alone may not be able to give us a position, but can we have a conference call with the board members to get their opinion? David and I can drive to Austin and conference in from your office."

"Yes, we can get a conference call set up with the board members to get their opinion," Huang acquiesced. "Cassandra will get some dates and pass them around."

As soon as the call ended, Treviño looked at Gonzalez and Saldaña and said as he shook his head, "Huang is the Director of the state's Chronic Disease and Prevention Department, and he doesn't know if the Texas CATCH program has evidence of lowering blood glucose?"

"Who is Larry Harkless?" Saldaña then asked.

"Harkless is to blacks what Sanchez is to Latinos," a disillusioned Treviño answered. "The type of person who, once they have a badge on their chest, forgets where they came from."

Indeed, Harkless continued to lobby hard against a bill that would support children and those living in poverty. Harkless was the past president of the South Texas Chapter of the American Diabetes Association (ADA), and when he found out that the ADA had provided a letter supporting HB 3618, he began calling Elizabeth Tobias, its current director. He left messages on her answering machine inquiring about the ADA's support of House Bill 3618—and Tobias sent Treviño the following e-mail wanting to know more about the matter:

> I'm curious—what was Texas Diabetes Council's role or opinion on this? Dr. Harkless called and left a couple of messages wanting to discuss my letter with him. We have not connected—just wanted to see if you could shed some light on this. Thanks

Treviño responded with an e-mail telling her of the $4 million the TDC gave the Texas CATCH program without there being any bidding or competing, and without the program having ever measured a blood sugar. He also sent her a copy of the NEEMA paper published three weeks prior in the *Journal of the National Medical Association*.

SAYING ONE THING, BUT DOING ANOTHER

It was a Tuesday morning in May 2007 when Saldaña and Treviño walked into the Texas Department of State Health Services (DSHS), formerly the Texas Department of Health. De Leon had set up a conference call meeting between Treviño, Saldaña, and (Hector) Gonzalez and the Texas Diabetes Council staff and board members.

As the invitees walked into the grand pink marble lobby, they noticed a large portrait of former Commissioner of Health, William Reyn Archer III, hanging on the left.

"Look, Dave," Treviño commented with a grin as he walked toward the portrait. "Texas is the only state where a commissioner makes public ethnic or racial slurs (see page 15), and the state hangs his picture to honor him."

The two men went up the elevator and walked down a hallway until they reached Huang's office. Waiting there were Huang and De Leon. The board members reached for the conference call were Harkless, Victor Gonzalez, Dora Rivas and two others whose name the SHRC representatives did not clearly hear. Hector Gonzalez also called in.

"I think we can do more by working together than by working against each other," Treviño said loudly for the benefit of all the callers. "We really want to be part of the Department of Chronic Disease and Prevention. What you do and what we do complement each other. Our intention is to work with you."

"So is ours," Huang replied. "The purpose of the Texas Diabetes Council is to work with everyone, and not exclude anyone."

"The reason I called in for this conference call," Hector Gonzalez jumped to the point, "is because Representative Guillen's office staff asked us to work with you. How can we get the support of the Texas Diabetes Council for House Bill 3618? Representative Guillen, and indeed all of us, value your position. What do we need to do to add House Bill 3618 to your list of bills that the Texas Diabetes Council supports?"

"The Department of State Health Services does not support one bill over another," Huang clarified.

• DR. ROBERTO P. TREVIÑO •

"Well, Ms. Margaret Pacillas was in Guillen's office representing the Texas Diabetes Council," Treviño said as he looked at Huang with a grimace. "According to a staff from his office, she had a problem with the bill."

"The Texas Diabetes Council is not the Department of State Health Services," Huang responded carefully.

Treviño knew that the TDC was an arm of the DSHS, and that Huang had both hands on the TDC operations. But Treviño tried not to be argumentative.

"Dr. Huang, how can we work together on this bill?" Treviño persisted.

"Well, our biggest problem with this bill is the money," Huang said, bringing up a new roadblock. "The total budget for the Department of Chronic Disease and Prevention is $7 million, and House Bill 3618 would take away from that budget."

"No, that's not correct," Saldaña responded quickly. "The bill comes with a fiscal note of $3 million, and that would come from another pool. It will not subtract from your budget. This money would be in addition to your budget."

"Oh," Huang responded. "That had not been made clear to us."

"Dr. Huang, since this is a diabetes prevention program, it needs to come through your department. We want to put you in control," Treviño said, trying to make it become more of a partnership.

"Well, if it doesn't take away from our budget, I'm okay with it," Huang agreed.

"Because the bill does request measurements, this is an opportunity for our center to work closely with the Texas Diabetes Council to track obesity rates in the schools," Treviño reminded everyone present on the call.

Dora Rivas, who was a TDC board member and had experience implementing the Texas CATCH program in Brownsville, interrupted the information flow because she had to excuse herself.

"I have another commitment and I need to get off the line but I've already made up my mind about supporting the work Dr. Treviño does," she said. "The biggest difference between the CATCH program and the Bienestar program is that the Bienestar staff measures health outcomes in all the schools they operate and the CATCH people do not. Before I took the position at Dallas ISD, I was the director of food services at Brownsville ISD. The CATCH people tried to implement their program in Brownsville ISD, and the two years I was there, I never saw them take a single measure to evaluate the effectiveness of their program.

Forgotten Children: A True Story of How Politicians Endanger Children

But when I hear about the Bienestar, it seems they're always measuring. And that's a great thing."

After she offered this praise and support, she hung up.

The call continued to go well from that point forward, with everyone sounding supportive of the bill.

Thinking that the TDC people were now supportive of House Bill 3618, Saldaña went to Guillen's office two days later to inform his office staff of the good news. But to Saldaña's surprise, Laura Salcedo had a new flyer released that morning by the TDC listing the bills they supported. House Bill 3618 was not on the list. Again, Huang had said one thing—and done another.

While this hypocrisy incensed Hector Gonzalez, Treviño, and Saldaña, they knew that the bill—although it would be hard—could continue moving forward without the support of state staffers.

TRICKY POLITICS

After HB 3618 was approved by the Border and International Affairs Committee, it was up to Speaker of the House Tom Craddick to refer the bill to the Calendars Committee. The Calendars Committee members would move the proposed bill to the house floor for a vote (second reading). If the Calendars Committee did not schedule the bill for a hearing, the bill would die.

It was May 2007, and Saldaña was in the SHRC program building waiting for Treviño with a newspaper section in his hand. As Treviño walked into the room, Saldaña looked up at Treviño and said, "Dr. Treviño, I have some bad news.

"What do you mean, 'bad news'?" Treviño asked quickly.

"To stay alive, House Bill 3618 needs Guillen and Craddick behind it, and a group of house representatives, lead by Jim Pitts (R-Waxahachie), Jim Keffer (R-Eastland) and Byron Cook (R-Corsicana), are about to oust Tom Craddick as Speaker of the House," Saldaña replied in a sad tone of voice. "Without Craddick, the bill will die."

"*Chingao*," ("damn"), Treviño whispered as he scratched his head.

"This is unbelievable," Saldaña said, justifiable angry. "The day we went to testify before the Borders Committee, I noticed men in expensive suits lobbying for the alcohol beverage, the telecom, and the oil industries and you know what? They'll probably get everything they want. But when it comes to the children of the poor, everything that will help them gets easily washed away by the political currents."

While Saldaña had accurately predicted the political battle that would come, the outcome he feared was not to be.

• DR. ROBERTO P. TREVIÑO •

Indeed, the projected battle got fierce and the two mostly Republican camps did go at each other in late May 2007. Craddick's opponents tried to remove him by calling a special session to vote to eject him from the chair of the Speaker. Craddick, in turn, refused to call for that special session, saying that as Speaker of the House, he alone had the authority to schedule sessions. As it turned out, his opponents never ended getting their way. Guillen and Craddick won, and got HB 3618 to the house floor. It went through its two readings (see chart in page 239) and at the end, it received 139 Yeas and 1 Nays.

The bill had gone over a hill; it now needed to go over a mountain— the Texas Senate.

Chapter 16

PROTECTING THE BORDER CHILDREN: THE SENATE

HURDLING FORWARD
HB 3618 had successfully hurdled past the house committee, house calendars, and house floor; now it was moving to the senate for approval.

Having gone this far was an accomplishment in and of itself. By this stage of the process, sixty percent of the bills proposed to Texas's house usually become dead in the water.

At the end of Wednesday, May 16th, 2007, Saldaña was leaving the Capitol. As he was exiting the first floor, Senator Judith Zaffirini (D-Laredo) and her aide, Jessica Ramos, were walking by him. When they noticed him, both gave him the "thumbs up" sign. He approached them to find out precisely what that signal was in reference to.

Zaffirini was an extremely successful representative of the people, having already spent twenty years in the senate. In addition, she was a member of the Health and Human Services (HHS) committee, and the Senate Finance committee, who had offered to carry, or move, HB 3618 through the Senate.

Now, with a huge smile on her face, Zaffirini reported, "Let Dr. Treviño and Dr. Gonzalez know they need to be ready to testify tomorrow at nine in the morning for the Health and Human Services Committee."

The hurdles for HB 3618 had only gotten higher and higher as it moved along in the approval process. The next hurdle would be a monumental one, as Jane Nelson was chairwoman of the HHS committee. Nelson had introduced Senate Bill 19 in the 2001 session, and allowed the CTN people to use her bill to claim exclusivity for the Texas CATCH program.

• DR. ROBERTO P. TREVIÑO •

Saldaña and Treviño arrived at the Texas Capitol at 8:30 a.m. on Thursday, May 17th, where they met up with Hector Gonzalez in the cafeteria. He was also planning to testify.

The three men walked over to Zaffirini's office, where the elegantly-dressed woman greeted them in a traditional black suit. When they sat down, she cautioned her guests to be sure not to use the Texas-Mexico border community as just research subjects through the bill. There would be no benefits to universities, and the community, just coming in and collecting data if the population, with its health problems, was left unchanged.

Dr. Gonzalez assured her that this was not the intention of this bill.

When they walked out of her office, the men went to the Senate gallery to observe the Senate legislative session. The gallery was like a nineteenth-century amphitheater. Spectators sat on the top to observe the senators quibbling on the floor below over bills and other matters of public concern.

While they were waiting, Gonzalez stepped out to receive a call. Gonzalez spent so long on the phone that Saldaña and Treviño walked outside to see if Gonzalez had any important information relevant to what was going to happen today.

When Gonzalez saw the two men approaching him, he gave them a look of dismay.

"That was Jessica Ramos on the phone," Gonzalez said, pausing to take a deep breath. "Senator Shapleigh wants to exclude El Paso from House Bill 3618."

"Shit!" exclaimed Saldaña. "Why on earth would he do that? This bill is going to bring much-needed help to children in his district."

"I told you guys to expect the worse, so don't be surprised by this," Treviño reminded Saldaña and Gonzalez. "Let's just go over to his office and find out why."

Shapleigh was not in, but Ruben Vogt, his legislative aide, was.

"Ruben, we were just informed that Senator Shapleigh wants to pull El Paso out of House Bill 3618," Saldaña explained. "Why would he do that?"

"El Paso is implementing the Texas CATCH program," Vogt said. "They came out with a study showing that they prevented obesity in El Paso children."

Treviño jumped in to explain the results. "Ruben, the author of that study, Karen Coleman, gave me a draft of the manuscript before it was published. Although the CATCH people gave $1.4 million to the four elementary schools in the program, only thirty-nine percent of

Forgotten Children: A True Story of How Politicians Endanger Children

the teachers actually implemented the Texas CATCH program on their campuses. They also had a low turnout when it came to participation by the food service staff and parents. According to Dr. Coleman, the reason for the poor participation was the lack of bilingual and culturally appropriate material. The senator needs to know this so that he can make better decisions for El Paso children."

Treviño then handed Vogt a copy of a PowerPoint presentation prepared by Coleman.

Vogt tried reaching Shapleigh right then to give him this news, but he was unsuccessful, so Saldaña, Treviño, and Gonzalez walked over to Representative Joe Pickett's office (D-El Paso).

Pickett was not happy when he found out Shapleigh was excluding El Paso, and he threatened to hold back some of Shapleigh's bills if Shapleigh did not support House Bill 3618.

Saldaña, Treviño, and Gonzalez then walked up to the Senate floor hoping to encounter Shapleigh. The three were standing in the Capitol rotunda when they saw Shapleigh walk by.

Treviño called him over and asked him, "Senator, why would you remove El Paso from House Bill 3618?"

Shapleigh stared at Treviño with disdain. "I have five years and millions of dollars invested in the Texas CATCH program. I am not going to let my reputation and investment be ruined by one house bill."

Shapleigh turned around and walked away without waiting for a response.

Treviño looked at Saldaña and Gonzalez and said, "And what about the children!"

Treviño quickly pursued Shapleigh, and knowing that Shapleigh was fluent in Spanish, said, *"Senador, y los niños que! El programa que usted apolla no le ha hecho provecho a los niños. El house bill del Representante Raymond propone traer programas con evidencia a El Paso. Por favor no lo bloque,"* ("Senator, and what about the children! The program you support has not given the children many benefits. Representative Raymond's house bill proposes to bring evidence-based programs to El Paso. Please, don't block it.") Treviño begged as he walked along side with him, but Shapleigh kept walking around the rotunda, keeping his face straight and ignoring Treviño.

"El Bienestar es el unico programa que a bajado el azucar a los niños y es bilingue. Por favor considere otros programas. Usted va hacer un gran error al no considerar otros programas mas efectivos y mas culturalmente apropiados." ("The Bienestar is the only program shown to decrease blood sugars in children and it is bilingual. Please consider

other programs. You will make a great mistake by not considering other more effective and more culturally-appropriate programs.")

Shapleigh's facial expression turned to one of anger, and he turned around to look at Treviño.

"Where are you from?" the senator snarled.

"From San Antonio," Treviño responded.

"Well, I'm from El Paso, so don't tell me what we need in El Paso."

With that, the senator walked right into the Senate gallery.

Treviño shook his head and turned around to walk back to where Saldaña and Gonzalez were waiting anxiously.

"What did he say?" Saldaña queried.

With a shake of his head and in a voice that visibly trembled, Treviño pronounced, "He doesn't give a shit about the children. He is more worried about his reputation."

The three men walked in silence back to the Capitol's cafeteria to wait for their turn to present.

STALLING IN THE SENATE

The Senate HHS committee started around seven o'clock in the evening. Members of the committee were Jane Nelson (Chair), Bob Deuell, M.D. (Vice-Chair), Kyle Janek, Robert Nichols, Dan Patrick, Eliot Shapleigh, Carlos Uresti, Royce West, and Judith Zaffirini.

As Chair, Jane Nelson started the meeting, and the guests began testifying for or against a multitude of bills. HB 3618 was scheduled to be heard around eight o'clock, but Nelson kept moving it down on the schedule. It was not until ten-thirty at night—after all the other bills had been heard—that she finally called up HB 3618.

The audience was gone; only a few committee members remained. By this point, Gonzalez, Saldaña, and Treviño were drained after what had already happened that day. But the men were determined to persevere.

Gonzalez went up first, and spoke passionately of the medical problems along the Texas-Mexico border, and the need for early age interventions. Then Saldaña shared his experience as a high school health education teacher, and the need that existed in the schools for more teacher-friendly school material. Treviño spoke of the diabetes medical treatment model being expensive, and how often it produced poor outcomes. He compared it against the better results observed in early age interventions.

After their presentations, the men went up to the front to answer questions. At this point, the room was nearly empty, and the few committee members left had no questions. Nelson adjourned the hearing, and the committee members stood up, and walked out the back door.

There were three potential outcomes from this hearing: the legislators would not vote on it and let it die; they would vote for it; or they would vote against it. The decision was usually made within the next work day of the hearing.

It was a depressing night for the bill's advocates. Because of the history between Nelson and the CTN, they were suspicious that Nelson was going to leave the bill without a vote, so that it would die in committee. And that to conceal her plan, she had moved the bill until last, to clear the chamber of audience and committee members.

When the meeting adjourned without a vote, Gonzalez informed Saldaña that if the bill did not go for a vote the following day, it would die. He advised him to return to Austin the next day to request a vote from HHS committee members. Gonzalez wanted the committee members to show the public if they considered the growing number of new cases of type 2 diabetes among youths living along the Texas-Mexico border to be a public health concern.

As requested, Saldaña drove back to the Texas Capitol the next day (Friday, May 18th), reaching the building by ten in the morning. The first office he visited was Nelson's, where he encountered Anna Libertino, Nelson's aide. He begged her to get the Chairwoman to have a vote on the bill. Libertino was taciturn, and did not offer an encouraging response.

Saldaña next met with Scott Kibbe, Deuell's aide. Saldaña hoped Deuell would have a better understanding of the disease and its potential treatments considering he was a physician.

Scott commented to Saldaña that the bill might not end up going for a vote, and his understanding was that this was because of the fiscal note that was attached.

Next Saldaña walked over to Zaffirini's office. As he walked into Zaffirini's office, Jessica Ramos was just walking out.

"Jessica, please ask Senator Zaffirini to get Senator Nelson to vote on House Bill 3618," Saldaña pleaded.

"David, I just got off the phone with Jo Cassandra Cuevas, Shapleigh's legislative aide," Ramos explained with a serious face and in a stern tone of voice. "Senator Shapleigh told her that we had to compromise."

"What does he mean by, 'compromise.'" Saldaña said with a sigh.

"Senator Shapleigh's office wants to leave out El Paso, and wants the language 'evidence-based' removed from the bill."

"We will do anything to keep this bill, for South Texas children, alive," Saldaña said in a resigned tone. "I will call Dr. Gonzalez and Dr. Treviño to amend the bill with the new language."

Saldaña called Dr. Gonzalez and Gonzalez agreed. Gonzalez's first objective was to provide the children of Laredo with some health program.

Saldaña then called Treviño.

"Dr. Treviño, I just met with Jessica Ramos, and she said Shapleigh wants to amend the bill to exclude El Paso and remove the words, 'evidence-based' from the bill."

At this point an argument ensued.

"It is up to Dr. Gonzalez but in my opinion, Shapleigh can remove El Paso from the bill but we should not lower the standards for those children," Treviño responded angrily.

"Dr. Treviño, the bill will die if we refuse."

"I'd rather it die than give the children watered-down ineffective programs," Treviño said clearly and unequivocally.

"Come on, Dr. Treviño," Saldaña argued, "I'm here trying to make the impossible happen! You are not being very helpful."

"David," Treviño shouted back, "of what use are health programs without proven results to the children?"

"If the bill doesn't go for a vote today, it will die. Our only chance is this amendment!" Saldaña yelled angrily.

Treviño finally conceded. "Okay, David, I will help by writing a draft amendment, and I will send it to Dr. Gonzalez for his approval."

"I know it's hard to compromise like this," Saldaña sympathized, "but we need to get the children *something*! The Capitol is filled with large corporate lobbyists competing for public money, but no one is here representing children living in poverty. We need to help them. So please send the draft to Laura Salcedo's e-mail address. I'll get it from her."

Treviño drafted the following amendment to HB 3618:

> In the best interest of Texas children this amendment specifies that funds will be appropriated to the participating school districts along the Texas-Mexico border so they can purchase an approved Texas Education Agency coordinated school health program of their choice. Because type 2 diabetes rates are increasing

along the Texas-Mexico border, selected programs will have <u>two years to demonstrate evidence that they have decreased blood glucose levels or diabetes rates</u> among the targeted high-risk children population.

Saldaña took the amended draft to Cuevas. He tried to convince her to convince Shapleigh not to pull out El Paso, because it was not in the best interest of children, but his plea fell on deaf ears. She too had her marching orders.

Saldaña walked over to Senator Carlos Uresti's office, where he talked to Diana Martinez, his aide. He asked her to ask Uresti to request a vote on the bill. But as Uresti was new in the Senate, he would not have the seniority to stand up to the icons—Nelson and Zaffirini.

Saldaña approached Senator Royce West's office next. He met up with his aide, David Quinn, who did not show much interest in requesting a vote. Zaffirini seemed like the only hope. He ran down to her office where he met with Amelia Crawford, another of Zaffirini's aides.

"Amelia, do you have any updates on House Bill 3618?" Saldaña said with desperation.

Crawford paused for a minute before she said with a sad face, "We just got information that the bill was not put on the schedule for a vote."

"Why not?" Saldaña asked, but then he saw Jessica Ramos walk out of a room. Knowing that Ramos was the right hand of Senator Zaffirini, Saldaña walked over to her and asked, "Could you please have Senator Zaffirini ask Senator Nelson to put the bill up for a vote? It's important that we see the position of the committee members on this bill."

Ramos's face was expressionless as she replied. "Senator Nelson does not want to call this bill for a vote. There is nothing we can do."

Saldaña immediately ran upstairs to the Senate Gallery. From the Gallery he saw Uresti down on the senate floor. When Uresti looked up and caught Saldaña's stare, Uresti shrugged and shook his head, indicating the bill was dying and nothing could be done.

Dejectedly, Saldaña walked downstairs to the Senate lobby. When he spied Van de Putte walking out of the gallery, his hopes were rekindled, and he moved forward quickly.

"Senator, can you check if the Health and Human Services Committee is going to vote on House Bill 3618?"

Van de Putte had the seniority to exert some pressure on the committee members, but she chose not to, responding instead, "Don't feel badly. You should see how many of my bills didn't get a vote."

Saldaña next placed a call to Anna Libertino, Nelson's aide. Only Jane Nelson could release the lever for a vote on the bill. "Anna, we need a vote on this bill," Saldaña persisted. "This bill is too important to the health of Texas-Mexico border children, and to do nothing would be harmful to their health."

"David, we already told you the Senator's decision. You need to respect that," she said flatly.

"Dr. Gonzalez and Dr. Treviño are requesting a vote on this bill and the Senator is refusing," Saldaña said, forcefully. "When a renowned authority on children's type 2 diabetes and a health department director speak, politicians need to listen. There is no way a politician can know more than physicians about diabetes in children."

"Are you suggesting that Senator Nelson doesn't listen to health experts when it comes to making decisions on children's health?" Libertino responded, clearly upset. "I know you're passionate about the bill, but that is just *your* opinion. There are many legislative issues that come into place when making a decision."

"It's not *my* opinion," Saldaña objected quickly. "It's the results of a large NIH trial showing there is a program out there decreasing blood sugars in high-risk children."

Despite his begging, pleading, and arguing, Saldaña got nowhere. The doors had closed on House Bill 3618.

DEAD IN THE WATER

Driving back that very evening to San Antonio, Saldaña placed a call to Treviño at around seven o'clock.

At that time, Treviño was sitting at La Margarita restaurant in El Mercado. The evening was beautiful so he and his wife, Maria del Carmen, were sitting outside in the patio to have their dinner.

They were waiting to place their order when Treviño received the call.

"Hey David, where are you?" Treviño asked first.

"I'm driving back," he replied in a weary tone of voice.

"How is the bill? Did they vote?" Treviño wondered.

"The bill is dead, Dr. Treviño."

Treviño jumped off his chair and walked into the grounds of the historical Mexican village El Mercado to avoid being overheard. He did not want his wife to worry unnecessarily about these political matters.

"It can't be!" he denied.

"It is."

"Did you talk to Zaffirini's staff?"

"Yes, they told me there's nothing they can do."

"How about Uresti?" Treviño pressed on.

"I saw him on the senate floor, and he just shook his head."

"Call Dr. Gonzalez; maybe he can get Raymond and Guillen to move on it?"

"I did. He couldn't even say a word when I told him the news. He's shell-shocked."

"How about Leticia Van de Putte? She's a heavy hitter," Treviño suggested.

"I spoke to her; all she offered was the following consolation: 'Look at all my bills that were killed'."

"'Look at all my bills that were killed'," Treviño echoed out loud. "What good does that do for children with diabetes? You would imagine she would be more sensitive seeing how often she has to prescribe diabetes drugs to the population!"

Treviño had run out of ideas, so the call fell silent for a while. Neither Saldaña nor Treviño wanted to hang up, though. They were hoping one or the other would come up with a solution to revive the bill.

"David, there's got to be a pulse," Treviño pressured.

"Dr. Treviño, it, is—a flatline."

Silence ensued again, but still, neither wanted to hang up. That would make everything seem even more final.

"Did you give Nelson the amendment? Did you talk to her people?"

"Yup. It was just a bluff. They already had their minds set, and they made us do all that extra work for nothing."

No one spoke for a while.

"Okay David, let's call it quits. Your conduct has been admirable. Doing all this from the bottom of your heart for these children, and taking it this far, should be considered a great accomplishment."

Saldaña did not say a word in response. The words were not going to make him feel better. He had been doing this for the children—and in his mind, he had failed.

YOU HAVEN'T HEARD THE LAST OF US.

The next morning was Saturday, May 19th and scheduled for this day was the end of the year *Tiendita* event, held on the grounds of the SHRC buildings.

The *Tiendita,* or "Little Store" in English, is an incentive system designed for the Bienestar and NEEMA children who participate in program activities and practice healthful behaviors. Throughout the program, Bienestar/NEEMA "bucks" are given to children who attend program activities or return sheets recording healthful behaviors. The children then can redeem the bucks at *La Tiendita* for merchandise. The merchandise is mostly donated new and used sports equipment, toys, school supplies, clothes, and shoes.

That day, the parking lots at SHRC were completely full with children and parents. As most program participants were from low-income families, it was a real treat for them to be able to redeem their play money with real merchandise.

When Saldaña and Treviño arrived around ten a.m. there was no time to discuss the matter of the dead bill. Help was needed in handling the crowds, and the men immediately jumped behind the counters to help "sell" merchandise. It was stimulating to see the children's faces filled with joy when their parents bought them the sports equipment or school supplies they wanted.

During the happy commotion, Treviño looked at Saldaña and promised, "We will move mountains for these children."

After the crowd diminished, Saldaña and Treviño, by instinct and without planning, went into their offices and started making phone calls and sending a barrage of e-mails to HHS committee members and their aides. The politicians still had not heard the last of Gonzalez, Saldaña, and Treviño.

Treviño sent the committee members the following e-mail:

> Pre-diabetes, blood glucose levels between 100-126 mg/dl, is a billable medical code. We estimate 4% of Texas-Mexico border children have pre-diabetes and they need medical attention. Society either pays $13,000 a child for medical care or pays $12 a child for an evidence-based health curriculum. But to leave these children without medical care would be substandard and unethical.

Gonzalez advised Saldaña to go back Monday and find another bill, relevant to the health issue at hand, where they could attach House Bill 3618. A way of resuscitating a demised bill is by a legislator agreeing to attach it to another bill that had already passed a Senate Committee, and it was ready for the senate floor for a vote.

Gonzalez also sent the following e-mail to the HHS committee members:

> For our children on the Texas-Mexico border this [youth-onset type 2 diabetes] is even more critical since up to 50% are underinsured, and without early detection and intervention at every opportunity, children become more vulnerable, adding to the health care burden. This is an opportunity to address a serious health care crisis.

Knowing only Nelson, as Chairwoman, could pull the lever for the bill's vote and hopefully passage, Treviño went directly to the source with the following e-mail:

> I am asking for a meeting with you in person so you can explain why a large number of children with pre-diabetes will be left untreated. I am open to any date on your calendar. Thanks

By Monday morning (May 21st), the computers of the HHS committee members and their aides were full of the men's e-mails. In addition, Saldaña was at the Capitol by seven forty-five that same morning. He wanted to make sure the aides opened up the messages, and gave them to their bosses.

His first visit was Nelson's office, where he met Amy Herzog, Nelson's chief of staff.

"Amy, Dr. Treviño and Dr. Gonzalez sent Senator Nelson an e-mail. It's very important that they receive those messages."

"David, we already—" she started saying when Saldaña abruptly interrupted.

"We need to have a medically-appropriate intervention for youth with type 2 diabetes along the Texas-Mexico border," Saldaña told her, with a stern voice and a serious face. "Dr. Treviño wants to schedule a meeting with Senator Nelson so she can tell him to his face why she won't put the bill up for a vote."

Herzog, looking somewhat intimidated by Saldaña's stern demeanor, replied, "I'll see what I can do."

"Dr. Gonzalez also wants a vote so he can see precisely which senator opposes putting an evidence-based health curriculum along the Texas-Mexico border," Saldaña persisted before their conversation ended.

Treviño also called Nelson's office and demanded to talk to Amy

• DR. ROBERTO P. TREVIÑO •

Herzog. Nelson's right hand reluctantly came to the phone.

"Ms. Herzog, I'm in my clinic this morning, and I've already seen eight patients with diabetes who have lost their eyesight, a limb, or kidney function. I'm here in the thick of it, treating all these complications while politicians are playing games with the lives of children. You need to get me an appointment with the Senator so she can tell me what plan the state has to treat youth-onset type 2 diabetes. I'm willing to drive up there right now."

Herzog had already been visited by Saldaña, and no doubt she did not want to incite another outburst.

"Yes, sir. I will let her know," she responded politely.

Treviño gave her his cell number so she could call him back directly.

In the meantime, Saldaña started running up and down the five-story staircase in the Capital building to continue driving home the need for a vote.

First he met with Martinez from Uresti's office. He told her the same thing he had told Herzog: "Open up your e-mail, and act upon Dr. Treviño's and Dr. Gonzalez's e-mails."

He then went to Deuell's office, where he met Scott Kibbe in the hallway. Saldaña handed Kibbe a copy of Treviño's e-mail, but Kibbe gave it back to Saldaña without reading it and raised his hands in a gesture of rejection.

"There is nothing I can do," Kibbe said, clearly upset. "You need to talk to Senator Zaffirini. The problem is the fiscal note that is attached."

"You need to show this to Dr. Deuell, and have him call Dr. Treviño," Saldaña insisted, shoving the e-mail right back into Kibbe's hands. "They need to talk physician to physician. He needs to explain how the state is going to care for all these children being diagnosed with type 2 diabetes along the Texas-Mexico border."

Then Saldaña spun around and walked away.

Around ten o'clock, Herzog called Treviño.

"Dr. Treviño, I talked to Senator Nelson, and she said that it was up to Senator Zaffirini."

"No, it's not, Amy," Treviño retorted, rebutting her suggestion. "Zaffirini supports this bill. It's Senator Nelson who is killing the bill."

Herzog paused, and with a trembling voice finally said, "Okay.... can you ask Senator Zaffirini to meet Senator Nelson on the senate floor?"

Treviño called Saldaña so that he could inform Zaffirini's staff that Nelson was ready to talk.

Saldaña rushed down the stairs to Zaffirini's office. He went up to a young lady named Jennifer, and asked for Jessica Ramos. But after Jennifer stepped into one of the offices, she came back immediately.

"Jessica can't talk to you. She's too busy."

Saldaña's hairs stood straight up. "Tell her that it's important that I talk to her. Senator Nelson is ready to talk to Senator Zaffirini about House Bill 3618."

"I'm sorry. She's too busy," Jennifer said, sitting down and starting to type. She refrained from giving Saldaña the courtesy of a direct look, but focused on the papers in front of her instead.

"We've got children with a disease that is going to kill them, and you're telling me that she's *too busy*," Saldaña said, raising his voice. "Let her know that the British Broadcast Channel (BBC) wants to broadcast a documentary on the NIH grant in Laredo. This is an opportunity for Senator Zaffirini to come out as a hero for children's health." [The BBC was interested in filming a documentary on the Bienestar study in Laredo.]

"I'm sorry, but—"

"If we don't get a vote, we are prepared to bring some media attention to this bill and, if necessary, attach it to a bill that has already passed in the Senate and going up for a vote in the House," Saldaña threatened. [A bill may start off in the Senate and then pass to the House for approval].

Jennifer looked up at Saldaña with an angry face, but did not respond.

Saldaña stormed out to the lobby to call Gonzalez and Treviño to see if perhaps they could get the word to Zaffirini to meet with Nelson.

Saldana had just received a call from Jorge Urby when he saw Ramos rushing toward him with an angry face. He asked Urby to hold on for a second.

"Don't you come into my office threatening my interns," she yelled furiously. "I don't want you stepping into our office anymore. You stay away. If we feel this bill is a good bill we will work it."

Her scolding left Saldaña speechless.

After she left, Ramos called Treviño to report, "Dr. Treviño, David came into our office and he was very rude with our staff. He also threatened to go to the media if Senator Zaffirini did not get this bill to a vote."

Treviño ignored the complaint and went right to the issue. "Did you inform Senator Zaffirini about meeting with Senator Nelson?"

She did not like that Treviño changed the subject, but answered appropriately. "She knows. She is going to meet with the Senator on the senate floor."

When Treviño got this favorable response from Ramos, he told her, "I'll talk to Dave and tell him to stay away."

Treviño called Saldaña immediately.

"David, you can't be pissing off these people! We need them on our wagon."

"Dr. Treviño, they needed to get off their asses," Saldaña said, unrepentant. "The bill was dead, and now it's being revived."

"Yes. In fact, Jessica just told me Senator Zaffirini will meet with Senator Nelson. They'll probably horse trade to get this bill to a vote."

"What do you mean by horse trading," Saldaña questioned.

"Zaffirini will support some of Nelson's bills if Nelson supports some of Zaffirini's bills," Treviño responded.

BATTLING ON ALL FRONTS

Saldaña also phoned Treviño to discuss another strategy.

"I'm still looking for a backup plan," Saldaña said. He was not willing to trust anyone or anything, even the meeting between Zaffirini and Nelson. "I'm going to visit Katharine Chambers, the chief of staff of Representative Pickett [co-author of House Bill 3618]. She had mentioned she was going to look into attaching House Bill 3618 to another, more viable one."

When Saldaña walked into Pickett's office, Chambers, a tall, attractive woman, greeted him with a big smile.

"David, I found a bill where we can attach our bill," she said with excitement. "But we have to attach our bill as an amendment immediately. There is no time to lose."

Saldaña's confidence about the bill going somewhere was boosted from Chambers' enthusiasm—and her idea. He nearly flipped when he heard she and Pickett would try to attach it to Nelson's Senate Bill 530—which increased physical activity in the schools. Once a bill receives approval in committee and goes to the senate floor, attachments to and amendments of the bill are more dependent on the senate floor than on the author alone—who in this case was Nelson. Although Nelson may not have liked it, it was still a chance to bypass her and carry House Bill 3618 further.

While Saldaña was with Chambers, she picked up the phone and called Lizette Montiel from Representative Raymond's office.

Forgotten Children: A True Story of How Politicians Endanger Children

"Hey Lizette, this is Katharine Chambers from Representative Pickett's office."

"Hi," responded Lizette with a dry tone of voice.

"I've been watching your bill, and it looks like it's slowed down. But it can be attached to Senate Bill 530 to save it," Chambers said in a charming, down-to earth manner. "We love your bill! In fact, it really rocks, girlfriend! Why don't you talk it over with your boss and tell him it was your idea?" she offered.

There were no indications of any enthusiasm for this proposal from Montiel.

As Chambers started giving the aide instructions of how to go about attaching a bill, Montiel interrupted her to say again in a dry tone, "I know the protocol."

"Oh, I apologize," Chambers said, backing down immediately, and not wanting to antagonize a potential partner in the fight to save House Bill 3618. "Well, let me know if we can do anything to help."

Later that morning, right before lunch, Saldaña received a call from Ramos.

"David, Senator Zaffirini wants to talk to you. She wants to meet you on the second floor just outside of the Senate Chamber," Ramos said solemnly.

Saldaña immediately called Treviño to inform him of the meeting.

"David, when you have her in front of you, call me," Treviño responded. "I need to talk to her."

"Dr. Treviño, I'm going to get chastised," Saldaña predicted despondently.

"David, I need to talk to her." Treviño emphasized, not interested in the possibility of Saldaña's scolding. He was only interested in Zaffirini's meeting with Nelson.

"Dr. Treviño, she is going to chastise me," Saldaña said yet again.

"You need to have your phone ready to dial when she is in front of you," Treviño continued, unperturbed.

Having gotten nowhere with Treviño, Saldaña went to the Senate Chamber and waited until Zaffirini came out with Ramos on her right side.

When the six-foot tall Saldaña walked up to her, he bent down to make sure he could hear what the four-foot-eight woman had to say to him.

"My staff tells me you have been intimidating them," she said smoothly. "Senator Nelson and I have been talking," she confirmed, "but we didn't have the votes. The votes now look more favorable. But let me tell you, it is almost unheard of for a bill to come this late and still be heard. Now, what's this I hear that you will do a negative campaign against me?" she said bluntly.

Saldaña's head, which had been bent down, shot straight up.

"I never said any such thing, Senator Zaffirini," Saldaña clarified, shocked that his words had been so misconstrued. "You are our champion! Why would I do that?"

But Zaffirini kept scolding Saldaña like a mother does to an unruly son.

"I also hear you've been saying rude things to Senator Nelson's staff."

"Well, I told them that they needed to listen to the experts who are treating type 2 diabetes in children," Saldaña replied, regaining his composure somewhat. "And that these children have a medical condition that needs a medical intervention."

"Let Dr. Gonzalez know that we are going to suspend the rules and take this bill for a vote," Zaffirini said, calmly, "and that we don't need your help anymore."

OSTRACIZED!

Saldaña had scheduled a late afternoon lunch meeting with Urby, former legislative aide to Representative Joaquin Castro, to tell him what had just transpired that day. Saldaña had no experience in the political process at the capitol, and frequently called Urby to ask questions.

"Was I wrong in pushing to get people to move on this bill?" Saldaña now wondered.

"It is Ramos's responsibility to get her constituents' bills moving, and to keep them informed," Urby offered in consolation. "There is nothing wrong in speaking out loud for the children."

"Do you think Zaffirini might sabotage this bill because of the pressure we placed, and my so-called 'rudeness' with her staff'?"

"At the end, this is her bill, and she will fight for it," Urby replied, knowing the inner workings of the political process. "It's a reflection on her."

Afterwards, Saldaña walked over to Guillen's office, but when he walked in, Laura Salcedo made a face as she whispered, "We got a call from the Mayor of Laredo's office to inform us that we are not allowed to talk to you."

Salcedo had been a great ally, and Saldaña did not want to get her in trouble. So he made a U-turn and went looking for another haven. He found one in Castro's office. He got himself set up there to receive e-mails from Dr. Gonzalez and Dr. Treviño, and to track the bill.

Later that same afternoon Treviño received a call from the Mayor of Laredo's office.

"Hi, this is Ronnie from the Mayor's office," a youngish-sounding voice said at the other end of the line. "We received a call from Senator Zaffirini's office. We need to inform you that Mr. David Saldaña is not allowed at Representatives Guillen and Raymond's or Senator Zaffirini's offices. We also prefer it if you too would stop calling their office. From now on, if either of you need anything, you must go through Dr. Gonzalez."

"But we are trying to get the children of Laredo a much needed health program," Treviño responded pleadingly.

"I'm sorry. The Senator does not want you and Mr. Saldaña around the Capitol."

"But the children of Laredo have no structured health curriculums in the schools; and now they will have an opportunity to receive one that is medically and culturally appropriate for them."

"I was told to give you that information and there is nothing I can do."

While Treviño certainly wasn't thrilled that he and Saldaña had been banned from the Capitol, Treviño was ecstatic that their efforts had helped resuscitate the bill. And, as Gonzalez could be a great spokesperson for the children, Treviño willingly backed off to comply with the orders.

THE CUT MAN

That evening, Treviño was working late at the SHRC when he received a call from Kloster. Treviño saw the name on the caller ID and thought Kloster was calling to congratulate them for resuscitating the bill.

"Dr. Treviño!" Kloster declared in a loud and angry voice after Treviño answered the phone. "We have looked at each other in the eye and made a gentleman's agreement. When I had you and the CATCH people in the same room [page 233], I made it clear that what was the past is past, and that we would start with a new set of rules. Well, you went behind my back and played politics with your program. Now you've put me in a difficult situation because of this screw-up."

Kloster continued berating Treviño for another five minutes, repeating essentially the same charges over and over.

Treviño remained mum as these charges were leveled against him. Finally he started pacing the room to think about how to end Kloster's tirade. This was a delicate situation because Kloster, as TEA's associate commissioner of school health programs, had the influence to find a way to remove the Bienestar program from school campuses. Treviño had to be very careful with his words.

In a soft and hesitant voice, Treviño said, "Jeff, you knew we were supporting this bill. In fact, I called and set an appointment with you in March to discuss the importance of this bill."

"Bullshit, Dr. Treviño, bullshit," was the angry retort. "My understanding was that this bill was going to go through the Department of State Health Services, not the Texas Education Agency."

Somewhere along the fourteen legislative steps, an amendment was made by a legislator that placed the bill under the TEA's coordinated school health programs. To Raymond and Guillen, the authors of House Bill 3618, it did not matter who operated the bill; what mattered was evidence-based programs operating along the Texas-Mexico border and accountability measures to determine its effectiveness.

"You knew this already, Jeff," Treviño said, gaining confidence and now raising his voice too. "I wasn't hiding anything! Why would I make an appointment and drive all the way to Austin on March 21 to inform you about this bill? Why would you be at the Border and International Affairs committee meeting on March 30 if it was not to answer questions about House Bill 3618?"

Kloster got quiet for a moment, but then became accusatory again. "What you did is no different than what you say the CATCH people did to you."

"There's a big difference, Jeff," Treviño said, firmly. "We don't have politicians writing in the name "Bienestar" in a draft, nor do we have bureaucrats interpreting the law as meaning the Bienestar program alone. With House Bill 3618, any program with high standards can come in and play."

"Don't give me that crap," Kloster said, unwilling to retreat. "The way that bill is written, only your program can participate. You're as big a politician as any of those in the capitol. You saw this as an opportunity to rake in money."

At this charge, Treviño became justifiably incensed.

"Jeff, I helped found a medical group that now has five clinics, sixteen physicians, and revenues of $6 million a year. If I want to rake in money, I go to the clinics and see patients. The government would rather pay me $80,000 a year to care for one patient on dialysis than pay me twelve dollars for one set of student's health textbooks. I'm losing money just taking the time to talk to you, but I do it anyway!" he retorted angrily.

Kloster appeared under some kind of pressure, as reflected in his following words. "We need to meet and we need to meet quickly. I need you and a representative from the Department of State Health Services in my office early tomorrow. What is the earliest you can be here?" Kloster asked.

"I can be there at 7:30 in the morning," Treviño promised.

"Well, you better get here because we need to talk," Kloster requested decisively before he hung up.

Treviño needed to release some of his own steam, so he called Saldaña. By then it was close to nine at night.

"David, Jeff Kloster just called and shitted all over me," said Treviño in a despondent tone of voice.

"Dr. Treviño, you can't afford to piss him off," Saldaña said in a loud tone of voice, more worried about Kloster and the power he wielded than about Treviño's feelings. "He's responsible for approving and disapproving school health programs at the TEA. He is the last guy you'd want to piss off."

"I know, and I agree! I had to swallow my pride and just take his heat," Treviño responded.

"What was he furious about?" Saldaña asked.

"I'm not precisely sure," Treviño said, still having a hard time trying to figure out what had just happened to piss Kloster off. "This is not the Jeff Kloster we know. He said we went behind his back and tried to slip the Bienestar into the bill."

"He knew we supported House Bill 3618," Saldaña said thoughtfully. "When we met with him, he seemed to know more about the bill than we did! So I don't understand what's going on either. How did the conversation end?"

"He wants to meet with us at 7:30 in the morning. Just you and I, and a representative from the Department of State Health Services."

Treviño and Saldaña arrived at the TEA at 7:20 a.m. on Tuesday, May 22, 2007. Waiting there for them were Kloster, Marissa Rathbone, and Anita Wheeler. Wheeler was the coordinator for the DSHS' School Health Services.

Kloster took the group to his office, where they sat down. He took out a tape recorder and placed it in the middle of the table. He introduced everyone in the meeting and picked up the conversation where he had left off the night before.

"Dr. Treviño, we had a gentlemen's agreement that we would play fair and not go behind each other's backs and play politics," Kloster said, breathing fast and his face getting red. "When you drove your bill into the legislative session, you broke that agreement. Now you've put me in a difficult situation."

"But Jeff—" Treviño tried to say, but Kloster interrupted.

"You listen to me," Kloster shouted. "This is my department and you will wait until I'm finished. Do you hear me?"

Treviño turned his face away from him and looked out the window, not answering. He couldn't believe he was being treated like this, but at the same time, he could not lose his temper. So he smiled instead as he reminded himself that he needed the TEA more than the TEA needed him.

"Do you hear me?" Kloster said, louder.

Although Treviño kept staring out the window, he nodded his head, not saying a word.

"I know you're a scientist but you're a politician too. Because of your politics, a fine man had to resign from the TEA," Kloster said, in reference to Fleming. "I'm not going to take that kind of shit here."

Treviño, with a derisive smile, turned his head to face Kloster and asked, "Can I talk now?"

"Yes, you can."

"I have e-mails showing you were kept informed about this bill," Treviño said. "You knew every step we took to support this bill. So it surprises me we're having this conversation."

"Yes, I did get the e-mails," Kloster acknowledged, "but it did not hit me until later that what you were doing was trying to secure a sole vendor bill."

"Jeff," Treviño said, raising his hand to stop him before he said anything else, "did the bill specify the name Dr. Treviño? Or did it have the name, Bienestar?"

Kloster shook his head negatively before he responded, "But the way it was written only your program could participate."

"What do you mean?" Treviño asked wrinkling his forehead.

"I mean, the words "bilingual" and "evidence-based" point only to your program."

"The bill was written with high standards to get those children the best school health programs available," Treviño replied quietly but firmly. "And if ours is the only program to have those standards, then only ours will participate."

"Dr. Treviño, you're the biggest politician I've ever met," Kloster pronounced, raising his voice again.

"Are you a politician?" Kloster asked Treviño.

Treviño did not answer this accusation.

"Are you a politician?" Kloster asked unrelentingly again.

Treviño narrowed his eyes and said, "If I am going to keep children from losing limbs and going blind, then yes, I'm the biggest politician you've ever met."

Saldaña saw the anger was escalating on both sides, and interjected. "Guys, we all want the same thing. We want the best health programs for the children. How do you suggest we accomplish that, Jeff?"

"House Bill 3618 has no business in the TEA's Coordinated School Health programs section (see page 241)," Kloster advised. "It should be removed from my department and be transferred to the Department of State Health Services. That's why I invited Ms. Wheeler to join us."

As Treviño needed to be in good standing with the TEA, he surrendered to Kloster's request.

"I agree, Jeff. This bill is more about treating a disease than about implementing an educational program. I have no problem putting it under the Department of State Health Services."

"Anita, do you have any problem with that?" Kloster asked.

"No, it's quite okay," she said. "We can bring it in."

"I will draft an amendment and deliver it to Senator Zaffirini later today," Kloster promised.

The meeting ended, and Kloster walked Treviño to the elevator. In a soft and friendlier voice Kloster said, "I hope you didn't take this personally."

Treviño turned to look at him and said, "Jeff, this is not about me. This is about the children who have no voice, and no one to speak for them."

SCREWED

The following day, the Senate's HHS committee voted unanimously to approve the bill, and on May 24th, 2007, the Senate passed it too. Many people, from those living in San Antonio to those based in Laredo, celebrated the passage. The staff of the SHRC and the City of Laredo Health Department staff were thrilled that a legislative bill that could deliver effective school health programs to children living in socially deprived communities along the Texas-Mexico border had passed in the Senate.

Yet Senator Raymond and Dr. Gonzalez still had three more hurdles for their bill to become law. They needed the Speaker of the House, the lieutenant governor, and the governor to sign it.

Because their previous pleas to the governor on behalf of the children of Texas had fallen on deaf ears, Treviño and Saldaña were skeptical that Perry would sign the bill. And when he did, it both surprised them and made them suspicious.

"David, call Representative Raymond's office and ask him if the $3 million fiscal note is still attached," Treviño asked quietly.

Saldaña went to place the call. When he returned to Treviño's office, he had a frightened look in his face.

"It's not," Saldaña said, visibly upset.

"Where is it?"

"His staff tried looking for it, but they couldn't find it," Saldaña answered.

"I'll call Anita Wheeler's office," Treviño said. "The Department of State Health Services is the fiscal agent, and they should know."

Treviño called Wheeler, but after she investigated she had no clue where the money had gone either.

Gonzalez called Zaffirini's office; Saldaña called Guillen's office. Neither of the legislators' offices reported knowing where the money was.

Gonzalez, Treviño, and Saldaña went down the list, calling politicians and bureaucrats; it seemed no one knew where the money had gone

No one knew until Deanna Hoelscher, a staff of Houston's UTSPH and member of the CTN, sent Gonzalez the following e-mail on June 4, 2007:

> I appreciate your email about the Bienestar program and your request to meet with me to further discuss the program and your results; however, I would first like to further clarify a few issues that you brought up in your email.
>
> The bill you have cited, HB 3618, is not associated with the Coordinated School program in Texas. As you know, the Texas Education Agency has approved four programs as Coordinated School Health Programs for elementary schools in Texas: CATCH, Bienestar, the Great Body Shop, and Healthy and Wise. All of these programs have been evaluated by the TEA and found to be appropriate for schools to implement to meet the current legislation. HB 3618 calls for a diabetes intervention pilot program and should not be associated with SB 19/1357/42 and SB 530 or the above referenced programs. As HB 3618 is an unfunded mandate and pilot

in nature, it is unclear how actions will proceed and how schools should act accordingly at this time. Certainly, one would want to know the outcome of the pilot test before issuing conclusive statements or recommendations to schools.

Funding to deliver evidence-based school health programs to high-risk children along the Texas-Mexico border had been stripped.

How could that happened? Who was responsible?

The final chapter will point to who may have been ultimately responsible for the events observed in this book.

• DR. ROBERTO P. TREVIÑO •

Chapter 17

WHO WAS RESPONSIBLE? INTEREST GROUPS, BUREAUCRATS OR POLITICIANS

This author's observation—based on people's acts, verbal communications, and documents—is that although children of color and those living in poverty in Texas had high rates of type 2 diabetes, they were isolated from a program shown to decrease blood sugars, thereby reducing the potential for controlling the onset of type 2 diabetes. These events occurred in Texas between the years 1997 and 2007.

What these children received instead was a program labeled, "a diabetes prevention program" despite its staff or trainers never having measured any participants' blood sugars. In addition, they received a health education program presented in a manner not relevant to their cultural lifestyle.

Who was responsible for this policy?

Policies are shaped by interest groups, bureaucrats, and politicians. Which of these three groups was ultimately responsible for endangering children of color and those living in poverty?

INTEREST GROUP

An *interest group* is an organized collection of people who seek to influence bureaucrats and politicians for the purpose of procuring public money and/or relaxing regulatory policies for their industry. The ability of interest groups to influence government is protected by the right to petition, which is in the First Amendment of the United States Constitution.

Examples of interest groups are lobby groups like the American Hospital Association, the American Medical Association, and the Pharmaceutical Research and Manufacturers of American. According to the OpenSecrets.org, the health care industry spent $2.3 billion between 1998 and 2006 to lobby U.S. bureaucrats and politicians. During this same time period, and among all lobby sectors, the health care industry was second only to the insurance industry in spending for lobbying activities.

The Social and Health Research Center and the CATCH Texas Network could be considered—to a much lesser degree—interest groups because they also sought to influence burcaucrats and politicians. Interest groups, for the most part, supply technical and scientific information to bureaucrats and politicians. This information is useful to government officials because it helps them make policy decisions based on evidence and best practices.

Since interest groups do not make the final decision of what laws to pass or what policies to implement, this group was less responsible than bureaucrats and politicians in depriving children at risk for diabetes of an effective diabetes control program.

BUREAUCRATS

Bureaucrats are non-elected officials employed by government institutions to staff and operate bureaus and departments designed to benefit the public interest. Bureaucracy is a cost to society, and society accepts this cost so long as bureaucrats perform their duties—which are to secure the well-being of the general public. Bureaucracy becomes inefficient when it implements policies or regulations that go against the public interest.

As revealed by this book, events occurred in which Texas bureaucrats implemented policies and regulations that went against the public interest, and favored a special interest. As examples: William Archer III, Commissioner of Health between 1997 and 2000, set grant review policies that eliminated a fair playing field in terms of competition, and instead set policies that favored the Texas CATCH program. The late Tommy Fleming, former Texas Education Agency Director of Health and Physical Activity, formed review committees to select coordinated school health programs with members stacked on the side of the Texas CATCH program. These are only two of many cases of bureaucratic malfeasance described in this book.

Although bureaucrats produced acts that went against the public interest, politicians are more at fault because they should have supervised and put a stop to these acts.

Forgotten Children: A True Story of How Politicians Endanger Children

POLITICIANS

Politicians are the chief executive officers (CEO) of the state. Politicians make and approve budgets, and hire and fire the head of government agencies. They are ultimately responsible for the acts of bureaucrats. The CEOs of the governmental agencies at the time of the events presented in this book were Former Governor and President George W. Bush (Bush Jr.). and Governor of Texas Rick Perry.

Bureaucrats, under the supervision of Bush Jr. and Perry, purposefully withheld from needy children of color and those living in poverty a program shown to decrease blood sugars, and approved and funded, through illicit means (as shown through the events in this book), one that did not. Perry, particularly, was informed about this misconduct on several occasions, but he decided to ignore the situation.

Motive: Eli Lilly and Company is the largest manufacturer of anti-diabetes drugs in the world, and the Bush family has had strong ties to Eli Lilly. A New York Times article, published on May 19, 1982, reported that George H. W. Bush (Bush Sr.) tried to arrange tax breaks for Eli Lilly even though he had a conflict of interest. Bush Sr. was a director of Eli Lilly, and Eli Lilly stocks were his most valuable stock holdings. Bush Sr. had been appointed to the Eli Lilly board by James C. Quayle, the father of former Vice-President Dan Quayle. The Quayle family owned controlling interest in Eli Lilly. The Supreme Court eventually ordered Bush Sr. to stop lobbying the IRS on behalf of Eli Lilly for tax breaks.

Bush Jr. was the clear front runner when it came to drug company contributions. According to the Center for Responsive Politics, drug manufacturers contributed $764,274 to the Bush Jr. Campaign in 2004. Former Board of Directors of Eli Lilly, or its affiliate companies, received key positions in the Bush Jr. administration. Donald Rumsfeld was named Secretary of Defense; Mitchell Daniels, Director of the Office of Management and Budget; Sidney Taurel, Homeland Security Advisory Council; and Randall Tobias, Global AIDS Coordinator. Going from the Bush Jr. administration to Eli Lilly was Alex Azar. Azar was the Deputy Secretary of Health and Human Services and then was named senior Vice-President of Corporate Affairs and Communications for Eli Lilly. The motive, therefore, to withhold the Bienestar/NEEMA school health programs from needy children might be money!

THE GENERAL PUBLIC'S RESPONSIBILITY

Bush Jr. and Perry were the CEOs, and the general public is the

Board of Directors that put them in office.

    This author's belief and conclusion is that the general public should question Bush Jr. and Perry about what has transpired. There needs to be an accounting for the shocking and unethical acts presented in this book.

Appendix A:
RECOMMENDED READINGS

1. Garica-Dominic, O., Wray, L.A., Treviño, R.P., Hernandez, A.E., Yin, Z., Ulbrecht, J.S. Indentifying barriers that hinder onsite parental involvement in a school-based health promotion program. *Health Promotion Practice 2009* (In Press).
2. The HEALTHY Study Group. Risk factors for type 2 diabetes in a sixth grade multiracial cohort. *The HEALTHY Study.* Diabetes Care 2009; 32:953-955.
3. Treviño, R.P., Fogt, D.L., Wyatt, T.J., Leal-Vasquez, L., Sosa, E., and Woods, C. Diabetes risk, low fitness, and energy insufficiency levels among children from poor families. *Journal of the American Dietetic Association* 2008; 108:1846-1853.
4. Shaw-Perry, M., Horner, C., Treviño, R.P., Sosa, E., Hernandez, I., and Bhardwaj, A. NEEMA: A school-based diabetes risk prevention program designed for African American children. *Journal of the National Medical Association* 2007; 99:368-375.
5. Treviño, R.P. The Bienestar school-based program for preventing diabetes in schoolchildren. *Therapeutic Strategies in the Intervention of Coronary Events* 2005; 1(4):10-13
6. Treviño, R.P. Social capital and health implications for working with minority and underserved populations. *The Health Education Monograph Series* 2005; 22(1): 13-18.
7. Treviño, R.P., Hernandez, A., Yin, Z., Garcia, O.A., and Hernandez I. Impact of bienestar on physical fitness in low-income Mexican-American children. *Hispanic*

Journal of Behavioral Sciences 2005; 25:120-132.

8. Treviño, R.P., Yin, Z., Hernandez, A., Hale, D., Garcia, O.A., and Mobley, C. Impact of the Bienestar school-based diabetes mellitus prevention program on fasting capillary glucose levels. *Archives of Pediatric and Adolescent Medicine* 2004; 158:911-917.

9. Trevino, R.P., Yin, Z., Garcia, O.A., Dempsey, L., Gonzalez, A., and Mobley, C. Bienestar's primary prevention of hyperglycemia: *A Randomized Controlled Trial. Diabete*s 2003; 52:A404.

10. Dempsey, L., Trevino, R.P., Garcia, O.A., Caballero, M., and Yin, Z. Mean fasting capillary glucose changes among low-income children participating in Bienestar *Diabetes* 2003; 52:A565.

11. Garcia, O.A., Trevino, R.P., Yin, Z., Hernandez, A., McConn, M., and Hale, D. Bienestar Health Program: a comprehensive approach to reversing hyperglycemia in low-income children. *Diabetes* 2003; 52:A403

12. Treviño, R.P., Dempsey, L., Garcia, O.A., Ramirez, G., and Yin, Z. Reversing hyperglycemia in low-income latino children participating in the Bienestar. *Diabetes* 2002; 51:A430.

13. Treviño, R.P., Hernandez, A., Yin, Z., and Mobley, C. Normalization of fasting capillary glucose in 4th grade children participating in the Bienestar program. *Diabetes* 2001; 50:A396.

14. Treviño, R.P., Marshall, R.M., Hale, D.E., Rodriquez, R., Baker, G., and Gomez, J. Diabetes risk factors in low-income Mexican-American children. *Diabetes Care* 1999; 22:202-207.

15. Treviño, R.P., Pugh, J.A., Hernandez, A.E., Menchaca, V.D., Ramirez, R.R., and Mendoza, M.A. Pilot study of the Bienestar health program: A diabetes risk-factor prevention program. *Journal of School Health* (1998) 68:62-67.

16. Trevino, R.P., Ramirez, R.R., Mobley, C., and Mendoza, M. A. A school-based overweight prevention program: The Bienestar Health Program. *Diabetes* 1996; 45:70A.

Forgotten Children: A True Story of How Politicians Endanger Children

• DR. ROBERTO P. TREVIÑO •